Bataille

'This collection fills a major gap in contemporary literature ... an indispensable examination and celebration of Georges Bataille ... a major publication.'

Mike Gane, *Loughborough University*

Georges Bataille's writings, focusing on eroticism and death, have come to dominate recent debates on subjectivity, on transgression, on sexual politics and community. They have made a profound impact on such thinkers as Derrida, Foucault, Barthes and Kristeva. Why is Bataille such an important figure in both intellectual debates and contemporary counter-culture? What use-value does his emotive discourse have today?

This collection, centred on Bataille's concept of the sacred – a radical, subversive negativity – brings together Bataille specialists from the United States, Britain, France and Canada and from a range of academic disciplines. Their essays demonstrate why Bataille is at the cutting edge of current discussions about the role of the forbidden in life and art, about politics and the notion of subjectivity, about the nature of community and about the value of a transgressive writing.

Contributors: Geoffrey Bennington, Jean-Michel Besnier, Leslie Anne Boldt-Irons, Briony Fer, Denis Hollier, Marie-Christine Lala, John Lechte, Alphonso Lingis, Michèle Richman, Allan Stoekl, Susan Rubin Suleiman and Sarah Wilson.

Carolyn Bailey Gill, the editor, teaches critical theory at London University.

Warwick Studies in European Philosophy
Edited by Andrew Benjamin
Senior Lecturer in Philosophy, University of Warwick

This series presents the best and most original work being done within the European philosophical tradition. The books included in the series seek not merely to reflect what is taking place within European philosophy, rather they will contribute to the growth and development of that plural tradition. Work written in the English language as well as translations into English are to be included, engaging the tradition at all levels ‒ whether by introductions that show the contemporary philosophical force of certain works, or in collections that explore an important thinker or topic, as well as in significant contributions that call for their own critical evaluation.

Bataille

Writing the sacred

Edited by Carolyn Bailey Gill

London and New York

First published 1995
by Routledge
11 New Fetter Lane, London EC4P 4EE

Transferred to Digital Printing 2004

Simultaneously published in the USA and Canada
by Routledge
29 West 35th Street, New York, NY 10001

Typeset in Times by Solidus (Bristol) Limited

British Library Cataloguing in Publication Data
A catalogue record for this book is available from the British Library.

Library of Congress Cataloging in Publication Data
Bataille: writing the sacred/edited by Carolyn Bailey Gill.
    p.   cm. – (Warwick studies in European philosophy)
Papers presented at the International Conference on Georges
Bataille in London, May 13–17, 1991.
Includes bibliographical references and index.
1. Bataille, Georges, 1897–1962 – Criticism and interpretation –
Congresses.   1. Gill, Carolyn Bailey, 1930–. II. Series.
PQ2603.A695Z585
848'.91209–dc20   94–13589
                                          CIP

ISBN 0–415–10122–0 (hbk)
ISBN 0–415–10123–9 (pbk)

Contents

Illustrations

Contributors

Geoffrey Bennington is Professor of French at the University of Sussex. He is the author of books on eighteenth-century French fiction, on Lyotard, Rousseau and, most recently, Jacques Derrida. He has written extensively on contemporary French thought and translated several works by Derrida and Lyotard.

Jean-Michel Besnier teaches Philosophy at the Université de Compiègne and is a member of the Centre de Recherches en Epistemologie Appliquée in Paris, as well as of the editorial boards of several French reviews. He has published a book on Georges Bataille, *La politique de l'impossible: L'intellectuel entre révolte et engagement*, and his most recent books are *Histoire de la philosophie moderne et contemporaine* and *L'humanisme déchiré*, both published in 1993.

Leslie Anne Boldt-Irons, who has taught in the United States, France and Canada, is currently Associate Professor of French at Brock University, Ontario. She published her English translation of Georges Bataille's *L'expérience intérieure* (State University of New York Press) in 1988 and has recently finished editing and translating a series of articles on Bataille for the same press.

Briony Fer teaches Art History at University College London and is particularly interested in Surrealism and psychoanalysis. She has recently co-written *Realism, Rationalism, Surrealism: Art between the wars* and is currently writing a book on abstract art.

Denis Hollier is Professor of French Literature at Yale University. Some of his books have been translated into English: *Against Architecture: The writings of Georges Bataille* (MIT Press, 1989), *The College of Sociology (1937–39)* (University of Minnesota Press, 1988) and *The Politics of Prose: Essay on Sartre* (University of Minnesota Press,

1986). He is the general editor of *New History of French Literature* (Harvard University Press, 1989).

Marie-Christine Lala is *maître de conferences* at the Université de Paris III – Sorbonne Nouvelle, where her research is concerned with the sciences of language and of literature. She has participated in conferences on Georges Bataille in Amsterdam, Rome, Freiburg, London and Paris, and was in charge of seminars at the Collège International de Philosophie from 1986–8.

John Lechte is Lecturer in Sociology at Macquarie University, Sydney. He is the author of a book on the writing of Australian history, articles on Rousseau and psychoanalysis, Joyce, Kafka, Foucault, Derrida and Kristeva, as well as on Bataille. His most recent publication is *Julia Kristeva*, published by Routledge in 1990.

Alphonso Lingis is Professor of Philosophy at Pennsylvania State University. He is the author of *Excesses, Libido: The French existential theories, Phenomenological Explanations, Deathbound Subjectivity, The Community of Those Who Have Nothing in Common* (University of Indiana Press, 1994) and the forthcoming *Abuses, Foreign Bodies* and *Sensation*.

Michèle Richman teaches French Literature and Culture at the University of Pennsylvania. She writes on anthropology and French modernism as well as on Bataille, Leiris and Barthes. Her first book, *Reading Georges Bataille: Beyond the gift* (1982), was the first full-length study of Bataille in English. She is currently preparing a study of Durkheim and the Collège de sociologie within the framework of French notions of otherness since the sixteenth century..

Allan Stoekl is Associate Professor of French and Comparative Literature at Pennsylvania State University. He is the author of *Politics, Writing, Mutilation: The cases of Bataille, Blanchot, Roussel, Leiris and Ponge* (University of Minnesota Press, 1985) and *Agonies of the Intellectual: Subjectivity, commitment, and the performative in the 20th century French tradition* (University of Nebraska Press, 1992). He has also edited and translated a Bataille anthology, *Visions of Excess: Selected writings of Georges Bataille, 1927–39* (University of Minnesota Press, 1985) and a collection of essays, *On Bataille* (*Yale French Studies*, 78, 1990). He is currently writing a series of essays on the relationship between posthistory and postmodernity, and translating Blanchot's novel *Le très-haut*.

Susan Rubin Suleiman is Professor of Romance and Comparative Literatures at Harvard University. She is the author of *Authoritarian Fictions: The ideological novel as a literary genre* (1983, re-issued 1993), *Subversive Intent: Gender, politics, and the avant-garde* (Harvard, 1990) and *Risking Who One Is: Encounters with contemporary art and literature* (Harvard, 1994).

Sarah Wilson was educated at Oxford and at the Courtauld Institute of Art, University of London, where she lectures in the 20th century field, specializing in French art after 1945. She is the author of substantial essays on Dufy, Leger, Picabia, Ernst and Fautrier, and a monograph *Matisse* (Ediciones Poligrafa/Rizzoli, 1992). Her *Calls to Realism: Art and politics in France, 1935–1955* is forthcoming from Yale University Press.

Acknowledgements

I wish to acknowledge financial assistance from the Ambassade de France, London, and the British Academy, who helped to bring some of the participants to the International Conference on Georges Bataille, in London, 13–17 May, 1991, at which many of the chapters in this volume were first given as lectures. Thanks also to the Architectural Association for their generosity and help in providing the venue for the conference. I am grateful to Laurel Brake, my co-organizer, of the Centre for Extra Mural Studies of Birkbeck College, University of London, for the opportunity of putting on the conference, and to Centre staff for their help with the practical matters connected with it.

I wish also to thank Professor Malcolm Bowie, of Oxford University, for his encouragement in publishing these papers, Andrew Benjamin, editor of the Warwick University series in European Philosophy, an enthusiastic supporter of the conference and of this project, and Adrian Driscoll, my editor at Routledge, for his commitment to the volume and for his patience. Thanks also to Susan Foale and Robert Williams, who provided help and advice.

Acknowledgement is made to Editions de Minuit, owner of the copyright of Denis Hollier's 'The use-value of the impossible', for permission to publish the English translation (first published in *October*, 60), and to the following for permission to reproduce illustrations: ADAGP, Paris and DACS, London for Joan Miró, *Peinture*, 1930 and *Composition*, 1930; Demart Pro Arte BV/DACS for Salvador Dali, *Le jeu lugubre*, 1929; Pierre Granville, Dijon, for Jean Fautrier, *L'homme ouvert*, 1928–9; Madeleine Malraux and Alain Malraux, Paris, for Jean Fautrier, *Enfer, Chant IV*, c. 1930, the vignette for *Madame Edwarda*, 1945, *La femme de ma vie*, 1948 and *Alleluiah, catéchisme de Dianus*, 1947; and Sami Tarica, Geneva, for Jean Fautrier, *Otage: La toute jeune fille*, 1943. The photograph *Greniers: Mannequins, débris et poussières* is reproduced by kind permission of the Courtauld Institute Book Library, London.

All requests for permission to reproduce Susan Rubin Suleiman's chapter should be addressed to the author.

A note on the translations

All French texts are quoted in English. Contributors have either made their own translations or quoted from existing English ones. Readers who wish to consult the full texts of the English translations of Bataille's works currently in print are referred to the following:

'Alleluiah, catéchisme de Dianus'	'Alleluia. The catechism of Dianus' in *Guilty*, trans. Bruce Boone with an introduction by Denis Hollier, Venice CA, The Lapis Press, 1988.
Le bleu du ciel	*Blue of Noon*, trans. Harry Mathews, New York, Marion Boyars, 1988.
Le coupable	*Guilty*, trans. Bruce Boone with an introduction by Denis Hollier, Venice CA, The Lapis Press, 1988.
L'erotisme	*Eroticism*, trans. Mary Dalwood, San Francisco, City Lights Books, 1986. *Eroticism*, trans. Mary Dalwood, New York, Marion Boyars, 1987.
L'expérience intérieure	*Inner Experience*, trans. and with an introduction by Leslie Anne Boldt, Albany, State University of New York Press, 1988.
'Hegel, la mort et la sacrifice'	'Hegel, death and sacrifice' in *On Bataille, Yale French Studies*, 78, ed. Allan Stoekl, New Haven, Yale University Press, 1990.
Histoire de l'oeil	*Story of the Eye*, trans. Joachim Neu-groschal, New York, Marion Boyars, 1979.

'La figure humaine' — 'Human face', trans. Annette Michelson, *October*, 36, spring 1986.

L'impossible — *The Impossible*, trans. Robert Hurley, San Francisco, City Lights Books, 1991.

Les larmes d'Eros — *The Tears of Eros*, trans. Peter Connor, San Francisco, City Lights Books, 1991.

La littérature et le mal — *Literature and Evil*, trans. Alastair Hamilton, New York, Marion Boyars, 1990.

Madame Edwarda — *My Mother, Madame Edwarda, The Dead Man*, trans. Austryn Wainhouse, New York, Marion Boyars, 1989.

'La notion de dépense' — 'The notion of expenditure' in *Visions of Excess: Selected writings 1927–39*, ed. and trans. Allan Stoekl, with Carl R. Lovitt and Donald M. Leslie Jr, Minneapolis, University of Minnesota Press, 1985.

La part maudite — *The Accursed Share*, trans. Robert Hurley, 2 vols, New York, Zone Books, 1991.

Sur Nietzsche — *On Nietzsche*, trans. Bruce Boone with an introduction by Sylvère Lotringer, New York, Paragon Books, 1992.

Théorie de la religion — *Theory of Religion*, trans. Robert Hurley, New York, Zone Books, 1989.

Introduction

The twentieth century has witnessed the appearance of a number of French writers and thinkers whose potential influence and importance, only detected in their own lifetime by a small circle of readers, is now slowly being revealed to the English-speaking world. Georges Bataille is such a writer. He is also a curious case of one whose work, while finding a larger public during the period of the journal *Tel Quel* and the debates in France around structuralism and post-structuralism, is today being re-read due to a second wave of interest in his writings, this time in English translation. This collection, a testament to the force and pertinence of his work, will undoubtedly attract for him new English-speaking readers.

The collection is gathered around Bataille's concept of a radical, subversive negativity which he called the sacred. The chapters address, in various ways, the central role of writing in Bataille's work in relation to this sacred zone. Highlighting the transgressive nature of this writing, they explore its implications today for a theory of community, for both general and sexual politics, and for philosophy. The chapters also contain new discussion on issues raised in Bataille's own writing in relation to key intellectual and artistic movements of this century, such as Surrealism and existentialism.

Chapters are arranged in terms of shared preoccupations and concerns, linked or juxtaposed in order to show certain kinds of relatedness without blurring the very real differences in approach or style exhibited by each one.

The collection begins with a Bataille-inspired meditation on the sacred by Alphonso Lingis. At the Mayan ruin of Copán, near the village of Chichicastenango, Honduras, Lingis powerfully evokes that realm of disorder, disintegration, sacrifice and death, where for Bataille the fundamental need for continuity and a sacred communication between beings is played out.

Chapters two and three address Bataille's relation to politics, to political action. From differing perspectives Jean-Michel Besnier and Susan Rubin Suleiman question the familiar view of a 'turning point' in Bataille's writing at the end of the 1930s, when Bataille has been seen to have withdrawn from political activity. Both insist instead on a continuity of preoccupations. Besnier claims that 'the surrender to events as to a joyful invitation' defines the very nature of Bataille as an intellectual (distinguishing him, for example, from Sartre): Bataille, he argues, is an *intellectuel pathétique*. Moreover, he insists that 'in privileging the ascetic experience (in *L'expérience intérieure* and later writings after the 1930s), the issue is the same, even if the quest is now a solitary one, sheltered from the solicitation of history.' The central concern, the desire to experience one's limits and the need to feel a continuity with the totality of existence, is unchanged. Suleiman sets Bataille's political writings of the 1930s against his erotic fictions of the same period, and traces in both his preoccupation with virility. By the end of that decade, and the turn inward, nothing has changed, she claims. Contestation is no longer a matter of outward action, it has become 'inner experience' but it is still apparently gendered. She takes up these matters within the complex interplay between oppositions of collaboration and resistance, and passivity and action.

Suleiman engages most directly with gender issues but a number of other chapters also take up these issues. Sarah Wilson notes the slippages between masculine and feminine significations in Bataille's work (and mirrored in Fautrier's). Briony Fer, while finding 'that Bataille's language erases feminine desire and pleasure', none the less sees dispersion of meaning and blurring: 'his formulation of a male sexual economy occupies the shadows where meaning and identity fail'. Suleiman too reminds us that *la déchirure* (variously translated as 'rending agony', 'laceration', 'inner sundering') which Bataille puts at the centre of *L'expérience intérieure*, is actively sought, and therefore is inflected in masculine terms. However, while insisting on the gendered nature of Bataille's articulation of this experience, she reminds us that in his erotic novels he bypasses the opposition between 'ordinary' masculinity and femininity. Ultimately, she suggests that Bataille might have been working towards a third term. Perhaps no serious attempt to come to terms with Bataille's theory of sexuality can ignore the radical form of his notion of sacrifice, which affects sacrificer as well as sacrificed and so arguably undercuts the notion of phallic mastery. Yet one is left with those insistent affirmations of virility which Suleiman discusses.

Geoffrey Bennington finds considerable agreement between Kant and

Bataille and raises a question about Bataille's distinction between general and restricted economy. Examining the status of excess or expenditure in Bataille's work, he attempts to show in what sense they are not an 'absolute exteriority'. Ultimately, he argues that general economy *is* restricted economy: it cannot be thought in any other way. His chapter has important implications for debates around the status of meaning and representation in Bataille's work.

Chapters five and six address questions of sacred communication. Michèle Richman, in an extended discussion on the Collège de sociologie, explores the effect on Bataille and his associates at the Collège of the Durkheimian notion of the sacred. She argues that Durkheim's sacred countered prevailing notions about crowd psychology developed, for instance, by Le Bon. She takes a different perspective on Bataille's concern with collectivities to that developed by Jean-Luc Nancy and Maurice Blanchot around community, arguing that Bataille 'reserved certain riddles for the sociological sphinx'. Allan Stoekl, on the other hand, takes up Bataille's relation to Hegel on the key issue of recognition. Given the importance of Bataille's Kojèvian reading of Hegel, Stoekl raises the important question of the meaning of Bataille's apparent neglect of the problematic of recognition. He attempts to answer this question through a close reading of *Madame Edwarda* in the light of the structure and the ritual substitutions of the Catholic mass. Is sacred expenditure simply more characteristic of mankind, in Bataille's view, than recognition? In *Madame Edwarda* Stoekl suggests that the anguish of absolute comicalness, which Bataille points us to in the famous preface to the narrative, is a form of recognition which is ceremonial rather than existential.

A group of chapters closely address Bataille's practice of writing by attending to his erotic fictions. Leslie Anne Boldt-Irons takes up Bataille's view of writing as an act of violent sacrifice. How does Bataille maintain the radical negativity that founds his writing and yet stay this side of the limit? What is the position of the (voyeuristic) reader in this violent writing? She argues that Bataille inscribed in his erotic fictions a dual structure of *mis-en-abyme/mis-en-abîme* which operates on the reader in the form of inner sacrifice.

Marie-Christine Lala is concerned with the deployment of the concept of *l'impossible* in a late work by that name. How can death, the void, the impossible, be spoken? Does not absence, in order to be intelligible, have to be present? Lala analyses strategies of a transgressive writing which reveal a radical, sacrificial negativity in Bataille's narratives, attributing much of the originality of his thought to the role he gave to the excluded Other, or *la part maudite*, in literary communication.

John Lechte takes up similar questions. Bataille's preference for metonymic over metaphoric substitution was another way of valuing the impossible over the possible and the imaginary, and separated him from the Surrealists, he argues. He confronts the quarrels between Bataille and Breton, examining the ground contested between them through the distinction between horizontal and vertical axes, which he correlates with immanence and transcendence as well as with metonymy and metaphor. Invoking the work of Julia Kristeva, Lechte examines issues of language and representation in a writing which puts language itself at risk, brings metaphor to a halt and is characterized by exhaustion and loss. Ultimately, Bataille is seen to be closer to a Freudian problematic than Breton, in spite of the privileged role psychoanalysis played for the Surrealists.

Denis Hollier also underlines differences with the Surrealists. *Documents*, says Hollier, wanted 'neither the imaginary nor the possible'. Hollier situates an anti-aesthetic ideology at the centre of Bataille's 1927–9 journal *Documents*, shared by both of the founding groups: the ethnographers and the avant-gardists. While both groups significantly prioritized use-value over exchange value (which it was claimed distinguished them, at a certain level, from the Surrealists), a gap emerged between them over the notion of the sacred. Bataille, urging the lifting of taboos, the inducing of expenditure, to bring about sacred communication, advocated the re-introduction of the excluded Other – the forbidden, the ugly, nauseating filth, spit – into ethnographic science.

It is not surprising that Bataille's work has been taken up by art historians, given his numerous writings on artists (his articles on Van Gogh, a book on Manet, to name just two) and his collaborations with contemporaries who illustrated his work. Briony Fer examines associated metaphors of dust and other kinds of decomposition, as well as chains of association suggested by dismemberment and mutilation, in Bataille's writing on Miró and Dali (it was of course in relation to Dali that the quarrel with Breton was played out). Referring to Miró's declared wish to 'undo painting' (which she relates to the sadistic impulse), Fer suggests that 'modern painting rehearses the cruelty of sacrifice on its own means of representation'. The effects with which she is concerned, therefore, are at the very centre of the origin and procedures of modern painting, rather than at its margins. Like Lechte, she attempts to elucidate connections with psychoanalysis and the relation to Freud.

Sarah Wilson traces Bataille's collaboration with the artist Jean Fautrier, the illustrator of two of Bataille's erotic fictions. She is concerned to investigate a relationship often ignored, or at least overshadowed by the more familiar Miró, Masson and Dali connections. She also confronts a period not usually explored, that of the 'crisis of Surrealism', a crisis occasioned by its collision with existentialism in the 1940s. Concerned to refute the recent attempt to elide the differences between Bataille's *informe* and *la peinture informel*, of which Fautrier was the acknowledged leader, she none the less sees a convergence in their obsession with the wound, at once celebratory and horrific, and their relation to historical events and 'a more existentialist ethos'.

Bataille's writings provoke. They are strange, difficult, often troubling, sometimes paradoxical: drenched in philosophical concepts, yet inimical to philosophy's totalizing gestures which he saw as philosophy's project. It is the act of writing which is conceived as the interruption of that project. Therefore it is not surprising that his works are being re-examined in connection with current arguments in critical theory about the relations between literature and philosophy. But there is more to the new wave of interest in his work than that. Bataille is becoming unavoidable for anyone interested in contemporary debates on the concept of alterity, on the notion of the subject, on the nature of community, on the relationship between representation and a particular theory of language, including its implications for gender politics, and generally on the relations between politics, literature and art.

Carolyn Bailey Gill

Note

1 All but three of the papers collected here were first presented at the International Conference on Georges Bataille, held in London on 13–17 May 1991. The chapters by Alphonso Lingis, Michèle Richman and Allan Stoekl were commissioned for this volume.

1 Chichicastenango

Alphonso Lingis

Copán, in Honduras, is celebrated by mesoamericanists as the most beautiful of all the Mayan ruins. Also the most intact; it and the river valley its people had cultivated had enigmatically been abandoned four centuries before the conquistadors arrived. Four centuries of tree roots had held and hidden its stones from the builders of colonial cities and churches. In this century archeologists from the North came to clear away the jungle and expose again its plazas, its temples, its great carved stelae. US ambassador John Stevens had personally acquired the entire city in 1840 for fifty dollars. It was discovered that the first priority was to redirect the river, which had shifted the direction of its force and had eroded the highest part of the city. Every summer teams from the North work to map out with the aid of helicopters and infra-red scanning the roads and buried ruins, to advance the excavation, to reassemble the walls overturned by the jungle, to dig up burial grounds and measure bones and teeth and subject them to radiation scanning. When they leave they continue to work, in university buildings filled with computers, over the data, publish monographs – historians, sociologists, linguists, agronomists, biologists. A veritable multinational corporate industry, transforming these ruins whose hewn shapes were effaced by five centuries of bacteria, lichens, roots and rain, into texts. Texts filed in microchips, reinstated in the great text of world civilization. Soon one will not have to come here at all, one will tap numbers into one's home modem and these ruins will be restored as a city, one will watch its priests and nobles circulating in hologram in one's own living room.

I bought a bagful of the latest publications, and went to have lunch in the village inn. The dining room was full of people, I had to wait long to be served. The others were finished as I began to eat; one of them stood up and began to give an account of the most recent findings by pathologists, who had studied the data derived from the burial sites, as to what these people fell ill of and died of. The others were taking notes, already busy on their future publications. Abruptly I recalled that Copán was the principal research site in Central America of the Physical Anthropology Department of my own university. I could not focus my mind on what he was saying in the noonday heat. I did not introduce myself. I walked to the site with my bag of literature. I studied the great stelae, thick figures cut in high relief, not idealized human bodies as in the art of what we call Classical antiquity, but their torsos studded with other figures, their limbs fitted between psychedelic protuberances, every inch of the space about and above them filled with enigmatic carvings. Soon I tired too of reading all the explanations before each marked site, I could do it this evening in my room. I contemplated the stelae much worn by the elements, craggy rocks re-cemented in the plazas now cleared and levelled, turned into parks. I strolled about the constructions which had sunk or whose upper layers had collapsed and had been reassembled; behind them the tangled jungle rustled with monkeys and birds. The once precision-cut stones no longer fitted together; sometimes cement had been needed to hold them. High staircases led from level to level of the city; one had to climb them on strictly designated paths, there were signs warning of the instability of either side. Wherever I looked I saw stones eroded, cracked, their relief effaced, lichens and bacteria gnawing at them. By the time the great text was completed, they would have subsided into a zone of the lithic strata of the planetary crust. The worshippers and the gods had vanished from these ruined temples centuries ago. The campesinos who had recently cultivated their milpas in these ancient plazas had been relocated elsewhere; now on the levelled lawns young mestizo men of the village who had been educated in English in government schools were reciting the explanations the scientists had summarized for them to the moneyed tourists. I became weary in the heat and damp of the afternoon; I sat down on a rock in the shade spread by an enormous ceiba tree that had grown on the highest point of the city walls, its trunk splayed at the bottom to send roots down in all directions, seeking the rock strata beneath over which the city had been built. I contemplated the multicoloured lichens spreading like acidic stains over the stones. The vegetation was dusty with tiny insects; I quickly gave up flailing them off, their minute stings drew nourishment from the torpor into which my body drifted. The theories – historical, sociological, religious – tangled in my mind, which could not sustain interest in them. Even images faded out. The ruins about me depopulated even of its ghosts. The clear-toned calls of unseen birds echoed in my skull. The wet humus and smell of rotting leaves rose to fill my inhalations. My eyes gazed unfocused, and the slight swaying of the trees and displacements of splatches of sunlight neutralized into a dense medium without colour and form. I don't know how long I remained in this lethargy; gradually I became aware not of eyes but of a look before me. The look was mild and fraternal. Little by little, about the look, a deer materialized, knee-deep in the vegetation. It was a soft grey as I had never seen on deer, with white belly and tail. It was so close I slowly shifted and reached out to touch it, but however I turned it always seemed to be the same distance from me. Little by little its grey turned to smoke and then charcoal as night fell. When I finally made my way to the entrance gate, it was locked; a high fence with five strands of barbed wire on top surrounded the site. I tore my clothes and cut my hands and legs getting over it.

The received judgement is that the Mayan civilization was the greatest of the Americas; its cities grand as Harappa, Memphis and Thebes, Rome, its agriculture so sophisticated that the unpopulated marshlands of Tikal and Chiapas once supported vast populations, its science – the Mayas discovered the zero a thousand years before Europe, they calculated Venus' year to within six seconds of what today's electron telescopes have fixed as exact – one of the greatest spiritual achievements of humanity. Where have they gone? Fully 50 per cent of the population of Guatemala today is pure Mayan stock; one can see them on market day in Chichicastenango.

Conquistador Pedro Alvarado contracted with one side, then another, of two rival Quiché nations in the high mountains of Guatemala, then betrayed them both. The remnant that remained of the smaller nation was put in *reducctiones* in the lowlands; that of the larger group was resettled in the ruins of the former capital of their rivals. The Aztecs conscripted in Pedro Alvarado's army called it Chichicastenango, the Place of the Nettles. The conquistadors garrisoned there had mansions of stone built. Franciscans arrived, and set the Indians working to construct an enormous church rising over a great flight of steps over the former Quiché sacred rock. The place was remote, the only road descended in rocky switchbacks down a deep gorge and then up again.

I went to Chichicastenango. By the entrance to the town there is a large billboard with the words 'Dios Familia Patria' and 'El Ejército es su Amigo'. Chichicastenango has hardly grown in five centuries; from the central plaza one can see the whole town, its streets stopped on all sides at the brink of gorges just four blocks away. But they are choked with people: market day. The plaza is filled with stands, down its narrow lanes blankets, hats, embroidered blouses and intricately woven skirts, iron picks and shovels and machetes, painted masks, fruits and vegetables, salt, are piled high. Some distance away, there is an empty lot where women are gossiping, holding in their fists the cords tied tightly to the rear legs of black pigs. Some of them have half a dozen pigs on leashes. The pigs pull and retreat, grubbing in their muck. In the streets Indians are still arriving, bent under huge baskets or heavy bundles of firewood. Many have walked the whole night. They are very small, with parched brown skin, the women dressed in extravagant colours, the men in dust-clogged trousers and wearing straw hats with the brims smartly turned up at the sides, down in front and back. In the central lanes of the plaza, women are cooking pans of beans and corn, vegetables, stir-frying chicken. The women converse in their melodious tongue in groups, laughing children chase one another around the stands. The men, alone or in groups, are getting drunk on chiché. One walks the lanes over the decaying husks of fruit, wrappings of leaves and twine, dirty plastic bags, broken bottles; in alleys and in doorways swept by the wind they pile up, splattered with urine, vomit, under swarming flies. Troops in combat dress carrying automatic rifles walk through the streets with impassive faces. Tourists under broad cloth hats panting from the sun and the dust are peering desultorily into the stands; occasionally one of them decides, after some confused bargaining, to buy something, the others gather protectively as she or he extracts some banknotes from a money-belt.

From the whitewashed tower of the church dedicated to Santo Tomás – Thomas the Doubter – the bells begin pealing. The church stands high in the sun over twenty feet of steps, the lower steps on one side are piled with bundles of gladioli and calla lilies around women whose blouses under lace mantillas blaze with crimson, royal blue, ochre. Above them in the thick smoke of sacrifices smouldering on the steps men are swinging incense-burners. I hear the high-pitched repetitive melodies of flutes dancing over the beat of drums; the officiants of the Indian communes are arriving, dressed in embroidered jackets and black knee-length trousers with elaborate head-dresses of plumes and animal fangs and carrying maces of burnished silver. The flower-women make a path for them and they climb the steps to the church entrance and disappear between men swinging incense-burners.

The main entrance is forbidden to those who do not know the secret Quiché formulas with which to invoke ancestral spirits; I make my way to the cloister on the right side of the church and enter through a side door. The church nave is long and high and filled with sticky perfumed smoke. Women are standing on the right side, men on the left; I cross over and move half-way up to the sanctuary. The centre aisle is open, every ten feet there is a small raised cement block upon which sacrifices, charred chickens and pieces of pigs, are smouldering in the midst of mandalas of flower petals. Over them men in workclothes are swinging incense-burners. A white-haired priest enters from the sacristy to begin the mass, the Indian officiants are already standing on both sides of the sanctuary with their hands closed over their maces. A marimba band in front of the altar rail begins to hammer out cadences. Men and women are continually stepping into the centre aisle, placing on the fires packets wrapped in leaves and consulting the crouched shamans who stand up and make wide-open-arm gesticulations in different directions before receiving the next supplicant. When the priest has reached the climax of the mass, the consecration of the bread and wine, he lifts the host and chalice high over his deeply bowed head; down the length of the centre aisle the shamans are occupied in making different kinds of ritual dances over their consultants. No one approaches the alter rail to take communion. When the mass is over the priest disappears into the sacristy; the Indian officiants descend from the sanctuary preceded by flutes and drums and leave from the main portal. I see along the side walls of the church only a few chapel altars; the carved statues of saints, completely black with soot, have been crowded upon them. On a few of these altars glass has been fitted over a painting, no doubt from the colonial epoch but barely discernible under the coat of greasy soot. I look down the length of the now empty church; with its blackened walls and ceiling and the charred statues of saints pushed together against the walls, its sooty windows with many broken panes, it looks like an old warehouse abandoned after a fire.

On the side of the plaza I notice a piece of cardboard with the word 'Museo' and an arrow on it. I find two rooms with handmade glass cases housing some broken pre-Columbian Quiché pots decorated with red pictures and designs, gold and jade pieces restrung into necklaces, incense-burners, strange deities like psychedelic visions congealed in brick-red clay. It turns out that this was the collection made by Padre Rossbach, whose faded photograph hangs in an aluminium frame on one wall. A sign says that he had been pastor of the Santo Tomás church from 1898 until his death in 1948. Campesinos brought him these things they had turned up with their ploughs, and he had told them not to sell them to the tourists. I looked at the photograph; Padre Rossbach looked German. In Central America, the ruling families still send one son to the seminary, they preside over the great basilicas with altars encrusted with gold in Guatemala City, Antigua, Tegucigalpa, San Pedro Sula, Managua. But aside from a few old priests drinking and fathering children in the mestizo and Indian towns, almost all the little churches in the mountains are boarded up. Those that have mass celebrated and children baptized in them are periodically tended by missionaries. These have come from missionary orders in Portugal, Ireland, the United

States. Such idealistic young men have now too become scarce. Those that came, and found themselves isolated for long months in dusty and famished villages, often heeded the Liberation Theology that was formulated originally in the favelas of Rio de Janeiro and has since been silenced by the Roman Curia. During the 1970s and 1980s, and in Guatemala especially during the dictatorship of Rios Montt, they were often the first to be massacred when the troops arrived in the Indian highlands. Even last year the priest was killed in nearby San Andrés, a village on the edge of Lake Atitlán much visited by tourists.

After eating some corn and beans in the plaza, I descended into the gorge on the east side of the town, crossed a small marsh and the now insignificant river, and looked into the forested hills that rise at once on the other side. From one of them I could make out a thin ribbon of smoke trailing into the blazing sky. I walked through milpas of parched cornstalks, and found a path into the trees. The path rose steeply and I trudged with slow steps like the old campesinos and had to stop several times until my heartbeat stabilized. On top, there was a circle of rough stones. Against it, a flat black rock about three feet high upon which one could see a face. It was roughly carved, one side much narrower than the other, the eyes not on the same level. They did not seem to look at me, and the expression was impassive. The stone had been broken across the face and cemented back together. Up against it there was a bundle of gladioli, not in a container of water, wilted. Within the circle of stones, and outside it, there were several piles of greasy ashes, still smouldering, and limp flower-heads laid in lines and circles. All around the dusty ground was littered with chicken feathers, all ragged, some spotted with black blood, the leaves under the trees were clotted with them. I sat down under a tree at the edge of the clearing. There were many long-needled pines in the forest, and the wind hummed in their thin branches. There was no other sound, even the locusts were silent in the heat of the day. After awhile I looked back at the shrine; there was now an old woman with one eye opaque laying a packet wrapped in leaves on the embers, and moving in a kind of slow dance. Then she turned and vanished into the forest as silently as she had come.

The noonday sky bleached out the forest and forced shut my eyes. I hear the sludges of my body pushed with uncertain pulses. The essential is that sweat, secretions, vapours depart from it. The body's thrusts are expulsions. Its orifices expel urine and excrement, also phlegm, mucus, tears, groans. The feelings that irradiate in me are discharged down its nerve fibres. The grey mass of my brain crystallizing insights, thoughts, projects, destinies, only to expel them. Everywhere we humans move we leave sweat, stains, urine, faecal matter. The organized constructions of our sentences flatten into bromides, erode into clichés, deteriorate into prattle, break into sighs, screams, sobbing and laughter in orgasm. What we call construction and creation is the uprooting of living things, the massacre of millions of paradisal ecosystems, the mindless trampling of minute creatures whose hearts throb with life. We level mountains to pave them with temples whose gods become forgotten, and markets settling into rotting husks and plastic bags. The beat of our life is relentless drives to discharge our forces in things left behind, our passions, charged with revulsion and awe, are excremental. Our blood shed, breast milk, menstrual blood, vaginal discharges, semen are what is sacred in us, surrounded from time immemorial with taboos and proscriptions. Bodies festering, ruins crumbling into a past that cannot be reinstated, ideas and ideals that are enshrined in a canon where they no longer light the virgin fires of first insight in our brains, extend the zone of the sacred across the mouldering hull of our planet.

Indians of Guatemala, driven to the high mountains by the ranchers who in the past twenty years have deforested the hills below for the raising of grass-fed cattle for hamburgers, Indians driven into Chiapas in Mexico during forty years of army rule, Indians dwarfed and stunted by chronic malnutrition. Indians stumbling all night under the weight of their handcraft, standing in lanes covered with debris and rotting vegetables, when night comes leaving under their heavy unsold bundles. Their Catholicism in disintegration, barely visible through the debris of Quiché myths and rituals of a civilization destroyed five centuries ago.

I was haunted all day by a sentiment I had felt nowhere in my country, in neo-Gothic cathedrals squeezed between high-rise buildings in cities or modernistic churches surrounded by spacious lawns and parking lots in the suburbs. A sentiment of the departed, the irrecuperable, the radically other. The sacred hovered inconceivably in the charred hull of the once-Catholic temple, in the broken idol in its circle of rough stones in the hill outside the town, in the grime of sacrificial stones and torn and bloodied chicken feathers, in the stunted bodies of Indians hunted down in these rocky heights by soldiers from the capital transported by helicopter. No, the sacred is this decomposition.

The sacred is what repels our advance. The taboos and proscriptions that demarcate it do not constitute its force of withdrawal. It is not the salvific but the inapprehendable, the unconceptualizable, the inassimilable, the irrecuperable.

One had to come this far, to this disheartening impasse of intellectual and conceptual activity. One had to come to this excretion of inassimilable elements. One had to come in a body breaking down in anguish, dejection, sobs, trances, laughter, spasms and discharges of orgasm.

Religion advances triumphantly over the decomposition of the sacred. It separates from its turgid ambiguity the covenant from the taboos, the celestial order from the intoxication with spilt blood, milk and semen, the sublime from the excremental. Its intelligence separates a celestial and divine order from the demoniacal world of decomposition. It levitates the sacred into an extra-cosmic empyrean, where a reign of intelligible providence and a paternal image of a personalized deity function to foster in humans exalted phantasms of indecomposable sufficiency. It consecrates the profanation of the world, given over to industry, information-processing, tourists bussed to the market of Indians while soldiers tread through the lanes with Uzis.

I got up and returned down the path and this time followed the river at the bottom of the gorge. Tangles of dirty plastic bags hissed in the scrub bushes. After a while I came upon the gate of the cemetery, which lay above on a height facing the city from the north. At the entrance there are stone and cement family mausoleums in which the creoles are buried. Behind them graves with simple headstones. And then more and more graves without even crosses or names, with only mounds of clay to mark them. Here and there on the rocky ground there are black smudges of ashes, with circles of flower petals. At the back of the cemetery there is a structure like a small chapel; it has been cracked by earthquake and most of the once-yellow stucco has crumbled off its bricks. Inside on the floor there is a large cross of raised cement: it is the grave of Padre Rossbach. Rays of light fall upon it from the half-collapsed roof. The floor is black with the tar-like grime of sacrificial fires, chicken feathers stuck to it or drifted into corners. There are wilted flower petals in lines and circles. The walls are completely caked with soot. At the back two men and a woman are bent over candles and packets wrapped in leaves. Padre Rossbach has been transformed into a Quiché ancestor, revered with rituals already centuries old when Christianity first arrived in this hemisphere . . .

I thought of his photograph. Germany was not sending Catholic missionaries to Central America, he must have been an American. I imagined a missionary order from a traditional area settled by Germans, Wisconsin or South Dakota. He came here to take over the Santo Tomás church, in a small town of creole landowners and Chinese merchants and thousands of Indians come from the mountains on market day. He learned Quiché, discovered in the Indian hamlets, their social order intact, the elected elders serving without salary, in fact having to expend all their resources to help in emergencies and to stage complex rituals. On market day they came to him with problems with the landowners and army. They brought offerings of corn and chickens, and sometimes old pottery they had had in their hamlets for generations. The Cardinal Archbishop in Guatemala City did not visit outposts of foreign missionary orders. There was no money to paint the church, repair the altars. There were no nuns to run a school. Little by little he let them come in their own garb, which the Franciscans five centuries ago had forbidden, knowing that the apparently decorative patterns were so many woven amulets invoking Mayan demons. He let the marimba players come in with their instruments, and when they began to play what were not hymns he did not stop them. He let them burn incense on the entrance steps, built over an ancient shrine. He himself took down altars which he was told were built over sacred stones. He ceased to demand they consecrate their unions in matrimony. He ceased to demand they come to tell him their sins in confessions. He let their officiants come with processions of flutes and drums into the sanctuary, the shamans to burn sacrifices in the centre aisle. One day a delegation of shamans showed him an ancient copy of the Popoh Vul, the great myth of the Quiché, which the world had believed lost irrevocably when Bishop de Landa in 1526 ordered all copies of the Mayan sacred writings to be burnt. They let him come to their meeting house night after night to copy it. He learned the sacred script, and was spending more time studying it and pondering its meaning than reading his breviary. The Quiché brought their children for baptism; it was the only one of the seven sacraments that were still performed in the Santo Tomás church. He must have opened his door to women who brought him chiché for the long cold nights, and received them in his bed – how many children called him padre? His last trip back to the motherhouse in the North American Midwest was before the war; his parents were gone and his relatives dispersed, and he found he had difficulty expressing simple things in English. He returned to the shamans he knew, who came with remedies and spells during his last illness. I thought of the afternoon of the first time I had come to Chichicastenango, eight years ago. I was sitting in the doorway of a building on the side of the plaza emptied by the sun, save for a few women who were tending pans of corn and beans over charcoal fires. A troupe of soldiers walked through. The steps of the Santo Tomás church were smoking from multiple sacrifices. A boy brought me a glass of water, and did not stop to talk. Then I heard the heavy beat of a drum, and a single flute repeating a thin succession of tones. A procession of Indians entered through a side street. I picked up my camera, but stopped cold. A peasant, perhaps thirty years of age, was stumbling behind them, under the dead weight of the body of a woman he was bearing on his back, her arms and legs limp across his steps. His wife. His grief bearing the weight of the dead – words as they formed in my mind that filled me with the shame of their hideous banality. The widowed peasant and his companions stopped at the steps of the Santo Tomás church and the shamans burnt fires and swung incense-burners before the entrance to the ancestors who dwell in the great rock below. They did not enter the church and the priest did not come to accompany them and bless the mountain grave to which they advanced. Now I thought that the unembalmed corpse of Padre Rossbach too had been borne on the back of some Indian who had loved him and whose heavy steps had not carried him up the steps to the altar of the Santo Tomás church.

It was dark and cold now in the crypt; the Indians had gone, leaving their smouldering fires. I was shaking, I did not know whether with sobs or with laughter.

The night had fallen and the town was dark with the mountain cold. The streets were empty; the campesinos were already dispersed in the mountains. Most of them must have sold nothing, they are bearing their now still heavier burdens back, to be packed up and carried again the next market day. The streets are ankle-deep in discarded husks and leave-wrappings, dog and human excrement. Down every lane I am startled by the rustling of vaguely visible transparent forms. I tell myself it is the wind whipping a snag of plastic bags, though each time I seem to catch sight of a half-decomposed cadaver fleeing through the night in a luminous shroud.

In a week I must leave, and return to the state university where big classrooms will be full of students preparing, with textbooks and computers, their futures in the gleaming technopoles of the First World. They are identifying, assimilating information. Their appetite is young and healthy, like their appetites in supermarkets big as warehouses piled with half a dozen kinds of apples, oranges, cheeses, prepared meats, fish, dozens of kinds of wine and liquors, unloaded from tractor-trailers from remote states, ships and jet aeroplanes from remote continents. Like the appetite they bring to shopping malls piled up with clothing, furniture, stereophonic sound systems, television sets and VCRs, computers, motorcycles, automobiles. The appetite they will bring to resorts selling snowmobiles, marinas selling yachts, real-estate agents selling condominiums and restaurant-chains. Everything abandoned in the onward advance or in death will be resold; everything worn out will be recycled. They are being trained by professors deciphering the genetic codes of living things, reducing the heterogeneity of snowflakes, gasses and rocks, asteroids and galaxies to classified series of concepts, laws, formulas. The tabooed and the prohibited, the excremental and the marvellous, will be conjured from the future; everything strange, departing, decomposing will be recuperated in the dragnets of knowledge. Their religion but one strand in the dragnets.

The working class created by the first industrial revolution is one that is deprived of the means to appropriate the materials and machinery of their labour. For them, industrial waste product, life does not consist in labour for the means to be freed of labour, but for the means to lose themselves in the violent discharges of orgasm. The students I will return to will be agents in the third, information-processing industrial revolution, they will not be workers.

The room was cold, there was nothing to do but take off my shoes and crawl under the blankets with my clothes on. I felt weary and sleep, as for the old, came slow and fitfully. From time to time I heard the slow steps of Indians outside. Warmth finally came to fill my bed, the warmth of secretions and sweat, of ejaculations and stains.

I would have liked one of them to come to me with chiché and to be received into my bed. Someone with face wrinkled by the mountain sun and hands gnarled by its labour.

2   Bataille, the emotive intellectual[1]

Jean-Michel Besnier

The question of the intellectual comes back at regular intervals. I don't know if it is a French speciality, but ever since the Dreyfus affair at the beginning of the century, we on the continent have continually involved and compromised our thinkers in current political debates. Some, like Michel Serres, are beginning to show impatience and to demand a right of incompetence in political matters. I tend to think that is so much the better in some cases, but basically I prefer the attitude of someone like Maurice Blanchot, who dreams instead of keeping for himself 'the right of the unexpected word', that is to say, the possibility of speaking only sparingly about current affairs, and without it appearing to be a duty.[2] In short, French intellectuals are probably still in mourning for Sartre.

No matter: the history of intellectuals, the history of their *engagement*, of their mistakes, of their slips or of their cowardice, constitutes an important chapter in the cultural and political history of the twentieth century. It is sometimes the pretext for historians of thought to hand out group marks, to condemn or to absolve this or that gaffe by virtue of their position as latest arrivals on the scene – more often than not having themselves defected from militant illusions. Georges Bataille is rarely forgotten at these ritual award ceremonies, and he is almost always unfairly treated. It is in order to set straight some of the prejudices about him that I would like to speak now, by describing him as an emotive intellectual. This category should, in my view, be added to those commonly used to describe the intellectuals whom Sartre saw as occupying themselves with that which didn't concern them: the critical intellectual, the revolutionary intellectual, the organic intellectual, the Messianic intellectual or, more prosaically, the expert. I will try to show that the label of emotive intellectual applies best to writers, philosophers, artists or scientists who are less concerned with bearing witness, judging or teaching than with joining with history, which bruises and moves them just as much as anyone else.

I said just now that Bataille was generally badly treated by the theoreticians of the intelligentsia. The essence of the judgements passed on him is effectively to classify him as an irresponsible thinker – irresponsible in the broad sense, that is, as a man who didn't think of changing the world or formulating regulating ideals, and who didn't burden himself with the duty of representing or being exemplary which comes necessarily with the profession of writer. This accusation might be convincing were it not accompanied by contradictory arguments, which I would like to begin by rapidly sketching out.

What does one readily say about Bataille when seeking to disqualify him as an intellectual? Broadly speaking, there are three charges, which don't seem very coherent:

1 Hostile to democracy in the 1930s, Bataille was seduced by Fascism, and even orchestrated the celebration of Nazi values within the Collège de sociologie and above all within the secret society *Acéphale*. (A book has just come out in France, *Les années souterraines* by Daniel Lindenberg, picking up on this already old thesis.)[3]

2 Although he had rubbed shoulders with Trotskyism at the beginning of the 1930s, Bataille proclaimed himself a hardline Stalinist during the cold war, the main evidence for which is his attitude to Kravchenko in 1948.

3 Bataille was a seeker after God, even though he didn't admit it, 'a new mystic', who would propose a desertion of History in favour of 'an ecstatic swoon'. We recognize here the well-known criticism by Sartre,[4] which has implicitly conditioned many mystico-religious readings of Bataille (for example, that of J.-C. Renard published in 1987 by Editions du Seuil).

Fascist, Stalinist, mystic – three labels of accusation which all in different ways denounce the influence wielded (even today) by the author of *La part maudite*. The serious reader of Bataille is condemned to an eternal advocacy in his defence – eternal because there are none so deaf as those who will not hear:

1 To exculpate Bataille of Nazism, he must repeat that the project which aimed 'to turn the weapons of Fascism back upon it' was obviously dangerous, but that it seemed to the moving force behind Contre-Attaque the only one capable of responding to the emergency in the context of moral and political degradation [*deliquescence*] of the pre-war years. The advocate will also add that Bataille dissolved Contre-Attaque precisely because he was aware of the misunderstanding to

which this ambition to defeat Fascism on its own terms could give rise. And the same advocate will conclude by citing, for example, the fate of Jules Monnerot who, unlike Bataille, remained fascinated by power to the point of seeing in Nazism a regenerative myth.

2   To set Bataille's Stalinism in context, he will need to recommend reading the final volume of *La part maudite* devoted to sovereignty,[5] and to underline the ambivalence of its author towards Stalin, that sovereign who exhausted himself in forbidding (even to himself) all joy [*jouissance*], that is to say all 'non-productive expenditure'; and who for that reason left himself open to the awakening of the same forces of opposition which in earlier times had risen against the tsars. At the very least, any honest reader will see that this book can only be interpreted as a critique of Communist society.

3   Finally, in order to reply to Sartre, it would be easy to cite the militancy of Bataille at the heart of Contre-Attaque and his intention 'to strike down capitalist authority and its political[6] institutions', and to translate words into 'action in the streets' (as he proposed to Kojève, who was terrified). After the war, Sartre doesn't say a word about this exhortation to mobilization, perhaps because he himself had not yet discovered *engagement* in the 1930s. Perhaps also because he felt no sympathy for the leftism of the movement led by Bataille, which denounced with one and the same gesture bourgeois moralism, electoral compromise and the power struggles of a Soviet Communist Party capable of making alliances with Western democracies on the pretext of the struggle against Fascism. Perhaps, finally, because he is deaf to the motives which lead Bataille to pursue, in *L'expérience intérieure*, an asceticism whose stakes can be described in the same vocabulary used before the war to talk about revolutionary mobilization. Because 'total existence' remained fairly and squarely the impossible aim of the Contre-Attaque militant who no more intended to join up with the project and sacrifice the present for some predetermined future than before. Sartre himself sometimes acted in bad faith. . .

Whatever the case may be, it is undeniable that Bataille refused to let the theme of Sartrian *engagement* be imposed upon him. He did not want his often stormy interventions in pre-war history to be interpreted as a way for the intellectual to pay for justice or freedom with his own soul. I would like to refer to two events to demonstrate this.

First, a dispute between Bataille and Caillois in 1939.[7] Irritated by the role Bataille gave to mysticism, to drama, to expenditure, to madness and to death, Roger Caillois stressed his own attachment to knowledge: *he* was an intellectual. The Collège de sociologie was in its last days, and Caillois deplored the fact that no one had been able to put theory into practice, which should have been the intellectual's true task. Bataille's response was pitiless:

> I too 'want to see myself as an intellectual' provided that I do not take it lightly – that is, provided that I do not give the impression of being 'upright' and 'honest' by renouncing my espousal of existence in its totality, on the pretext of restricting myself to knowledge, or by letting it be imagined that it is possible scientifically to overcome 'the unpredictable course of things'.
>
> (Letter to Roger Caillois, 20 July 1939)

What is clear is this: the intellectual is obliged to lie to himself – he must tell himself that his erudition equips him to act in full possession of the facts, and that he can transform the world through it. There is in that the arrogance of the intellectuals[8] converted to history. Bataille is manifestly -humbler while at the same time more demanding, because he declares that, for his part, he cannot honestly deny 'the total man' by turning his back on the damned part [*la part maudite*] which continues to haunt humanity (in the form of drama, madness, the sacred, eroticism and violence). If the intellectual defines himself as a man who puts his knowledge at the service of history, one must denounce in him if not an impostor then at least the victim of an illusion which risks sustaining the one-dimensional character of social existence, and as a consequence the impotence in the face of the excess which in 1939 threatens to submerge Europe.

The second incident I want to mention took place after the war, when René Char undertook an enquiry into the relationship between literature and politics: an enquiry on the theme, 'Are there incompatibilities?' Replying to this question, it is to Sartre that Bataille addresses himself in order to signify his absolute resistance to the arguments for the *engagement* of intellectuals, even in the service of 'freedom through socialism' (as proposed by Sartre's manifesto, 'Situation de l'ecrivain en 1947', in 'Qu'est-ce que la littérature?'). I would like to quote part of Bataille's response:

> The incompatibility of 'literature and *engagement*, which entails obligation, is precisely that of opposites. The *engagé* intellectual never wrote anything that wasn't a lie, or that went beyond *engagement* itself.
>
> (*OC*, XII, 23)

Once more, then, it is of lying that the intellectual stands accused: he lies if he takes up his pen in the service of a cause imposed on him from the outside – which Bataille makes clear by explaining that, in his opinion, one should never write to order in the same way that one never throws oneself into action motivated by a feeling of responsibility or obligation. Writing, like personal involvement in history, appears as 'the effect of a passion, of an unquenchable desire' – never as the product of a reasoned choice, except that of resolving oneself to inauthenticity. In other words, literature is fundamentally sovereign: it doesn't serve any master, any value. That is why it is 'diabolical', and reveals the impossible in man. 'I don't doubt', writes Bataille, 'that by distancing oneself from that which reassures, we approach that divine moment which dies in us, which already possesses the strangeness of a laugh, the beauty of an anguished silence.' The reply to Sartre does not depend on circumstance, and doesn't betray any sign of personal animosity towards the author of *Un nouveau mystique*, who defined literature as 'a profession requiring an apprenticeship, sustained effort, professional conscience and a sense of responsibilities'.[9] Already in 1944, in an article in *Combat* (*OC*, XI, 12–13), Bataille denounced the propaganda literature organized by the Fascists and countered it with an ideal of inutility as well as his contempt for prejudices and commands: 'I write authentically on one condition: taking account of no one and nothing, trampling on the rules.' His conclusion was clear. The writer is the person who must reveal 'to the solitude of everyone an intangible part which no one will ever enslave'; so he teaches only one thing – 'the refusal of servility' – in this context, hatred of propaganda. 'That is why he is not on the bandwagon of the mob, and he knows how to die in solitude.'

So before, during and after the war Bataille shows himself to be equally disobedient to the idea of a reasoned *engagement* in action and anxious to make a place for that which can only elude the specialists of knowledge – the disobedience of all rules, the chaos of emotions, or if one prefers, the heterogeneity from which humanity ineluctably rises and to which it can constantly return.

If one forgets what these two incidents I have just cited show us, one can understand nothing of the way in which Bataille grabbed hold of the political history of his time. But equally, one understands nothing of the paradoxical attitude of the many men of letters and other intellectuals who launched themselves into the struggles of their time. That is what I wanted to show in my book *La politique de l'impossible*[10] with particular regard to Maurice Blanchot, Paul Nizan and the Surrealists, but also in relation to Maurice Clavel, Michel Foucault and to the

French Maoists of 1968: Sartre's theorizing of *engagement* is clearly incapable of explaining the pendulum swings from right to left or from left to right which mark the successive political alignments of many of the participants of pre-war France. It does not allow us to understand the intensity and the excesses of those who plainly feel the desire to be incorporated in the body of history more strongly than that of carrying out a political manifesto. Excess, enthusiasm, the fascination for limit-situations, for crowd phenomena, for the Apocalypse or death from which the new and the unheard-of could rise – all of this can be found in the struggles of Blanchot or the young Nizan, the Surrealists' lyricism of the uncontrollable, the revolutionary metaphors of someone like Clavel, the pro-Khomeini tendency of Michel Foucault, or the mysticism without salvation of the Maoists. All of this can be found, too, in the seduction of Sartre (in *Critique de la raison dialectique*) by the violence which gives birth to History, by those 'perfect moments' which dissolve the series in the '*groupe-en-fusion*'. In all of these examples, we are dealing with a version of the intellectual which is entirely alien to the register of responsible, exemplary *engagement*. These intellectuals do not baulk at the idea that they could slip [*déraper*], because the essential thing for them seems to be to let themselves be taken over by emotions, by inspiration and by the sublime – in short, by the irrational which fuses together the supercharged masses.

It is this attitude I call that of the emotive intellectual, and which I feel describes better than Sartre the mode in which many of the great names of contemporary literature and philosophy have been involved in history. (I have said nothing of Heidegger, but it will be clear that it is in this sense that I understand his aberrant adhesion to the Nazi madness.) Whether it was a question for them of escaping from the sentiment of decline, from disgust or from boredom, they surrendered to events as to a joyful invitation. At the high points of our recent history, they made excess their profession, evil their temptation and encouraged pathos to the extent of wishing for the Apocalypse. In short, Bataille was far from being the only one at the end of the 1930s to want to join with the elemental forces whose absence was causing democracy to wither – forces, precisely, which could spring from revolutionary sentiments, from a return to myth or from a quest for the sacred in all its forms. The emotive intellectual pursues every occasion which facilitates pathos, as though he more than anyone else felt isolated, abstracted. It is in this sense that he doesn't hesitate sometimes to celebrate the cult of irresponsibility as an antidote to the rationalism he is supposed to represent in the eyes of the world. Far from claiming to change the world, he is struggling to escape the inertia and cowardice of politics. Hence the haste shown by Bataille and before him by the followers of people like Georges Sorel to reject planning, manifestos and in general anything resembling an ideal. He wants 'being without delay', and if he abandons himself to action it is like others giving into alcohol or to lust. He wants 'to be there with no other aim than to exist', and it is this which seems most subversive – that which Bataille will soon describe as sovereignty. In any case, poles apart from what Sartre's message is in 1947, he is indifferent to any ethics of salvation and as a consequence to political ideologies, those 'secular religions' which all promise a final reconciliation. The emotive intellectual conceives his life entirely at the moment of tragedy; that is his strength or his weakness, depending upon your view. In any case, it is what will save him after the war from parading under the banner of *engagement* raised by Sartre.

Seeking to understand the intellectual context which made Bataille such a striking example of the emotive intellectual, I have given particular importance to the double reference in his work to Hegel and to Nietzsche. It seems to me that from the collision of the influences of Hegel and Nietzsche came the paradoxical result in Bataille of a will to action associated with a fatality which was demobilizing.

In the chaos of the 1930s, Bataille among many others was taken by Nietzsche, that is to say by the invitation to reopen the possibilities offered by a world without God. The appeal to danger, to adventure, to war – the joy of chaos – worked for him as a stimulant, and an entire aesthetics of pathos seems to have arisen from it. One cannot understand Bataille well if one does not take his integral Nietzscheanism seriously, if one forgets, for example, that one of his essential political gestures was to want to 'wrest Nietzsche from the grip of the Nazis' – that is to say, to preserve the symbol of the irreducibility (of heterogeneity) of thought against the totalitarian enterprise. If Nietzsche could be saved from Nazism then sovereignty is impossible: we can see that, in these terms, it was clearly for him an entirely political gesture.

But in Bataille, Nietzsche meets Hegel, and at a very early stage, as I have tried to show in my book. At the moment when Bataille went to listen to the earth-shattering lectures of Kojève, he was already studying closely the work of the 'philosopher of the system'

If the thought of Nietzsche could be an incitement to explore the virgin territory of history, to invent the myth of the future and to shatter the idols to let new possibilities appear, the teaching of Hegel was stifling. Certainly, the representation of history which appeared in Kojève's teaching was impressive: struggle, toil, anguish and death ruled in this vision, and that must have helped to make Kojève's teaching credible to a generation brought up amid the sound and fury. But in the final analysis, Kojève revealed that Hegel was right – that history had ended, that there was no longer any point in waiting for some new possibility, and that it would be better to reconcile oneself to the present. We well know the effect on Kojève's audience: on Bataille, on Queneau, on Aron and on so many others. It was an unbearable and obvious fact – there is nothing left to do. All that remains is to live, as much as possible like a man – that is to say, through art, through love, or through the game.

Of course, I am merely sketching out here the collision of these two conflicting necessities which had characterized Bataille's thought since before the war. We know how this double necessity found its expression in terms of rupture, of paradox, of anguish: how *Le bleu du ciel*, for example, transposes it into a sad hero incapable of taking quite seriously the revolution before his eyes. The famous letter to Kojève of 6 December 1937 in which Bataille expresses his exhaustion merits a long commentary, which I am unable to undertake here. In it, Bataille describes himself as an animal screaming with its foot in a trap, as a 'negativity without a cause' – that is to say, a desire to act (all action being negation in Hegel's view) which suffers from no longer being able to reach its goal because history is over. What was he to do with this surplus not foreseen by Hegel? How was he to cope with the rebellion which was by definition without prospects for the future, where the only outcome was tragedy? The only way out, said Bataille, was the impossible; that is to say that the only possible *engagement* is emotive.

Unreconciled with the world, Bataille consents to be a member of the category of intellectuals: but, convinced of the impossibility of a transparency that would be entirely satisfying, he can only consent on the level of pathos. Hence, the vertigo which seizes him, the will to wholehearted and endless action – to keep alight that flame which makes existence a rupture and a paradox. Acting for no reason at all (because all the cards have already been played), all one can do is call upon the emptiness which will henceforth sustain history. All of this is in order to try to escape from insignificance, to raise oneself to the level of the impossible. Hence, too, Bataille's tendency passionately to counter the unfinished nature of everything as the condition of human existence. In an essay in *Critique* devoted to Camus he underlines this in these terms: 'Life, the world, are nothing in my eyes if not capriciousness.' Which means that there can never be lasting satisfaction. The result is that the only conceivable good consists in never being still, and not in fighting the obstacles to a final reconciliation, as a Sartrian intellectual would do. One has reason never to be satisfied and one has reason also to abandon the illusion that there could be a remedy for this situation.

Bataille's work always gives one the impression of functioning as a 'continual fight of honour'. Hegel is right. Everything has already been done. But Hegel left to one side the essential thing on which one must wager: The open wound that is my life, the erotic desire for the other, the tears or laughter that distance us – the sacrifice which unites men beyond the discontinuities sustained by societies where reason supposedly rules. In short, action has perhaps become futile and illusory, but what still remains is to live to the full extent of those states, or rather those ecstasies which are the reverse side of and the objection to a complete rationality dreamed by the philosophers. What remains, then, speaking like Bataille, is to confront in oneself the feeling of being 'a savage impossibility', the pain of existence confined to limits which one can only desire eternally to transgress.

What I describe here fairly schematically could explain how the fascination with revolutionary action of an earlier time finally gave way to a desire for asceticism permeated with the will to live and to communicate. This transition seems to be in place during Bataille's time at the Collège, at the time of *L'expérience intérieure*, but, I stress, does not in my opinion constitute a turning point, for Bataille did not come to deny himself. Privileging action obviously meant taking existence to its boiling point or, to put it another way, experiencing one's limits and feeling the fundamental continuity which fuses individuals together. In privileging the ascetic experience, the issue is the same, even if the quest is from now on a solitary one, sheltered from the solicitation of history. The figure of the sovereign sums up this transition and gives the emotive intellectual his most striking features.

The sovereign inherits the aspiration to total existence which Bataille continually demanded as the source of his 'tattered humanism'. The figure imposes itself in his work more or less at the time when the ambition to live gets the upper hand over that of action; when Bataille himself admits to no longer being a man of action and feels the loss of all energy. So, at the advent of war, this existential figure of the sovereign lends his features to the man at the end of history, and in general to a humanity which recognizes itself as incomplete at the same time as being at the end of the line. One must add that, in the political context, the sovereign also incarnates the horror of power which blindly wants the end.

I have tried to show in my *La politique de l'impossible* in what way this sovereign differs from the citizen of a homogeneous universal state described by Kojève; and I have underlined, in this sense, that if he too escapes the pair of master–slave which determines the historical process, that is because he does not act, and is therefore responsible for no project or no historical initiative. There remains the fact that, unlike the citizen of Kojève, the sovereign remains in irreconcilability – which gives him his pathos. He is a solitary who calls on communication not as a need (which would presuppose that history was still possible) but in the mode of excess. He lives in tragic fashion the 'paradox of surplus [*excedent*]' in his own person, that is to say, the tortures of negativity without a cause. This exposes him to looking for the summits – those paroxystic experiences like so many escape routes to expenditure and communication – mystic, erotic, ecstatic; the experience of the sovereign operates at the limits; in other words like the revolution in times past it challenges all limits, invites 'the putting into play of life in all its capriciousness' (*OC*, XII, 199) and engages for that reason in a process of communal and sacramental unity.

In this sense it is clear that the term 'emotive intellectual' can still describe the man who takes on or lets himself be possessed by all the situations offered to this experience of limitlessness. If it is impossible to formulate a plan to achieve sovereignty, one can nevertheless open oneself to it by confronting the element of the impossible in oneself and in other people, that element which the tragic history of the twentieth century reveals so clearly. That is enough to explain the fact that Bataille never turned away from the unhappiness and promises of his time and that it was right to call him an intellectual. Auschwitz and Hiroshima have touched the very core of his being just as much as for people like Adorno or Aron, showing the excess which lies at the heart of humanity and polarizes it – often for the worse. In order to understand the paradoxes of sovereignty and its politics of the impossible, which consists of an approach to the world from the point of view of chaos, one asks oneself how Bataille was able to give the impression that he was a follower of Stalinism – up to the point where he was even suspected of being under the orders of Moscow, like any organic intellectual – the Bataille who nevertheless confirmed the common ground between the sovereign and the rebel.

In order to save him, on this point, from the title of 'pitiful intellectual', we must put things back in context – in January 1948, in *Critique* (reprinted in the third part of *Le part maudite*) Bataille evokes the book of Kravchenko, *J'ai choisi la liberté*. He does so after having described the Communist ideal to which he seems to subscribe: Communism aims to restore man to himself as against capitalism which alienates him. In that, it is not wrong to say that it is in the service of sovereignty, and that it works towards the whole man. The workers' movements which rally to the cause of Communism aptly express the 'taste for living without delay' (*OC*, VII, 145) which characterizes the sovereign. So it is clear that Bataille feels consistent in declaring his interest for Communism. I have mentioned elsewhere the book by Dionys Mascolo, *Le communisme: revolution et communication*, published in 1953, which shares with *La part maudite* the hope that man will be restored to himself through the realization of Marx's programme. But Bataille doesn't stop there: he knows that life in the USSR is not all roses, and that there is a long way between the ideal and the real. Before attaining sovereignty, one must accumulate, that is to say, produce. In fact, the Russia of 1917 had to give itself over to a class which despised extravagant wastage in order to preserve resources for equipping the country. Whence the need, in Bataille's view, to confront the 'paradox of a proletariat reduced to forcing itself stubbornly to renounce life in order to make life possible' (p. 147). In other words, Communism is obliged to deny itself in order to bring itself about; and the intellectual is obliged to cover up all that contradicts his beliefs while at the same time affirming that it is by contradicting his beliefs that they have the best chance of being realized. Sartre said that the intellectual is often obliged to think against himself. I don't see how Bataille could disagree!

This, then, is the context in which Kravchenko's book is discussed: Russia was working to create a surplus which would not serve consumption and joy [*jouissance*], but which was reinvested to create new means of production. Thus everyone should immediately recognize that, at that time, 'Soviet Communism (had) resolutely shut out the principle of non-productive expenditure' (p. 149). From that starting point, one can read Kravchenko's *J'ai choisi la liberté* and welcome the terrible description he gives of a universe totally subjected to the norms of work and which resorts to executions and deportations to achieve that end. Bataille doesn't claim that the dissident is a liar, but he accuses him of not understanding the inevitable character of this endless race for production without loss. Thus, as far as the author of *La part maudite* is concerned, his book is 'without theoretical value', because it does not recognize the inevitable necessity of Stalinism.

I certainly don't want to push this justification too far: Bataille certainly deserved to be criticized, and it was regrettable that (in 1948) he no longer felt inclined to denounce in Stalin the 'cold monster' which in 1932 he called upon the world to oppose in the same way as Hitler or Mussolini: 'Stalin – the shadow, the chill cast by that name alone on all revolutionary hope' (*OC*, I, 332). I think that it is now clear that the figure of the emotive intellectual which I use to describe Bataille expresses quite well the vulnerability to contradiction to which he gave in, no doubt too easily on this occasion. Another clue to this consent to paradox, which seems perverse in the context of a critique of totalitarianism, is the statement which ends an article entitled 'Le mensonge politique', still in 1948:

> Man cannot be treated as an object. And that is why he is a Communist. (But one must add: Communism can, to begin with, only complete and generalize to begin this reduction to the object, and it is for this reason that man fights Communism to the death.)
>
> (*OC*, XI, 338)

At a time when the cold war claimed to impose upon everyone the need to take sides, one must admit that Bataille's attitude could irritate and even scandalize.

I think that, to prevent 'emotive' being equated with 'impotent', 'cowardly', 'incoherent' or 'blind', it is valuable to read the third volume of *La part maudite*, begun in 1953 and published posthumously under the title *Sovereignty* (*OC*, VIII). I do not intend to comment on this work, the heart of which is devoted to a critique of Communist society, except to say that here Bataille is incontestably anti-Stalin, and that he expresses in straightforward terms a rejection of Communism, which he accuses of putting an end to non-productive prodigality. In this book, Bataille proclaims himself to be 'a stranger to Communism' – guilty, in his eyes, of abolishing all difference and forbidding sovereignty, a criticism he was already making in *Critique* in 1950: 'The Communists can neither unequivocally condemn nor tolerate the sovereign attitude, where the present life frees itself from, and loses interest in, the life to come.' In short, Stalin was able to mislead people for a while: henceforth he is seen as an impostor. He was a man of power, not a sovereign. His legitimacy lay in his army, just as the Communist Party was founded on a military organization. That has nothing to do with sovereignty, the conditions for which the emotive intellectual seeks to define: 'The sovereign in its true sense is passive, and military command on the contrary is the definitive form of activity' (*OC*, VII, 393). Bataille continues that what in his view marks the incompatibility of the sovereignty he is seeking with Stalin's regime is that 'there is in Communism a danger, which consists of the impossibility of accumulation being applied to any end except war' (p. 394). That is precisely the risk: that the surplus is invested in the expenditure of war and that it conspires to total annihilation. The awareness of this menace proves at least that Bataille has still not rid himself of a sense of responsibility; as is shown, moreover, by the criticism he addresses to Caillois – who had, in the appendix to the reprinted *L'homme et le sacre*, described war as the modern equivalent to the paroxysm of archaic celebrations: 'This interpretation is shocking, but there is no point in closing one's eyes: it lacks understanding both of the sacred and of war. And to be blunt it essentially lacks understanding of contemporary man.' Taking the form of war, the sacred would in fact threaten man with total annihilation, which would precipitate a resolution to which the sacred is, on the contrary, the definitive contradiction.

Finally, we come back to the essential point: the intellectual is emotive because he expects only the worst, without being able to be satisfied with how things are: always between revolt and resignation, never engaged, at any rate. At the end of his life Bataille seemed to me to be comparable with Adorno, who offers a view of the intellectual preoccupied with resisting the barbarization of the modern world, of the intellectual who makes a point of honour out of refusing to play the game. Here I can only point to the pages I have devoted to this comparison in *La politique de l'impossible*.[11]

I would like to end by referring to the sense of a phrase of Bataille's which is often called upon because it seems to sum up on its own the gulf that separates its author from the *engagé* intellectual like Sartre: 'The world of lovers is no less true than that of politics. It even absorbs the totality of existence, which politics cannot do.' Bataille wrote this at a time when he was battling ferociously against Fascism, and he was trying to polarize the forces which bourgeois individualism had let dissipate. That was the time of public declarations on the international crisis, and of the misdeeds of systematic pacifism. The celebration of the world of lovers has thus probably little to do with the justification for demobilization or the praise of private life. If we interpret it with reference to *Le bleu du ciel*, written at the same time, it gives a striking expression of the emotion (pathos) to which Bataille dedicated himself: namely, on the one hand, the aspiration to embrace the totality of existence – to which the worlds of art and politics and science are all equally alien; on the other, the subversion which, beyond all limits, offers the communal and sacramental unity for which humanity feels an irresistible nostalgia. In short, the strength of lovers clearly signifies the inadequacy and even imposture of the politics in which, according to Sartre, the intellectual ought to participate: it is certainly not a question of achieving power, but of keeping as close as possible to the emotion which fills the individual and then overflows into society in its first moments. At the time of *Acéphale*, that society which was secret but not plotting (in the sense of seeking to seize power), Bataille hoped in this way to get a foretaste of the mystery of the social bond, and perceive in the same gesture the sense of awakening of the Great Politics for which Nietzsche so longed.[12] Was ever an intellectual more demanding?

Translated by Alisdair McIntosh

Notes

1 *Translator's note (TN):* In French, 'Bataille, intellectuel pathétique.'
2 Cf. Maurice Blanchot, 'Les intellectuels en question. Ebauche d'une réflexion', *Le Débat*, Paris, Gallimard, 29 March, 1984.
3 Daniel Lindenberg, *Les années souterraines*, Paris, La Découverte, 1990.
4 Cf. Jean-Paul Sartre, 'Un nouveau mystique', *Situations*, I, Paris, Gallimard, 1947.
5 See Georges Bataille, *Oeuvres complètes*, VIII, Paris, Gallimard, 1976. Hereafter referred to as *OC*, followed by volume and page number.
6 *TN: politiciennes:* pejorative, connoting cynicism etc.
7 See Georges Bataille, *Lettres à Roger Caillois (4 août 1935–4 février 1959)*, selected and edited by J.-P. Le Bouler, Romillé, Editions Folle Avoine, 1987.
8 *TN: clercs:* cf. Julien Benda, *La Trahison des clercs.*
9 Jean-Paul Sartre, 'Qu' est-ce que la littérature?', *Situations*, II, Paris, Gallimard, 1948, 265.
10 Jean-Michel Besnier, *La politique de l'impossible: L'intellectuel entre révolte et engagement*, Paris, La Découverte, 1988.
11 Cf. ibid., 191–5.
12 On this point, see, for example, Karl Jaspers, *Nietzsche: Introduction a sa philosophie* (1936), Paris, Gallimard, 1950.

3 Bataille in the street

The search for virility in the 1930s

Susan Rubin Suleiman

To whom do the streets belong? This question, formulated by Susan Buck-Morss in an article on Walter Benjamin, will serve as the starting point for an itinerary among some of Bataille's writings between 1930 and 1941. The itinerary will be labyrinthine, because following Bataille is never a simple process; but also because that decade was particularly tortuous in its historical unfolding, and I want to read Bataille's texts with and against the history of the 1930s. I will argue that as the decade moved toward its disastrous close, Bataille's thinking about politics and action turned increasingly inward; and that, rather than constituting a major break in his thought, this inward turn – culminating in the publication of *L'expérience intérieure* in 1943 – offered a solution, albeit a paradoxical one, to the 'outward' questions of politics and action that had preoccupied him throughout the 1930s. As to what this has to do with virility – wait and see.

Ambiguities of the street

'Streets are the dwelling place of the collective', wrote Walter Benjamin in the late 1920s.[1] In this early note for his *Passagen-Werk*, Benjamin celebrated the street as the home of the crowd, 'eternally restless, eternally moving', where the proletariat might 'awake' to itself as a revolutionary subject. By the late 1920s, the street could claim a glorious history as the site of revolutionary uprisings all over Europe, even if, like the Paris Commune, many of those revolutions failed. Buck-Morss notes, however, that Benjamin was aware of another side to the 'restless' collective: what he called its 'unconscious, dreaming state', the state which – as became all too clear after 1933 – was most receptive to the 'political phantasmagoria of fascism' (p. 117). After 1933, any attempt to think politically about the street had to grapple with its profound ambiguity: for to its long-accrued connotations of 'progressive' revolutionary action, there now had to be added the disturbingly regressive connotations of mass psychology. Marxists had to recognize that the street was not only the place of socialist revolution leading toward a new dawn, but the place of Nazi marches and torchlight parades, exploiting the darkest human longings for violence, war and death.

The ambiguities of the street did not (do not) end there, however; for if it is the privileged site of collective action and mass manifestations, whether of the Right or Left, the street is also the site of private needs, curiosities, obsessions. 'Only those for whom poverty and vice turn the city into a landscape in which they stray from dark till sunrise know it in a way denied to me', wrote Benjamin about his sheltered youth in Berlin.[2] The penniless vagrant seeking a place to sleep, the wealthy prowler in search of erotic thrills, the bar crawler, the criminal, the prostitute, the poet – these too are denizens of the street, and what distinguishes these night people is that they move alone. Not necessarily literally, but spiritually and metaphysically, they are alone.

From street to street

It was just five o'clock and the sun was burning hot. In the middle of the street, I would have liked to speak to the others; I was lost in the middle of a blind crowd. I felt as dull and as impotent [*impuissant*] as a baby.[3]

At the corner of a street, anguish, a dirty dizzying anguish, undid me (maybe because I had just seen two furtive whores on the staircase of a toilet) ... I began to wander down those receptive streets which run from the Carrefour Poissonnière to the rue Saint-Denis. The solitude and darkness made me completely drunk. The night was naked in the deserted streets and I wanted to strip myself as naked as she: I took off my pants and hung them on my arm. I would have liked to tie the coolness of the night over my legs, a heady sense of freedom carried me forward. I felt myself growing bigger. I was holding my erect member in my hand.[4]

These two passages, taken from Bataille's erotic fictions, were written six years apart (*Le bleu du ciel*, although not published until 1957, was written in 1935; *Madame Edwarda* was written and first published in an extremely limited edition, under the pseudonym Pierre Angélique, in 1941). Both may be called secret works, unavowed by their author at the time of writing, except to his close friends. Maurice Blanchot has spoken of a 'communication diurne' and a 'communication nocturne' in Bataille's writing.[5] These two works belong to the nocturnal category.

The relation of each of these nightworks to the 'daytime works' – the political or philosophical essays – Bataille was writing around the same time is, however, interestingly different; and the two nightworks themselves are significantly different from each other, despite a certain family resemblance. This is evident in the above passages: in the first, the solitary narrator is surrounded by a crowd, but feels all the more alone and lost. The sun, way past noon, is still burning hot (we are in a southern city, Barcelona); and although he is a grown man, the narrator, Troppmann, feels reduced to the powerlessness of a baby. In the second passage, the narrator is also an anguished soul alone in the street, this time literally as well as spiritually. He is wandering in Paris, in the neighbourhood André Breton had celebrated in *Nadja* thirteen years earlier – deserted now, not the bustling place of Breton's fateful encounter. In paradoxical contrast to Troppmann, this narrator's anguish leads to a triumphant, if transgressive, virility: in the cool of the night, he walks the street half naked, holding his erect penis before him – like a lance, perhaps, or a gun.

Despite his persistent anguish and obsession with 'undoing' ('l'angoisse . . . me décomposa', 'anguish undid me'), the narrator of *Madame Edwarda* is a potent male; soon after this opening passage he will enter a brothel and 'go upstairs' like any other John. Of course, that is not all he will do, for *Madame Edwarda* is no ordinary piece of pornography. As Bataille explained years later, it is the work without which the central section of his major philosophical work, *L'expérience intérieure*, which he was writing at the same time, could not be properly understood.[6] In both works, virility is an important preoccupation, as it is in Bataille's political essays of the 1930s and in *Le bleu du ciel*, where the sexual and political imbrications of that word are explored with particular acuity.

Being Troppmann, or How not to lose your head in the noonday sun

The narrator of *Le bleu du ciel*, despite the plethora promised by his name, is suffering from a generalized impotence; it is as if the crisis he is undergoing, at once political and sexual, had ironically transformed him into 'Trop-peu-mann', not enough of a man. Sexually, he is in crisis because, having met the 'most beautiful and exciting woman' of his life, he finds himself impotent despite efforts that exhaust him (pp. 404–5). He remains impotent with this woman (whose name, emblematically, is split: Dorothea/Dirty) until close to the end of the novel, when he is finally able to make love to her on All Souls Day (*le jour des morts*) in the mud above a cemetery in Germany. But his frantic lovemaking above the tombs seems more like an exception than the attainment of a new norm – a sudden surge of power, not a steady stream.

Politically, Troppmann's crisis occurs in a European context. The year is 1934: he is in Vienna the day after the assassination of Chancellor Dollfuss by the Nazis in late July; after that in Paris, where he suffers from nightmares and falls ill before leaving for Barcelona in late September, just in time to witness the preparation of the workers' uprising – and then its crushing by government troops. (Although Troppmann does not mention it, the troops that crushed the Catalan revolt of October 1934 were led by a certain General Franco.) Finally, after leaving Barcelona (where he has been joined by his 'impossible' lover Dorothea), he and Dirty travel to Frankfurt where he watches, with a mixture of fascination and 'black irony', a parade of Nazi youth marching to military music under the leadership of a 'kid degenerately thin, with the sulky face of a fish', who moves a huge baton up and down in front of him like an obscene penis (p. 486).

Although Troppmann is evidently a Marxist and was involved in various political projects before his illness in Paris, once he is in Barcelona he is unable to muster anything but a touristic interest in the revolutionary action around him. Just before the passage I first quoted, when he walks in the crowd, reduced to solitude and impotence beneath the burning sun, we read the following sentence: 'I hated the curiosity which was pushing me to participate, from very far, in the civil war' (his participation consists in having offered his car to another French Marxist intellectual who is actively involved in the uprising). A few lines before that, we read: 'I could not deny to myself that I had a guilty conscience toward the workers. It was unimportant, it made no sense, but I was all the more depressed because my guilty conscience toward Lazare was of the same order' (p. 448). Lazare is yet another French Marxist intellectual in Barcelona, a young woman who simultaneously fascinates and repels Troppmann because of her political passion and authority – and also because he finds her sexually unattractive, an ugly 'dirty virgin' in contrast to the beautiful, exciting Dirty. (The model for Lazare is said to be Simone Weil, whom Bataille frequented in left-wing circles around 1934.)

Troppmann's association of the workers with Lazare evokes a crucial earlier scene that occurred while he was still in Paris. Just before falling ill, but already in a feverish state, Troppmann visits Lazare in her apartment, which she shares with her stepfather, a professor of philosophy. The discussion centres on what Melou, the stepfather, calls the 'anguishing dilemma' confronting intellectuals once they have admitted 'the collapse of socialist hopes': 'Should we isolate ourselves in silence? Or should we, on the contrary, join the workers in their last acts of resistance, thus accepting an implacable and fruitless death [*une mort implacable et stérile*]?' Troppmann, in a state of shock, feels unable to respond. Finally, he asks Lazare to show him the toilet, where he proceeds to 'piss for a long time' and tries to vomit by shoving two fingers down his throat. Slightly relieved, he comes back and confronts Lazare and Melou: if they really believe the working class is 'screwed' (*foutue*), why are they still 'Communists ... or socialists ... or whatever?' Lazare answers: 'Come what may, we must be on the side of the oppressed.' This infuriates Troppmann, who thinks to himself: 'Sure enough, she's a Christian!' The stepfather's reply, though not Christian, is also in the idealist register. He compares himself to a peasant working on his land despite the gathering storm: stubborn, and at the same time sublime, the peasant 'will raise his arms for nothing toward the sky ... waiting for the lightning to strike'. Troppmann, seeing in Melou's own upraised arm 'the perfect image of a frightful despair', feels ready to cry and rushes away (pp. 422–5).

Returning home, he falls seriously ill; but first he has a terrifying dream: on a stage he sees a corpse transformed into an armoured marble statue of Minerva, 'upright and warlike (*dressée et agressive*) beneath her helmet' (p. 419). Brandishing a marble scimitar (*cimeterre*), the 'crazed' Minerva, suddenly a giant, notices him in the 'alley' (*ruelle*) from where he is watching:

> I had then become small, and when she noticed me she saw that I was afraid ... Suddenly, she came down and threw herself on me, twirling her macabre weapon crazily, with increasing vigour. It was about to come down: I was paralyzed with horror.
>
> (*OC*, III, 420)

Not the least interesting thing about this dream is that Troppmann recounts and interprets it *before* he recounts his meeting with Lazare and her stepfather, even though he subsequently makes clear that it occurred on the night *after* that meeting (p. 420: 'that meeting resembled a nightmare, even more depressing than that dream, which I was to have the following night.'). Giving us a premature interpretation, Troppmann sees only his sexual dilemma in the dream: 'I understood that, in this dream, Dirty, having become crazy and at the same time dead, had taken on the clothes and the aspect of the Commander's statue' (p. 420). Alluding to the Don Juan theme with which the novel began (a two-page monologue by an unidentified voice who could be Don Juan, evoking his encounter with the Commander in the cemetery

– *cimetière/cimeterre*), Troppmann offers an exclusively Oedipal interpretation of the dream, and consequently of his own impotence. A
desired woman who is at the same time a vengeful father is a powerful
deterrent to sexual performance.

This psychosexual interpretation, although highly plausible, fore-
closes another, more obviously political interpretation that Troppmann
would have been obliged to make if he had recounted the dream in
its chronological place, *after* the visit with Lazare and Melou. By
deferring his telling of the political discussion until after the telling
and interpretation of the dream, Troppmann avoids having to notice
that the virgin goddess who seeks to castrate him evokes the 'dirty
virgin' Lazare as much as the sexual, silken Dirty. Lazare and her
stepfather (the Commander, Zeus, Father-God?) have foretold the
'implacable and fruitless death' of intellectuals who support the
working class. If the working class is 'foutue', it will be the revolution,
not a dead Commander's statue, that will kill Troppmann, as well as
anyone else who may wish to 'join the workers in their last acts of
resistance'..

Note that the anxiety of the Oedipal/Don Juan plot, which Troppmann
sees in the dream, is not rendered irrelevant by the political interpretation; to propose the sexual anxiety as the only one, however, as
Troppmann does, is to deny the 'other story', the story of political
uprisings and their failure. Walking the streets of Barcelona just before
the workers' insurrection (which he knows is doomed to fail), Troppmann tells himself that he cannot deny his feelings of guilt toward the
workers and toward Lazare – for Lazare, as is made clear in an earlier
scene, has the courage of her 'Christian' idealist convictions, even to the
point of being willing to die for them. Troppmann, on the other hand,
cowers before the upraised arm; and beneath the burning sun, he feels
as helpless as a baby. On the day the insurrection begins and the sound
of machine-guns and cannons fills the air, he does not venture into the
street, but stays in his hotel room and watches from the window. Dirty,
who has joined him and to whom he still cannot make love, goads him
ironically: 'If only you could lose your head!' ('Si seulement tu pouvais
perdre la tête!' – p. 477).

Decapitation is a symbolic castration, if Freud is to be believed;
but Troppmann is already symbolically castrated, so his decapitation
would be redundant. (Troppmann, incidentally, was the name of a
mass murderer beheaded in Paris in 1870.) Unless, of course, 'losing
his head' *restored* his potency, according to that characteristically
Bataillian equation which states that a violent loss of control is the
precondition of *jouissance*, a radical letting go. Bataille would start

to explore the political and philosophical connotations of potency as headlessness the year after writing *Le bleu du ciel*, when he founded the secret society of *Acéphale*. But in *Le bleu du ciel*, the male character who 'loses his head' is simply killed, not made potent: Michel, the revolutionary intellectual to whom Troppmann offered his car, is spurned in love, goes out into the street and is shot. The woman who spurned him blames herself and Troppmann: 'I was horrible . . . The way you were with me . . . he lost his head' (pp. 478–9). But Troppmann had already predicted Michel's death much earlier (p. 448), independently of love: 'If there's an uprising, he'll be in the moon, as usual. He'll get himself stupidly killed.' ('Dans une émeute, il sera comme il est d'ordinaire, dans la lune, il se fera bêtement tuer.')

Michel, being 'in the moon', gets killed in the noonday sun. But I am tempted to say *by* the noonday sun for, as Leo Bersani has noted, there is a powerful network of associations in the novel between the sun and murderous violence.[7] Troppmann, recalling a childhood memory of seeing slaughtered sheep in a butcher's van moving in the 'blazing sun' ('en plein soleil'), associates the sun with red, and blood. In the passage I first quoted, the burning sun seems to be at least partly responsible for his feeling of infantile powerlessness. This configuration is repeated later, when Troppmann sees a 'va-nu-pieds', a 'man in rags', staring at him in the street: 'He had an insolent air, in the sun, a solar air [*un aspect solaire*] . . . I would have liked to have that frightful air, that solar air like him, instead of resembling a child who never knows what he wants' (p. 468).

Troppmann's Oedipal anxieties are closely related, as his nightmare in Paris suggested, to his political anxieties. In both cases, the son's virility in the face of a powerful, castrating father (sun) is at stake. Bersani, commenting on this link, writes: 'Bataille suggests that the political is always related to the sexual, but their interconnectedness implies no priority on one side or the other.'[8] Bataille appeals to Bersani because he refuses 'the culture of redemption', a theory of sublimation that opposes the 'high' realm of the political to the 'low' realm of sex.

Bersani offers a powerful reading of *Le bleu du ciel*, but his framework is more philosophical than historical (despite his essay's title, 'Literature and History'). He does not ignore the novel's concern with politics, and comments perceptively on the closing scene of the marching Nazi youth observed by Troppmann. His conclusions, however, are phrased in general and somewhat abstract terms:

For Bataille, a false perspective on Nazism gives an account of it … cut off from the desiring energies that produced it … In its avoidance of this reifying seriousness about History and Politics, Bataille's art of vertiginous replications is designed to make us feel that we are already everywhere in history, and that an ethos of political engagement is grounded in the illusion that we have not produced the violence against which we struggle.

(p. 120)

As a philosophical summing up that emphasizes the ambiguity of Bataille's thought (his 'vertiginous replications' allow the sun, for example, to be associated with both the workers' uprising and the marching Nazis), this strikes me as right. What Bersani's reading overlooks is the specific historical moment in which *Le bleu du ciel* was written, and the concrete problems of action and politics that Bataille was trying, both in that novel and in his public life and writings of the 1930s, to work through. He was not only trying to arrive at philosophical truths during those years; he was also trying to *act* in a specific historical situation that looked, after 1933, more and more bleak. The scene between Troppmann and Lazare and Melou, which Bersani's reading ignores, is not an abstract discussion – it presents the dilemma faced by anti-Fascist and Marxist intellectuals (especially those not enrolled in the Communist Party) throughout the 1930s, and with particular urgency from 1933 on. Troppmann's sense of powerlessness must be understood in a historical context, which was also that of Bataille. Bataille's biographer, Michel Surya, speculates that *Le bleu du ciel* remained unpublished in 1935 because it was in too much contradiction with Bataille's political activities and writings at the time:

> If it had been published, the book would have created a scandal: one could hardly find a more violent contestation, a more sarcastic questioning of the very thing Bataille was known for in Paris … as a militant of the extreme left, convinced of the urgent necessity to fight the progressive rise of fascism with all the intellectual forces at his disposal.[9]

What is required, then, is to read *Le bleu du ciel* in the context of Bataille's political and philosophical writings of the 1930s. Rather than attempting a general overview of those writings,[10] I will follow a single thread: Bataille's uses of the word 'virility' in some of the major texts. This choice is justified not only by Bataille's continuing preoccupation with virility – both the word and the concept – but also by the fact that so many other political writers of the 1930s were fixated on it, regardless of their ideological allegiance. From Malraux's celebration of 'virile fraternity' to Drieu La Rochelle's glorification of 'the great white virile God', virility figured as an absolute value to writers of the Left as of the Right. The question was, how to attain virility – indeed, how exactly to define it?

My contention is that Bataille moved during the 1930s from an outward, action-oriented definition of virility to an inward one, and that this move was intimately related to the evolution of European politics during that decade; furthermore, that it acquired a particular relevance and resonance in Nazi-occupied France.

From virile action to virile inaction

For 'virilité' (from Latin *vir*, 'man'), the *Petit Robert* dictionary gives the following definitions: 'Set of attributes and physical and sexual characteristics of man; capacity for generation, sexual potency in man; virile, energetic character. Synonym: vigour; Antonyms: impotence, coldness.' For the adjective 'virile,' the dictionary gives: 'Characteristic of man; male, masculine; characteristic of the adult man; possessing the moral traits attributed especially to man: active, energetic, courageous. Antonyms: effeminate, feminine.' Virility is thus a moral, political and sexual virtue: to be virile is to be active, energetic and courageous in matters private and public, and to be potent sexually. The contrary of virility is powerlessness, or else femininity. In this equation, femininity carries a negative charge, although it is not clear whether femininity in general or only femininity in men (effeminateness) is considered negative. The question may be academic, however; whether in men or generally, femininity is opposed to the manly virtues of courage, energy, effectiveness. Bataille emphasizes the sexual and moral connotations of virility in 'The "lugubrious game"' (1929), devoted to Dali's painting by that name, and in 'Sacrificial mutilation and the severed ear of Vincent Van Gogh' (1930). In another early essay, 'Le lion châtré' ('The castrated lion', 1929), a polemic against André Breton, his attack on Breton's lack of virility is both political and sexual.[11] But it was in another polemic against Breton, the now famous 'old mole' essay written around 1930 (though not published until 1968), that Bataille fully exploited the political implications of the word. The essay was written at a time when many European intellectuals were becoming critically concerned with political action, prompted by the rise of Fascism and a general historical unease.

On the very first page of the 'old mole' essay, one finds the following statement: 'To whatever extent the unhappy bourgeois has maintained a human vulgarity, a certain taste for virility, disaffection with his own class quickly turns into stubborn hatred.'[12] That the democratic bourgeois regime lacks virility, and prevents men from fulfilling theirs, will be one of Bataille's themes throughout these years. In the 'old mole' essay, his solution is classically Marxist (as is the image of the old mole): the bourgeois intellectual who holds his manhood dear must throw in his lot with the lower classes. Bataille even criticizes Nietzsche, one of his personal heroes, for not having seen that

> there is only one solution to the difficulties that gave play to the violence of his language, namely, the renunciation of all moral values associated with class superiority, the renunciation of all that deprives 'distinguished' men of the virility of the proletarian [*la virilité prolétarienne*].
>
> (*Visions of Excess*, p. 37)

Did Bataille assume that all workers were more 'virile' by definition, the way some white people mythologize the sexual prowess of black men? He does not say. In fact, he says very little in the essay about the virile proletariat. What preoccupies him is less the desired end than its possible failure – not virility, but castration. 'The sun ... castrates all that enters into conflict with it (Icarus, Prometheus, the Mithraic bull)' (p. 34). After this, the adjective 'Icarian' recurs insistently; Bataille uses it to designate all enterprises, from revolutionary idealism to Surrealism, that seek to soar 'toward the heavens from which it seems it will be easy to curse this base world (but from which we know above all with what derisive ease a man is cast)' (p. 42). As the parenthetical remark emphasizes, the 'Icarian' adventurer is naively unaware that he risks losing his head – or else, he is aware, but is driven by a pathological desire for 'a brutal and immediate punishment', an unconscious 'réflexe de castration' (p. 39; *OC*, I, 103).

Taking this essay into account, one understands why Troppmann is outraged by Lazare's idealism and Melou's sublime imagery. If the proletariat is 'foutue', as they claim, then proletarian uprisings too can become Icarian adventures, and the bourgeois intellectual who counted on proletarian virility had better think again. Can even the old mole be castrated? That was not a possibility Bataille entertained in 1930, but by 1935, when he wrote *Le bleu du ciel*, things had changed. The biggest change was the rise of the German eagle.

The eagle as a sexual and political symbol of virility occupies a crucial place in the 'old mole' essay, making his appearance in two paragraphs that are worth quoting at length:

The eagle's hooked beak, which cuts all that enters into competition with it and cannot be cut, suggests its sovereign virility. Thus the eagle has formed an alliance with the sun, which castrates all that enters into conflict with it ... Politically the eagle is identified with imperialism, that is, with the unconstrained development of individual authoritarian power, triumphant over all obstacles ...

Revolutionary idealism tends to make of the revolution an eagle above eagles, a *supereagle* striking down authoritarian imperialism, an idea as radiant as an adolescent eloquently seizing power for the benefit of Utopian enlightenment. This detour naturally leads to the failure of the revolution and, with the help of military Fascism, the satisfaction of the elevated need for idealism. The Napoleonic epic represents its least ridiculous development: the castration of an Icarian revolution, shameless imperialism exploiting the revolutionary urge.

(*Visions of Excess*, p. 34)

Although Bataille establishes his distance from 'authoritarian imperialism', he recognizes the appeal of the eagle as a symbol of power, and is willing to grant Napoleon epic stature despite his 'castration' of the French Revolution. With the rise of the German eagle after 1933, Bataille admitted not only his own attraction to its power, but analysed, in extremely persuasive terms, the psychological appeal of Fascism as a mass movement.[13]

What to do? Interestingly (or, one might argue, tragically), it did not occur to Bataille or to other intellectuals on the revolutionary Left to start defending the bourgeois democracies against the threat of Fascism. The democracies were in any case 'foutue' and ought to be, as far as Bataille was concerned (in this, he and Breton shared the same view). The solution lay elsewhere: the proletarian revolution had to appropriate the arms of its enemy and 'use for the liberation of the exploited the weapons that had been forged to enchain them more'.[14] The proletarian revolution had to learn how to 'exalt' men and move them in and into the street as the Fascists did, but in order to achieve different aims. This was the argument of Bataille's 1933 essay (published less than a year after Hitler became Chancellor of the Reich), 'The psychological structure of Fascism'. It was also the argument he developed, in various forms, during the brief attempt to forge a dissident Marxist militant movement (outside the French Communist Party) that reconciled him temporarily with Breton and the Surrealists: Contre-Attaque, which lasted roughly from October 1935 to May 1936. Bataille, alone or in collaboration, wrote most of the tracts and manifestos distributed by the group, and spoke at several public meetings. The idea of a 'counter-attack' and common action on the Left had gained momentum in France in early 1934, in response to the Fascist riots of 6 February. The Popular Front, uniting Socialists, Communists and Radicals, was a counter-attack too but, in Bataille's eyes, it was too timid and parliamentary. Contre-Attaque, as Bataille saw it, was a virile Popular Front, a Popular Front with (to put it crudely but aptly) balls.

In the hortatory essay entitled 'Popular Front in the Street' (first given as a speech at a Contre-Attaque rally in November 1935), Bataille used the sexual vocabulary quite consciously. Parliamentary democracy offered nothing other than

> the horror of human impotence. We want to confront this horror directly. We address ourselves to the direct and violent drives which … can contribute to the surge of power that will liberate men from the absurd swindlers who lead them … The will to be done with impotence implies, in our eyes, scorn for this phrase-mongering.[15]

Enough words, actions are what count. Actions in the street:

> What drives the crowds into the street is the emotion directly aroused by striking events in the atmosphere of a storm, it is the contagious emotion that, from house to house, from suburb to suburb, suddenly turns a hesitating man into a frenzied being [*un homme hors de soi*].
>
> (p. 162)

Jean-Michel Besnier, commenting on 'Popular Front in the street' and more generally on this phase in Bataille's thought, suggests that, despite the call to arms in the street, Bataille was always more interested in a certain state of exaltation than in political action; according to Besnier, Bataille's politics during the 1930s was 'a politics of the impossible which underpins revolutionary action while it resolutely rejects the goal of a takeover of political power'.[16] I agree with Besnier that Bataille's projected politics was a 'politics of the impossible' for many reasons, not the least of which was the problem of being a non-Communist revolutionary intellectual in the 1930s; but I disagree about the question of political power *as Bataille conceived it at the time of Contre-Attaque.* His writings during that brief period suggest that he did envisage a 'takeover of political power', including the use of authority and discipline. To be sure, he qualified the meanings of those terms: they were not those of 'father, fatherland, boss' (*père, patrie, patron*), the basis of the 'old patriarchal society'. Rather, the new revolutionary discipline would displace the 'servile discipline of Fascism' and the authority of a single master would be replaced by 'ALL acting as MASTERS'.[17]

These rousing public writings could hardly be further from the vacillations and impotence of Troppmann. It was as if, in reaction to the anxieties and premonitions expressed in *Le bleu du ciel*, Bataille sought to affirm, by means of his own 'surge of power', the possibilities of virile revolutionary action. Toward the beginning of 'Popular Front in the street' he evokes the mass demonstration of 12 February 1934 (the Left's response to the riots of 6 February) which, according to him, marked the real beginning of the Popular Front:

> Most of us, comrades, were in the street that day and can recall the emotion that overcame us when the Communist marchers, coming out of the rue des Pyrénées, turned into the Cours de Vincennes and took up the entire width of the street: this massive group was preceded by a line of a hundred workers, shoulder to shoulder and arm in arm, marching with unprecedented slowness and singing the *Internationale*. Many among you, no doubt, can remember the huge old bald worker, with a reddish face and heavy white moustache, who walked slowly, one step at a time, in front of that moving human wall, holding high a red flag.
>
> (*Visions of Excess*, p. 163)

The huge old bald worker holding the red flag strikes me as Bataille's hopeful (illusory, impossible?) counter-image to the closing figure of *Le bleu du ciel*, the 'degenerately skinny' Nazi kid manipulating his huge baton–penis. However, the black irony of that novel, rather than the red rhetoric of the Popular Front essay, proved to be premonitory. By the time the essay was published (in the first and only issue of *Cahiers de Contre-Attaque*, May 1936) Contre-Attaque as a movement was dead, and there were not many to mourn it – not even Bataille, who probably realized that the programme of mass armed action in the street, appropriating the means of Fascism for other ends, had come dangerously close to Fascism *tout court*.[18] The Popular Front, although triumphant at the polls in 1936, would soon be caught up in parliamentary politics and would fall a year later. In March 1936, Hitler occupied the Rhineland; in July, Franco's troops launched their assault against the Spanish Republic.

What was a man to do?

By the summer of 1936, Bataille had founded the secret society of *Acéphale*, whose rituals, unknown in their details to this day, were practised not in the street but in an ancient forest.[19] The public side of *Acéphale* was a journal by the same name, written largely by Bataille, published irregularly from 1937 to 1939; and the Collège de sociologie, founded by Bataille and Roger Caillois in 1937 and active until July 1939. Denis Hollier has characterized the Collège as an attempt at 'sociological activism' and Caillois later claimed that Bataille's ambition for the Collège was much more than that of a 'groupe de recherche'.[20] Yet there is no doubt that by the time he founded the Collège, Bataille's idea of action had little to do with politics in any ordinary sense, or even in the extraordinary sense of Contre-Attaque. If one can speak of activism as part of his ambition for the Collège de sociologie, it was an activism founded in ritual and myth, unfolding between the 'sacred space' and the bedroom: 'The world of lovers is no less *true* than that of politics', he wrote in one of his key texts for the Collège.[21] Significantly, the essay begins with a note stating that his purpose is to show how 'the results of sociology can appear as responses to the most virile concerns [*des réponses aux soucis les plus virils*]'. He is still preoccupied with virility, but virility has become less a matter of action than of 'total existence', the opposite of 'acting, depicting, or measuring' (p. 228).

We see here one manifestation of the inward turn in Bataille's thought. Some would argue that his thought had been 'inward' even at the height of his politically activist period and that it is artificial to impose 'turns' on it. Bataille's chief preoccupations and obsessions endure from one end of his writing to the other; in that sense, he is a singularly single-minded thinker. Yet I would insist that no thought exists outside history. Between the defeat of the Republicans in Spain (foreseeable by the spring of 1938) and the Nazi Occupation of France, the problem of virile action continued to preoccupy Bataille; but the definition of virile action shifted.

One of the essays he wrote for the last issue of *Acéphale*, 'The practice of joy before death' ('La pratique de la joie devant la mort', published in June 1939), prefigures some of the major themes Bataille would elaborate in the grim autumn of 1941, in *Madame Edwarda* and *L'expérience intérieure*:

> He alone is happy who, having experienced vertigo to the point of trembling in his bones, to the point of being incapable of measuring the extent of his fall, suddenly finds the unhoped-for strength to turn his agony into a joy capable of freezing and transfiguring those who meet it.[22]

Whatever battles Bataille might have envisaged, a few years earlier, as unfolding in the street, have now been transferred exclusively to the interior, both spatially and existentially. Bataille uses (for the first time, or close to it) the word 'mysticism' to describe his preoccupation – specifying that although his vocabulary may be Christian, his thought is not: 'The mystical existence of the one whose "joy before death" has become inner violence can never attain the satisfying beatitude of the Christian who gives himself a foretaste of eternity' (p. 236). Unlike the Christian mystic, the man of 'inner violence' is not an ascetic: 'those who would be afraid of nude girls or whisky would have little to do with "joy before death". Only a shameless, indecent saintliness can lead to a sufficiently happy *loss of self*' (p. 237).

From here to the brothel of *Madame Edwarda*, where the man of inner violence meets the whore in whom he will recognize the indecent saintliness he calls God, it is but a step.

Virility: it's how you look at it

The inward turn in Bataille's thought became more pronounced as the outward events around him became more violent. By the autumn of 1941, when he wrote *Madame Edwarda* and began working on 'Le supplice', the Nazis were fully established in Paris, executing hostages, rounding up Jews and carrying on other 'routine' activities (such as dynamiting synagogues).[23] Bataille's inward turn provided a philosophical solution, albeit a paradoxical one, to the political and existential problems he had been struggling with since the early 1930s, chief among them that of effective, virile action.

Why was the solution paradoxical? Let me, going fast, cite two passages from 'Le supplice' and suggest the outlines of a commentary. The first deals with the problem of virility, though not as it relates to politics; rather, to poetry:

To go to the end of man, it is necessary, at a certain point, to no longer suffer fate but to seize it [*non pas subir mais forcer le sort*]. The opposite, poetic nonchalance, the passive attitude, the distaste for a virile, decisive reaction – that is literary decadence (pretty pessimism). Rimbaud's damnation: he had to turn his back on the possible he attained, in order to rediscover a power of decision intact in himself. The access to the extreme has as its condition the hatred not of poetry, but of poetic femininity (absence of decisiveness, the poet is woman, invention and words violate him). I oppose to poetry the experience of the possible. It is less a matter of contemplation than of laceration [*déchirement*]. Yet it is a 'mystical experience' I am speaking about. (Rimbaud tried it, but without the tenacity he later put into trying to amass a fortune. To his experience, he gave a poetic solution; in general, he did not know the simplicity that affirms – half-baked schemes in some letters – he chose feminine evasiveness, aesthetics, the involuntary and uncertain mode of expression.)[24]

One of the difficulties in interpreting this passage (besides its maddeningly paratactic style) is that Bataille's meanings for crucial words like 'poetic', 'poetry' and 'possible' vary not only from this text to others, but also, occasionally, from sentence to sentence. What I offer, therefore, is a necessarily tentative reading, although I firmly believe in it.

Rimbaud obsesses Bataille because he gave up poetry for action. Bataille, on the contrary, is trying to elaborate a mode of experience and a kind of action ('going to the extreme') that will not necessarily reject poetry, only the 'feminine' aspects of poetry. Opposed to 'feminine evasiveness' is the virile man who seeks the extreme, the 'experience of the possible' – and also seeks to find a language to express that experience. One might expect Bataille to mock the merely 'possible' in the name of the extreme, but in this passage the 'experience of the possible' is itself envisaged as an acceding to the extreme, in both language and existence. Rimbaud's 'damnation' was that he could not envisage, or practise, a poetry other than a 'feminine' one; in order to 'rediscover a [masculine] power of decision' in himself, he had to give up writing.

Remembering the anguished protagonist of *Madame Edwarda* and his broken, fragmented style of writing (the style of 'Le supplice' is no less shattered), one might ask where is his 'power of decision', his 'simplicity which affirms'? To ask that, however, is to misunderstand Bataille profoundly – for the chief characteristic of the inner experience is not visible action, but *déchirement*, an inner sundering. But how, one may ask, does this sundering differ from 'poetic femininity', the 'passive attitude' of the poet who is violated by words? The difference is that the hero of the inner experience *actively engages himself* in 'la déchirure'. He is dominant and virile (Bataille will later say, 'sovereign') because he actively chooses his sundering.

But seen from the outside, how can one distinguish between a hero of inner experience and an ordinary loser, or a wealthy prowler in search of erotic thrills? *Précisément*, one cannot. Seen from the outside, the protagonist of *Madame Edwarda* is just one more client with a few weird tastes, like engaging in oral sex in public or getting a kick out of watching his girl make it in the back of a taxi with a burly proletarian cabbie. It is only because he *writes* his inner experience that we know the philosophical stakes involved in his eroticism, know the anguish he is suffering, and know too that he dominates his suffering by the act of engaging himself in it. Bataille thus redefines the *poète maudit* in sovereign terms, and implicitly claims that status. Where Rimbaud stumbled, abandoning poetry for virile action (or what he considered as such), Bataille has pursued the quest, practising virile action in the inner experience and in its writing. Between gun-running in Abyssinia and the inner experience, which is the more virile?

The second passage I want to comment on is very brief: 'I arrive at this position: the inner experience is the opposite of action. Nothing more' (p. 59). Is the inner experience passivity (after all), or the boredom of the leisure class? No. Once again, it is a matter of understanding a paradoxical negation as affirmation: when Bataille says 'action', he means 'project' ('"Action" is totally dependent on the project'); and when he says 'project', he means the *'deferral of living to later'*, *'la remise de l'existence à plus tard'* (p. 59, his emphasis). The man who refuses 'action' (Bataille places the word in quotation marks to indicate his distance from its conventional definition, linked to the notion of project) is therefore the only one who really lives in the present: 'The inner experience is the denunciation of respite [*la dénonciation de la trêve*], it is being [*l'être*] without delay.' The principle of inner experience, finally – paradoxically – comes down to this: 'to exit by means of a project from the realm of the project' (p. 60). It is not difficult to understand why Sartre, reviewing *L'expérience intérieure* at its publication in 1943, found it totally 'unusable' – 'cette expérience inutilisable'.[25] The philosopher of the project *par excellence*, Sartre saw in Bataille's book only the portrait of a paradoxical individual (he calls him a madman), not a programme.

Viewing *L'expérience intérieure* historically, one could arrive at a quite negative judgement: in the France of 1941, did not the inner experience, for all its lacerations, offer the writer obsessed with virility the comforts of an alibi? Why try to resist, why act in the street, when you could be just as virile sitting at home, or in a brothel, experiencing the extreme on the inside? This, however, is no doubt too simple a view. Besides, if the inner experience excused one from 'vulgar' action such as joining the Resistance, it could also protect one from active collaboration with the enemy. Bypassing the opposition between resistance and collaboration, as he bypassed in his fiction the opposition between 'ordinary' masculinity and femininity (the protagonist of *Madame Edwarda* has more in common with the ecstatic whore than with the burly taxi driver), Bataille may have been working toward a salutary third term. Years later, in the beginning of the cold war, when the reigning opposition was between the United States and the Soviet Union, he would propose the third term of neutrality – recognizing that 'neutrality means, without any doubt, the refusal of all action, a resolute distance from all political undertakings'.[26]

Bataille's paradoxes make him interesting, in his political theories as in his pornography. It has been claimed that his attitude toward Fascism was troublingly equivocal. Dénis Hollier, confronting that claim, has argued on the contrary that the equivocal nature of Bataille's thought saved him from Fascism: 'A little equivocation gets close to fascism, a lot of it moves away from it.'[27] That is because Fascism, like other political ideologies, abhors the equivocal.

Because I am persuaded by this argument, it is in the name of equivocation that I fault Bataille, finally, for his obsession with virility – the word as much as the concept. As a concept, virility took shifting forms in Bataille's thought. His continued use of the word, however, locked him into values and into a sexual politics that can only be called conformist, in his time and ours. Rhetorically, 'virility' carries with it too much old baggage. Bataille's male protagonists may be sexually equivocal, possessing feminine traits and female soulmates; but his rhetoric of virility does not follow them.

Notes

1 Quoted in Susan Buck-Morss, 'The flâneur, the sandwichman and the whore: The politics of loitering,' *New German Critique*, 39, autumn 1986, 114. The question about the streets is on the same page of this very rich essay. Hereafter, page references are cited in parentheses in the text.
2 *One-Way Street and Other Writings*, London, NLB, 1979. Quoted in Buck-Morss, 114.
3 Georges Bataille, *Le bleu du ciel*, in *Oeuvres complètes* (*OC*), III, Paris, Gallimard, 1971, 449. Further page references to this edition are given in parentheses in the text. Unless otherwise stated, all translations from the French are my own.
4 Bataille, *Madame Edwarda*, in *OC*, III, 19.
5 Maurice Blanchot, *La communauté inavouable*, Paris, Minuit, 1983, 39.
6 See *OC*, III, 491.
7 Leo Bersani, 'Literature and History' in *The Culture of Redemption*, Cambridge, Mass., Harvard University Press, 1990.
8 Ibid., 117. Hereafter, page references are cited in parentheses in the text.
9 Michel Surya, *Georges Bataille: La mort à l'oeuvre*, Paris, Librairie Séguier, 1987, 222.
10 For comprehensive studies, see Jean-Michel Besnier, *La politique de l'impossible*, Paris, La Découverte, 1988 and Francis Marmande, *Georges Bataille politique*, Lyon, Presses Universitaires de Lyon, 1985. As always with Bataille, the interpretations of his positions vary considerably.

44 *Susan Rubin Suleiman*

11 These essays are in *OC*, I; the first two have been published in English in Bataille, *Visions of Excess: Selected Writings, 1927–39*, ed. and trans. Allan Stoekl, with Carl R. Lovitt and Donald M. Leslie, Jr, Minneapolis, University of Minnesota Press, 1985.

12 Bataille, 'The "Old Mole" and the prefix *sur* in the words *Surhomme* and *Surrealist*' in *Visions of Excess*, 32. Hereafter, page references are cited in parentheses in the text.

13 'The psychological structure of Fascism' (1933) in *Visions of Excess*. Bataille's relation to Fascism has been much discussed lately (see note 27). He himself, in his 'Autobiographical note' written in 1958, noted his 'fascination' with Fascism in the mid-1930s (*OC*, VII).

14 Bataille, 'Vers la révolution réelle' in *OC*, I, 422.

15 Bataille, 'Popular Front in the street' in *Visions of Excess*, 161–2. Hereafter, page references to this essay are cited in parentheses in the text.

16 Jean-Michel Besnier, 'Georges Bataille in the 1930s: A politics of the impossible', *Yale French Studies*, 78 (1990), 180. See also Besnier, *La politique de l'impossible*, 114.

17 See '"Contre-Attaque": Appel à l'action' in *OC*, I, 396. The refusal of 'the old patriarchal society' is in '"Contre-Attaque": La patrie et la famille' (leaflet advertising a meeting), *OC*, I, 393. All of Bataille's *Contre-Attaque* texts are in *OC*, I, 379–432.

18 Bataille suggests this in his 'Autobiographical note', *OC*, VII.

19 Many rumours have circulated about the secret rituals of *Acéphale* in the forest of Saint-Nom-la-Bretêche. For a reliable account, see Surya, *Georges Bataille*, 253–8.

20 See *Le Collège de sociologie*, ed. Denis Hollier, Paris, Gallimard, 1979, 31.

21 'The sorcerer's apprentice' in *Visions of Excess*, 229–32. This essay was first published in 1938 in the *Nouvelle Revue Française* as part of an introduction to the Collège de sociologie, along with essays by Caillois and Michel Leiris. Reprinted in *Le Collège de sociologie* and in *OC*, I, 523–37.

22 'The practice of joy before death' in *Visions of Excess*, 236. Hereafter, page numbers are cited in parentheses in the text.

23 Bataille was living in Paris throughout 1941; he wrote *Madame Edwarda* in September–October. In late September, three Communist deputies were executed, as were a number of hostages in reprisal against the Resistance. The infamous 'Jewish exhibition', *Le Juif et la France*, organized by a Nazi-sponsored Institute with the support of the Vichy Government, opened in late September. On 3 October, six Paris synagogues were dynamited. All these dates are cited by Michel Surya, *Georges Bataille*, 501–2. See also Michael Marrus and Robert Paxton, *Vichy France and the Jews*, New York, Basic Books, 1981.

24 Bataille, *L'expérience intérieure* in *OC*, V, 53. Hereafter, page references are cited in parentheses in the text.

25 J.-P. Sartre, 'Un nouveau mystique' in *Situations*, I, Paris, Gallimard, 1947, 187.

26 'Du sens d'une neutralité morale dans la guerre russo-américaine'. Review of Raymond Aron's *Le grand schisme*, *Critique*, 1948; reprinted in *OC*, XI, 374n.

27 Denis Hollier, 'On equivocation (between literature and politics)', *October*, 55 (winter 1990), 12. Hollier cites an essay by Carlo Ginzburg which accuses Bataille of being dangerously close to Fascist and Nazi ideologies; a similar criticism is found in Daniel Lindenberg's *Les années souterraines*, Paris, La Découverte, 1990. In terms of Zeev Sternhell's analysis, Bataille could qualify as one of the many French intellectuals of the 1930s who were 'fascists without knowing it': Sternhell, *Ni droite ni gauche: L'idéologie fasciste en France*, Paris, Seuil, 1983, 311. Bernard Sichère's two-part article, 'Bataille et les fascistes', *La Règle du jeu*, 8 and 9 (September 1992 and January 1993), is somewhat inconclusive.

4 Introduction to economics I

Because the world is round

Geoffrey Bennington

In his *avant-propos*, Bataille begins by presenting not so much *La part maudite* itself[1] as his own earlier difficulty in presenting it, before the work was completed, while he was working on it. 'A work of political economy', carefully enclosed in quotation marks in the text, those marks not just called for by the fact that he is here quoting his own earlier, embarrassed but apparently necessary ('j'étais *gêné d'avoir à dire*' – my emphasis) description of his work in progress in these terms. If this *is* political economy, then political economy turns out to have a much broader frame of reference than might previously have been imagined (which might make political economists feel better), but on the other hand it seems to lose its boundary line or frontier and filter out or spill over into a wide and rather vague area we might call philosophical anthropology (which might not make political economists feel so good after all). 'General economy', says Bataille, still quoting his own earlier embarrassed descriptions of the book, is economy in which expenditure becomes an object of study prior to the production (and exchange) that political economists take as their primary object. This trouble over disciplinary boundaries, this excess of the object to be described over its usual description, means necessarily that Bataille's book must in principle be *itself* an excessive object in terms of traditional descriptions; an example, then, of what it tries to describe, an excessive object about an excessive object, and this Bataille is perfectly lucid about, although he tends to personalize and anthropologize this strictly logical problem as a subjective problem of writing (such a move is always a principle of the existential pathos infusing Bataille's work in general, leading him to derive what is ultimately an ethics from what is immediately a logic):

> To the extent that I envisaged the object of my study, I could not personally refuse the effervescence in which I discovered the

inevitable end and value of the cold and calculated operation. My research aimed at the acquisition of knowledge and required coldness and calculation, but the knowledge acquired was that of an error implied in the coldness inherent in any calculation. In other terms, my work tended first of all to *increase* the sum of human resources, but its results taught me that accumulation was merely a delay, a retreat before the inevitable outcome, in which accumulated wealth has value only instantaneously. Writing the book in which I said that energy can in the end only be wasted, I myself was using my energy, my time, my labour: my research responded in a fundamental way to the desire to increase the sum of goods acquired for humanity. Shall I say that in these conditions I could sometimes do no other than respond to the truth of my book and could not continue writing it?

(*La part maudite*, pp. 50–1)

This, then, should be, or should have been, a book *of* general economy, reading the genitive both ways, a book that should exemplify the truth of its object, a book that 'the author would not have written if he had followed its lesson to the letter' (p. 51), a book impossible to write, an unreadable book. This set-up again generates a certain displaced pathos which dictates the idea that the reader must have a certain 'courage' in reading the text, and the assertion that the folding back of the object of research onto the process of research itself necessarily leads to an opposition of an exuberant 'freedom of mind' to the 'fear and anxious search for a solution' (p. 52) which, apparently, characterizes traditional work.

But, in so far as Bataille thinks that he has discovered the principle of a philosophical anthropology, we should perhaps not be surprised that he formulates these questions in primarily anthropological terms, assuming, at least transitionally, 'the desire to increase the sum of goods acquired for humanity' as the correct description of the restricted economy of intellectual labour. I want to suggest that this is unnecessary, an unnecessary luxury – aware that in this suggestion I am running up against an italicized assertion in this same *avant-propos*, namely that '*it is not necessity but its contrary, "luxury", that poses their fundamental problems to living matter and to mankind*' (p. 52). But the point is to suggest that Bataille's 'unnecessary luxury' (the signs of which are the constant references to metaphysical values such as 'life', 'energy', 'humanity', 'the sovereignty of mankind in the living world' (p. 61), the 'instant' of consummation (p. 96) and so on) is in fact, on his own terms, generated by a certain giving in to a falsely perceived necessity, namely the supposed necessity that it be luxury and not necessity that poses these very problems. In its most abstract form, this suggestion would say that 'general economy' is not the other of 'restricted economy', but is *no other than* restricted economy; that there is no general economy except as the economy of restricted economy; that general economy is the economy of its own restriction – and that this is necessity and not luxury. What is necessary is not the fact that luxury and not necessity be the truth of economy: the necessity of necessity is not luxury, as Bataille claims, but rather the luxury of necessity is still necessity. Another way of putting this is that general economy is the economy of general *and* restricted economy, and that this is part of the economy of restriction. These slightly brutal formulations certainly bespeak a necessity of violence which is not different from what Bataille does in writing his violent text: but they tend to contest the thematization (and therefore violent loss) of that violence in terms of sacrifice and expenditure and transgression that constantly return Bataille to a naturalism and a humanism after all.

Bataille's formal point is simple enough, and again the redoubling of that point at the level of the 'method' of his text is probably the quickest way of grasping it: traditional economics isolates particular domains for study, and when it tries to ask questions about the general milieu in which those domains are isolated and particularized, it always treats that general domain as just another particular domain. But that particular domain is necessarily situated in a general milieu which it cannot by definition *comprehend*. Put in this way, the problem is that of the logical structure of the frontier, and recalls the general principle of Hegel's critique of Kant: any drawing of a frontier presupposes a beyond of that frontier (and therefore the immediate transgression of it) which cannot be understood in the terms of the area on the *inside* of the frontier. It is in terms of this logic that I want to pursue Bataille a little, in an attempt to distinguish (in a way to be specified) what I, with some·trepidation, call an 'absolute exteriority' which I think is entailed by the logic of the frontier, from what Bataille calls by various names, of which 'dépense' is the most obvious in the context of *La part maudite*.

Bataille's argument for the necessity of luxury goes as follows: any circumscribed system receives more 'energy' from its surrounding milieu than it can profitably use up in simply maintaining its existence. Part of the excess (the 'luxury' with respect to what is strictly necessary) can be used in the growth of that system, but when that growth reaches its limit (for reasons to be specified), then the excess must be lost or destroyed or consumed without profit. The premise of this argument, and it is an empirical premise, is that there clearly *is* such an excess, precisely because there *are* systems (essentially living organisms) that

obviously receive more energy than they require for mere subsistance
– and this is proved by the *fact* that they do *in fact* grow (and reproduce:
Bataille thinks of reproduction as a form of growth rather than a form
of maintenance). There is in the first instance an excess of energy over
the requirements of maintenance, and this is used up in growth, and we
know this because *there is in fact* growth. The source of this excess
energy is the sun, which founds and funds the whole economy by being
pure gift of energy without return. (This pure gift of solar energy at one
end of the system is – economically – balanced at the other by the
description of what Bataille thinks of as the 'intimate' world of the
sovereign subject, described as *night* (p. 96).) Growth, and what Bataille
calls 'turbulence' (produced by the excess of the excess, the excess of
energy over that part of the excess that can be transformed into growth),
account for the excess up to a certain point or limit (or frontier).
Organisms grow and reproduce as much as they can. They encounter a
limit to growth and reproduction in the growth and reproduction of other
organisms or groups of organisms, and this encounter is limiting
because (moving, as Bataille always wanted to, from the circumscribed
system to its general milieu) the total available space for expansion is
itself limited:

> The immediate limitation, for each individual, for each group, is
> given by the other individuals and other groups. But the terrestrial
> globe (or more exactly the *biosphere* which corresponds to the space
> accessible to life) is the only real limit. The *individual* or the group
> can be reduced by the other individual or the other group. But the
> global volume of living nature is not changed by this: in the end, it
> is the size of terrestrial space which limits global growth.
>
> (*La part maudite*, p. 67)

The sun, as pure gift, *is* pure gift to the extent that it stands outside this
finite terrestrial system (but can only be conceived of as *pure* gift from
within that system: Bataille's account is itself limited by this tell-
urocentrism and eventually anthropocentrism – if we really attempt to
talk about the general economy of energy in the cosmos, the sun cannot
of course be thought of in this essentially traditional and even
metaphysical way).

I want to pause for a moment over this point. In order to talk about
excess, expenditure or transgression, Bataille needs to posit limits (on
this point, as on so many others, his physics and metaphysics are not
essentially different from those of the Marquis de Sade). Limits as
restrictions to growth (the determination of growth as finite) are
produced only because the world is round. A formally identical point

informs Kant's political writings, where it works in the service of an argument about the inevitability of perpetual peace, whereas in Bataille it is part of an argument about the inevitability of excess and therefore violence. Nature's purpose, according to Kant, is that man achieve, through the trials of discord, the full rational development of his faculties. War, which is one of the forms of discord, and which occurs, as it does in Bataille, when groups encounter a limit set by another group, tends to disperse mankind over the whole surface of the planet (Aristotle too links war to separation, of the whole into sub-human parts – the separated individual must, says Aristotle, be a lover of *polemos* – even Rousseau's claim that the state of nature would naturally be a state of peace depends on an argument about dispersion), to spread people even into those inhospitable regions which nature nonetheless takes care to provide with camels, reindeer, driftwood and the like.[2] We can link this tendency to dispersion to the right Kant says I have to make my neighbour move from my vicinity if he refuses to enter into a lawful civil union with me – there must be somewhere for him to move to. We might wonder how Kant, contrary to Bataille, can argue that such a dispersion as a result of discord leads, or should lead, to nature's end, viz. a state of perpetual peace. Why should war not go on forever or, conversely, why should mankind not just continue to disperse in order to flee war without however entering into a lawful state of right (and therefore remaining in an essentially warlike state of nature – Kant sets up an asymmetrical relationship whereby potential war is already war, and peace is only really peace once it is perpetual). The answer lies, precisely as in Bataille, in the planet or the globe, the shape of which seems to have an almost transcendental status in this argument:[3] dispersion reaches its limit when those fleeing or moving eastwards, for example, come back out in the west, or vice versa. The earth has a finite and continuous surface, and this disallows any possibility that dispersion, and therefore war, in Kant's view, be the fate of mankind for ever.

It seems to me that this argument is not in fact dependent upon the earth's sphericity, which might strike us as an uncomfortable element of contingency in what ought to have a transcendental quality to it. In the *Metaphysic of Morals*, where the argument from sphericity is to be found explicitly stated, Kant, as is often the case when he is seeking to fix a properly philosophical and dignified sense to a word, provides a Latin version in brackets, here 'globus terraqueous'.[4] But we might wonder what effect could be had on Kant by an argument that the earth is not in fact a globe at all:

As already said, however, de Selby provides some genuine mental sustenance if read objectively for what there is to read. In the *Layman's Atlas* he deals explicitly with bereavement, old age, sin, death and the other saliencies of existence. It is true that he allows them only some six lines but this is due to his devastating assertion that they are all 'unnecessary'. Astonishing as it may seem, he makes this statement as a direct corollary to his discovery that the earth, far from being a sphere, is 'sausage-shaped' ...

Standing at a point on the postulated spherical earth, he says, one appears to have four main directions in which to move, viz., north, south, east and west. But it does not take much thought to see that there really appear to be only two since north and south are meaningless terms in relation to a spheroid and can connote motion in only *one* direction; so also with east and west. One can reach any point on the north–south band by travelling in either 'direction', the only apparent difference in the two 'routes' being extraneous considerations of time and distance, both already shown to be illusory. North–south is therefore one direction and east–west apparently another. Instead of four directions there are only two. It can be safely inferred, de Selby says [a footnote here suggests that this is 'possibly the one weak spot in the argument'] that there is a further similar fallacy inherent here and that there is in fact only one possible direction properly so-called, because if one leaves any point on the globe, moving and continuing to move in any 'direction', one ultimately reaches the point of departure again.

The application of this conclusion to his theory that 'the earth is a sausage' is illuminating. He attributes the idea that the earth is spherical to the fact that human beings are continually moving in only one known direction (though convinced that they are free to move in any direction) and that this one direction is really round the circular circumference of an earth which is in fact sausage-shaped. It can scarcely be contested that if multi-directionality be admitted to be a fallacy, the sphericity of the earth is another fallacy – that would inevitably follow from it. De Selby likens the position of a human on the earth to that of a man on a tight-wire who must continue walking along the wire or perish, being, however, free in all other respects. Movement in this restricted orbit results in the permanent hallucination known conventionally as 'life' with its innumerable concomitant limitations, afflictions and anomalies. If a way can be found, says de Selby, of discovering the 'second direction', i.e., along the 'barrel' of the sausage, a world of entirely new sensation and experience will be open to humanity. New and unimaginable dimensions will supersede the present order and the manifold 'unnecessaries' of 'one-dimensional' existence will disappear.[5]

Presumably even if de Selby turned out to be right and the earth *were* sausage-shaped, Kant would still want to maintain his argument, which seems to require no more than a closed finite surface (though probably not one with a 'hidden' dimension of this kind). But we might want more seriously to reproach Kant – and indeed Bataille – here for not envisaging the possibility of interplanetary or even intergalactic travel in the starry sky above my head. The fact that Kant, and even Bataille, did not know of the real possibility of space travel is a contingent matter that should not affect a transcendental argument. Perhaps nature's views on mankind – in Kant – and the inevitable pressure of growth – in Bataille – destine it not only to inhabit all parts of the terrestrial globe but eventually all parts of the universe too. Oddly enough, Kant is not silent on the possibility of other planets being habitable (the question of the possible plurality of inhabited worlds is of course a good eighteenth-century *topos*), though he only seems to envisage the possibility of their having *native* inhabitants rather than people forced to inhabit them by fleeing from war elsewhere: in a footnote to his 'Idea for a Universal History from a Cosmopolitan Point of View', Kant says:

We do not know how it is with the inhabitants of other planets and with their nature, but if we ourselves execute this commission of nature well, we may surely flatter ourselves that we occupy no mean status among our neighbours in the cosmos. Perhaps their position is such that each individual can fulfil his destiny completely within his own lifetime. With us it is otherwise; only the species as a whole can hope for this.[6]

As there is no *a priori* reason why the dispersion of mankind should not extend beyond the confines of the earth to the rest of the cosmos, into that famous 'final frontier' called space, then Kant's argument about how the dispersion inspired by war necessarily leads to new encounters and eventually to peace negotiations ought to be expandable into this domain too. Kant is of course very interested in the cosmos, in the 'starry sky above my head' which is, famously, described in emphasized print at the end of the *Critique of Practical Reason* as one of the two things (along with the 'moral law within me') which fill the soul with an ever new and ever growing admiration. In the essay on Theory and Practice, Kant describes man as 'a being designed to stand upright and to scan the heavens'.[7]

But extending the argument into the cosmos like this seems extremely perilous, in Kant's own terms: for just as the argument about the earth depends, if not on its sphericity, then at least on its finitude, so the extension of that argument into the cosmos would have to assume that the cosmos too is closed and finite, and that people fleeing from war in one 'direction' would eventually come back round to their starting point. But such an assumption of the finitude of the cosmos could not be made without further ado, in view of the arguments laid out in the 'Antinomy of pure reason' section in the *Critique of Pure Reason.*

Bataille's 'general economy', then, is in fact restricted, as is Kant's, by a closure identified with the spherical form of the earth, or at least by its being a closed finite surface. Within that closure, for both Kant and Bataille, mankind is sovereign, and Bataille's taking dilapidation of objects in all its forms as a mark of that sovereignty makes sense only within that closure. As Sade came to realize, however,[8] destruction and dilapidation are *always* recuperable as restricted moves within the general or sovereign (an)economy they attempt to signal but cannot reach. Bataille knows this too: in his discussion of the gift and the potlatch, for example, he consistently shows that *there is no gift,*[9] and to that extent no loss, no excess, no transgression or dilapidation that does not generate surplus value within the system it attempts to exceed: and indeed that this surplus value *just is* what is called by names such as loss, excess, dilapidation and so on. For example: 'The gift has the virtue of being an overcoming [*dépassement*] of the giving subject, but in exchange for the object given, the subject appropriates this over-coming' (*La part maudite*, 107), or, more generally, 'the dilapidation of energy is always the opposite of a *thing,* but ... it only enters into consideration once it has entered *the order of things,* once it has been changed into a *thing*' (p. 106), or, in terms of the 'intimacy' we have already seen, the night standing opposite the solar gift: 'intimacy is never truly cleared of external elements, without which it could not be *signified*' (p. 165).

These *a priori* statements suggest that necessity consists in the fact that luxury 'exists' only as always already restricted into the signification of its failure to be excessive. This restriction or, as Derrida would call it, stricture or striction, means that the attempted generalization of economy beyond the bounds of the restricted is itself part of the economy of restriction, or of economy *as* restriction. There is only ever exchange and signification, even in the thermodynamics of solar energy.

This leads to two essentially fictional limits in Bataille's system. On the one hand, he admits as a merely 'theoretical' (i.e. fictional) possibility (which he dismisses on the grounds that things are not in fact like that) that an equal pressure of energy across the surface of the globe might lead to a state of rest, in which growth comes to a halt and is replaced simply by loss of heat (*La part maudite*, 71): this would correspond in Kant to the perpetual peace he starts out thinking of as the inevitable outcome of frontier violence in the international politics produced by the shape of the globe, and ends up realizing would be the worst possible outcome of that violence, the deathly peace of cemeteries.[10] At the other end of the system, as it were, is the equally theoretical (fictional) limit of an infinite violence linked to an infinite and instantaneous expenditure of energy, still thematized in the terms of a sort of existential anthropology:

> If I no longer care about 'what will be' but about 'what is', what reason have I for keeping anything in reserve? I can immediately, in disorder, go in for an instantaneous consummation of all the goods at my disposal. This useless consummation is *what pleases me*, as soon as care for tomorrow is lifted. And if I thus consume without measure, I reveal to my peers what I am *intimately*: consummation is the way in which *separate* beings communicate. Everything is transparent, everything is open and everything is infinite among those who consume intensely. But then nothing counts, violence is liberated and is unleashed without limits, to the extent that heat increases.
>
> (*La part maudite*, p. 96)

That these limits are fictions implies that we are always left in fact *in the middle*, in the rhythmic restriction of gift to exchange and of excess to surplus value or profit. This rhythm (Bataille sometimes calls it, rather than the impossible excess itself, 'turbulence', or, like Rousseau, 'effervescence') is also what guarantees that Kant's initial teleological optimism about the inevitability of perpetual peace is cut through by the recognition of the necessity, on the contrary, of perpetual frontiers and therefore of violence, without end, but always within limits. This violence cannot, without resolving into the death of perpetual peace, be absolute or infinite, but is never ending. This is why, in spite of Bataille, there is no lesson (or political or economic programme) to be drawn from his book, and why the book itself is written and readable in spite of the fantasized lesson that would make it impossible to write, and which generates the pathos of its supposed difficulty. This is why, happily, *there is no sovereignty* and why Bataille's best lesson is just that.

In a sense, these points are purely logical and therefore need give rise to no assignable or predictable emotional or physiological state, excesses and transgressions notwithstanding. *This* is necessity, not luxury but the perpetual economy of luxury, what is sometimes called 'thought'. Thought is not intimate or subjective, neither pure light nor pure night: it befalls me in a violence which is never absolute nor absolutely ordinary, from an absolute exteriority that is neither inside nor outside. It necessarily occurs at disciplinary boundaries but promises neither abolition nor reinforcement of such boundaries. It is, of course, excessive with respect to regulated exchange, but this excess cannot by definition be inhabited, and is therefore not a provider of lessons or truths. It is a perpetual 'Introduction to Economics', never itself, never *in* an economy, always becoming economical.

Notes

1 *La part maudite*, Paris, Editions de Minuit, 1967. All references are to this edition. All translations mine. Further page references to this edition are given in the text.

2 Kant talks a lot about nature in his political writings, but it would probably not be easy to extract from them a simple statement about natural boundaries. On the one hand, Kant recognizes at the very least that there are divisions which seem natural enough: 'The community of man is divided by uninhabitable parts of the earth's surface such as oceans and deserts ...' (*Kant's Political Writings*, ed. Reiss, Cambridge, Cambridge University Press 1970, 106), but immediately points out the means of crossing such boundaries or frontier-zones: '...but even then, the ship or the camel (the ship of the desert) make it possible for them to approach their fellows over these ownerless tracts, and to utilise as a means of social intercourse that right to the earth's surface which the human race shares in common' (ibid.).

This is part of a more general, and rather touching, doctrine about natural providence (itself carefully divided, and given the added gravitas of Latin terminology into 'original' providence (*providentia conditrix*), in so far as it is active from the earliest times onwards, 'ruling' providence (*providentia gubernatrix*), in so far as it keeps nature running according to purposive laws, and 'guiding' providence (*providentia directrix*), in so far as it has an aim in view that mankind could not foresee (p. 108n). This view of nature can seem at first rather pastoral and childish: isn't it *wonderful*, exclaims Kant, that moss can grow in the Arctic wastes, so that reindeer can scrape it up and eat it, so that Eskimos can eat the reindeer or harness them? Isn't it *marvellous* that the desert is home to the camel (second mention of the camel, though no joke here about the ship of the desert – Kant's obviously rather taken with the camel in a way that invites speculation: you can of course learn a lot from the animals invoked by philosophers; Locke, for example, is all monkeys and parrots), so that men can travel through the wastes and not leave them unused? Isn't it *fantastic* that apart from the reindeer, Arctic inhabitants have seals and walruses and whales so as to provide food and warmth? Isn't it *just incredible* that ocean streams carry driftwood to just those places where trees don't grow, so that the inhabitants can build boats and dwellings (this one is mentioned twice too). It's all too easy to laugh at this, remembering Pangloss's admiration that men should have two legs so that they could wear trousers, or that the top of the ears should be in line with the bridge of the nose so that they can wear spectacles, or Bernadin de St-Pierre marvelling at the design of the orange, naturally divided into segments so that it could be eaten *en famille.*

3   This apparently transcendental status of the shape of the earth would run into some trouble in the light of the antinomies of Kant's *Critique of Pure Reason.*

4   See *Kant's Political Writings*, 172. On the use of 'a dead and learned language', see the *Critique of Judgement*, §17, note.

5   Flann O'Brien, *The Third Policeman*, London, Picador, 1974, 81–3.

6   *Kant's Political Writings*, 47n.

7   *Kant's Political Writings*, 63. Kant also invokes the cosmos in the eighth proposition of his essay 'Idea for a Universal History from a Cosmopolitan Point of View', but in a purely analogical way, wondering how he can justify the teleological optimism that informs his arguments: 'The real test is whether experience can discover anything to indicate a purposeful natural process of this kind. In my opinion, it can discover a little; for this cycle of events seems to take so long a time to complete, that the small part of it traversed by mankind up till now [a page earlier Kant had confidently talked about humanity being 'a little beyond the half-way mark'] does not allow us to determine with certainty the shape of the whole cycle, and the relation of its parts to the whole. It is no easier than it is to determine, from all hitherto available astronomical observations, the path which our sun with its whole swarm of satellites is following within the vast system of the fixed stars; although from the general premise that the universe is constituted as a system and from the little that has been learnt by observation, we can conclude with sufficient certainty that a movement of this kind does exist in reality' (ibid., 50).

8   Cf. my analysis in *Sententiousness and the Novel: Laying down the law in eighteenth-century French fiction*, Cambridge, Cambridge University Press, 1985, Ch. 5, §12, 202–8.

9   Cf. Jacques Derrida, *Donner le temps I: La fausse monnaie*, Paris, Galilée, 1991.

10   Kant also envisages (only, like Bataille, to reject the possibility) a perpetual peace coming about by random means: 'Whether we should firstly expect that the states, by an Epicurean concourse of efficient causes, should enter by random collisions (like those of small material particles) into all kinds of formations which are again destroyed by new collisions, until they arrive by chance at a formation which can survive in its existing form (a lucky accident which is hardly ever likely to occur [but which nothing seems to exclude in principle, just as nothing appears to exclude in principle Bataille's 'equal pressure' scenario]); or whether we should assume as a second possibility that nature in this case follows a regular course in leading our species gradually upwards from the lower level of animality to the highest level of humanity through forcing man to employ an art which is nonetheless his own, and hence that nature develops man's

original capacities by a perfectly regular process within this apparently disorderly arrangement; or whether we should rather accept the third possibility that nothing at all, or at least nothing rational, will anywhere emerge from all these actions and counter-actions among men as a whole, that things will remain as they have always been, and that it would thus be impossible to predict whether the discord which is so natural to our species is not preparing the way for a hell of evils to overtake us, however civilised our condition, in that nature, by barbaric devastation, might perhaps again destroy this civilised state and all the cultural progress hitherto achieved [and now there's an abrupt return of the first possibility in a parenthesis] (a fate against which it would be impossible to guard under a rule of blind chance [and now a further complication, as this general possibility, which seemed above to carry the possibility, however improbably, of generating order from chaos, is identified with an apparently much more specific moment of the analysis, viz. the state of nature] with which the state of lawless freedom is in fact identical, unless we assume that the latter is secretly guided by the wisdom of nature [we shall have more to say about secrets in due course]) these three possibilities [i.e. apparent order by random means, order by naturally purposive means and no order at all] boil down to the question of whether it is rational to assume that the order of nature is purposive in its parts but purposeless as a whole' (*Kant's Political Writings*, 48).

5 The sacred group
A Durkheimian perspective on the Collège de sociologie (1937–39)

Michèle Richman

Introduction

Assessments of the Collège de sociologie (1937–9) as a group reflect the particular challenges posed by a socio-historical phenomenon eccentric to standard disciplinary criteria. Some detractors dismiss as puerile and/ or impossible the very premise of surpassing conventional boundaries of intellectual exchange in order to generate political and social activity.[1] Another perspective holds that the deliberate provocation of such overflows of energy constitutes a flirtation with violence, a potentially dangerous swerve toward the impulses that feed Fascism. While the Collège itself was exonerated from any overt collusion,[2] the belated French confrontation with the intellectual sources of anti-Semitism and racism in the 1930s has encouraged postwar historians to place the entire period under suspicion. Especially targeted is the pervasive tendency among the 'non-conformistes des années trente',[3] disaffected from parliamentary politics, institutionalized religion and university-based knowledge, to channel their discontent into the formation of elective groups. Even the Collège's appeal to anthropology, whether references to Dumézil or its allegedly 'particular'[4] enlistment of Durkheim, has singled it out for rebuke. Thus, despite evidence to the contrary,[5] the history of the Collège has been ascribed an 'exemplary' status (*sic*), based on its allegedly shared fascination for National Socialism with 'vast sectors of the French intelligentsia'.[6]

Within the Collège itself, acknowledged antecedents in the nineteenth century were generally elitist, conspiratorial, 'secret' societies, with such literary incarnations as Balzac's *Histoire des Treize*, whereas the most elaborately detailed appreciation of their potentially political role was presented by Hans Mayer's historical account of the evolution of secret societies in Germany. In France, advocates for the restoration of groups, who perceive them as mediators between the individual and the all-powerful State, have been identified as conservative. Indeed, because 'The history of freedom has been written largely in terms of the individual'[7] arguments for the pre-eminence of the group offered by De Bonald, Maistre and even Comte, were automatically at odds with the liberal tradition in which the individual was often consecrated as a heroic *conscience libre*, standing for innovation and progress against collective tyranny and oppression. But whereas the French counter-revolutionary position appears as a scandalous aberration of little concrete *political* consequence, 'the ideas of this school of writers have measurably affected the subsequent social thought of France ... It nonetheless provided the basis of a new science of society, sociology'.[8]

By the end of the nineteenth century, French reflections on the group bifurcated: into the positive endorsements of 'solidarism' within the syndicalist and socialist movements on one side, and the crowd psychologies of Tarde and Le Bon, whose explicit political agenda was the denunciation of socialism as a manifestation of 'mass hysteria', on the other. From within the same social, historical and epistemological framework of *fin-de-siècle* France, modern sociology emerged under the aegis of Emile Durkheim. Friend of Jaurès, committed Dreyfusard and socialist, Durkheim was dedicated to resolving the problem of social solidarity and cohesion in terms consonant with his republicanism and individualism. Renowned by the 1900s for his texts on the *Division of Labour* (1893), *Suicide* (1897) and the *Rules of Sociological Method* (1895), Durkheim surprised the academic world by devoting the latter part of his career to a demonstration of the collective basis of all civilization. Most controversially, he enlisted as his evidence the effervescent ceremonies of Australian aborigines.

Durkheim's dogmatic insistence that sociology expunge all vestiges of psychologism, so that social facts might be explained only by other social facts, has often been dismissed as unduly rigid disciplinary protectionism. But recent scholarship has revealed the extent to which French psychology at the close of the nineteenth century was dominated by a model of the unconscious derided by one historian of psycho-analysis in France as 'l'inconscient à la française'.[9] Alluding to the steadfast resistance to any 'Germanic', i.e. Freudian, psychoanalytic revision, Roudinesco points out that this view of the unconscious served as a politically expedient reproduction of racist, classist and sexist biases disguised as science. For, as Le Bon argued in his immensely popular *La psychologie des foules* (1895), hereditary and racial elements constitute the most 'stable' dimension of the unconscious. At the antipodes of the rational Cartesian cogito, this unconscious is formed from a substrate of hereditary influences. And while the majority of anyone's daily actions may be determined by 'secret causes' emanating from the unconscious, their effect is nowhere more potent nor detrimental than in crowds, when the controlling power of individual volition becomes subordinate to the suggestive influence of the hypnotized masses.

One explanation for Le Bon's appeal, outside the scientific community's general disdain, resides in the fact that its basic premises regarding the nefarious effects of crowd comportment – irrationality, lowered intellectual capacity of each individual, propensity to violence, the hypnotic influence of the leader over his followers – helped to justify the systematic and violent repression of political demonstrations vilified as 'crowd' or mass gatherings.[10] Moreover, the pseudo-scientific hypnotic model of suggestive influence effectively diverted attention away from the historical context of the group gatherings and the social pathologies prompting them.[11] Most disturbing has been the persistence of Le Bon's analyses, so that even his oblique influence facilitates a tendency to generalize from the crowd to all group or collective behaviour. The rare exception to this trend within the academic social sciences was Durkheim, whose democratic allegiances were indisputable. Yet his enthusiasm for effervescent assemblies as precursors to change has tended to be down-played in standard sociological accounts.[12] While the neglect of Durkheimian effervescence by traditional sociology may in part be attributed to its elusive nature – its resistance to conventional categories and methods of representation – it is also possible to argue that it has suffered from its historical proximity to the sensationalistic crowd psychology of Le Bon (1895). Ironically, by the 1920s, Freud refers to Le Bon's 'deservedly famous'[13] treatise for his own speculations on group psychology, whereas Durkheim's very different positions are not mentioned.

Within the Collège, however, Durkheim becomes an essential source, and his descriptions of collective effusion associated with sacred rites and rituals in the *Formes élémentaires de la vie religieuse* (1912) provide a common reference for their ethnological appreciation of the sacred as well as a means for tracking its presence in modern society. But by the 1930s, the mass ceremonies in Germany made Durkheim's emphasis on collective representations and experiences increasingly problematic to appreciate. Mauss himself recognized the dangers of the French school's version of collective phenomena, while defending his uncle against accusations that Durkheim's early endorsement of corporate associations may have served as a model for Mussolini's Fascii.[14]

By highlighting the historical parallels between the turn of the century crises concentrated in the Dreyfus Affair and the 1930s prewar period of the Collège, I hope to demonstrate that representations of the group phenomenon as a catalyst for social change were *over-determined* by those specific contexts. Durkheim's precedent will be reconsidered in view of its reprise (and modification) by the Collège, although the overarching goal of this presentation is neither to justify nor legitimate the Collège's activities by means of the reference to the French school of sociology.[15] Rather, it considers how recourse to 'sociologie', especially when conjugated with an appreciation of the sacred, facilitated a rethinking of the nature of collective experience in contemporary society.

Another aim of this historical perspective on collective thought is to break the stranglehold on the development of social psychology effected by the early crowd psychologies. As one study concluded, 'the initial crowd psychologies and their disqualification of the masses represent another example of a "missed opportunity" ... of *locating social psychological inquiry explicitly at the crossroads of the sociopolitical and individual levels*'.[16] In his introduction to a recent edition of Le Bon, André Akoun argues that the enduring interest in *La psychologie des foules* is partially motivated by Freud's re-reading of Le Bon, with readers seeking not so much an account of the structure and behaviour of groups *per se*, but rather 'the discovery of a new sort of question: the relation of desire to the social field'.[17] The 'Freudian Revolution' rendered such questions possible by introducing a dynamic conceptualization of the unconscious in relation to the social by conceiving of its new object as 'neither the individual psyche nor the collective crowd'.[18] Moreover, by evacuating the notions of heredity, degeneration, organicism, race or instinct characteristic of *l'inconscient à la française*, the Freudian unconscious emerges as a 'field', where drives, repression and transfers exert their respective influence.

But Freud's major innovation within the domain of mass psychology – the model of *identification* rather than hypnotic suggestion – does not obviate his general endorsement of Le Bon's portrait of the crowd. For both, the pivotal issue is the distinction between the moral and intellectual consequences of group influence. Le Bon's 'law' points to the inversion brought about between affect (subsuming morality) and intellect. Whereas the emotions are heightened to the point of inspiring great acts of sacrifice and self-abnegation, the debasement of logical thought processes prompts Freud to invoke in comparison the 'primitive mentality', the child's lack of cognitive sophistication and/or the neurotic's subjugation to emotion. The individual's subordination to the group allegedly causes him to share with these other categories a tolerance for contradictory notions, a devaluation of truth as final goal and a logic dominated by images. The one trait of the crowd expunged by Freud though favoured by Le Bon is its so-called femininity. The following characterization is indicative of the period's fascination with female (*sic*) hysteria: 'Crowds everywhere are feminine; but the most feminine of all are the Latin ones.'[19]

Finally, even when Le Bon and Freud acknowledge the heroism of the group as inaccessible to the individual dominated by personal interest, the ethical *élan* is debunked by both as a temporary phenomenon. Le Bon's political motives are transparent: to undermine the growing enthusiasm for socialism, pervasive even among those he claims stand to lose most from it! It is especially interesting to see how he approaches the series of revolutions that rocked France during the nineteenth century. Le Bon argues that the changes wrought by the popular revolts were merely superficial modifications that left basic structures intact; Durkheim, however, evaluates the surge of effervescence accompanying historical conjunctures as evidence of their revolutionary potential.

Durkheim's position can be explained by the fact that his references to the *assemblée* or *rassemblement* preclude *la foule* as the group responsible for lynchings. Yet his differences with Le Bon reside less in the descriptions of the outward manifestations of the crowd behaviour than in the value he ascribes to its specific characteristics. More precisely, he praises *moral* conviction as highly as intellectual achievement, since it is the basis for social cohesion. Furthermore, his descriptions of the transformative effects of the collectivity on thought processes are charged with admiration for 'the way collective thought changes everything that it touches ... In a word, *society* substitutes for the world revealed to us by our senses a different world that is the projection of the ideals created by society itself'.[20] Society, for Durkheim, is a virtually ubiquitous force or host of influences, whose 'unconscious' effects can nonetheless be discerned, measured and analysed by the sociologist. Polemically poised to contravene the eighteenth-century bias that the individual was the ultimate object of knowledge, sociology must demonstrate the existence of a *sui generis* 'social' reality exhibiting laws all its own. From his earliest writings, Durkheim revised the individual versus society conflictual model to a view of *homo duplex* as both self and other, with greatest emphasis on the multiple dimensions of social determinism. His most singular rethinking of 'society', however, resides in his perception of social formations that defy standard sociological categorization. Beyond the fragmentation, atomization and even dissolution of traditional forms deplored by his contemporaries, Durkheim discerned within the effusion of intellectual activity stimulated by the new socialism, for instance, signs of transformation. One sociologist was therefore prompted to insist upon the innovative contribution of Durkheim's new 'topique', located between the social and the political, which will re-emerge in the project of the Collège.[21]

But whereas Durkheim described how, under the effect of 'some great collective shock'[22] individuals gather more frequently, exchange ideas more intensely and thus generate collective ideals and actions, the challenge to form a Collège was posed by the perception of a 'moral panic' among the French population confronted with the prospect of imminent war and possible death. Recognizing that death is the primary cause for movements of attraction and repulsion, and that the need to mediate encounters with it is what prompts the consecration of sacred places, persons or things, the Collège united under the banner of a common interest in a 'sacred sociology'. One of the Collège's founding declarations claims that an understanding of how 'the primordial longings and conflicts of the individual condition'[23] are projected into the social arena will provide insights into the pathology of a phenomenon other disciplines would not venture to approach. Previous studies of Bataille's theoretical as well as experiential preoccupation with collectivities have primarily focused on the role of community in orienting his investigations. Community is generally associated with a longing for intimacy and connectedness without the negative associations of submission to an authoritarian leader or violent goals associated with the stereotyped behaviour of the 'crowd' or 'masses'. Yet Bataille reserved certain riddles for the sociological sphinx. The following sections consider how it is that the group becomes the site for exploring facets of human nature appreciable only within a collective context, situated under the sign of a sacred sociology.

Reading the sacred

Mid-way through his lengthy *Formes élémentaires de la vie religieuse* (1912) Emile Durkheim illustrates the general opposition between the sacred and the profane by means of its particularly violent dramatization among Australian aborigines. Periodically, clans are called together to celebrate a snake or fire ceremony, so that the dull and torpid existence of the dispersed phase of social life is transformed into a concentrated exaltation of collective energies. The exceptional intensity of the effervescence indeed fosters the sense of having reached a qualitatively different order of being: individuals feel, think and behave in new and unpredictable ways, so much so that for the 'être nouveau', 'everything is just as though he really were transported into a special world, entirely different from the one where he ordinarily lives, and into an environment filled with exceptionally intense forces that take hold of him and metamorphose him'.[24] How, questions Durkheim, when experiences such as these are repeated each day for weeks at a time, could one avoid concluding that the universe is divided into two heterogeneous, mutually incompatible worlds:

> One is that where his daily life drags wearily along; but he cannot penetrate into the other without at once entering into relations with extraordinary powers that excite him to the point of frenzy. The first is the profane world, the second, that of sacred things.[25]

Such Nietzschean verve from the founder of modern French sociology, viewed as the staid bourgeois moralist of Third Republic ideology, could not fail to surprise supporters as well as detractors. When *Elementary Forms* appeared in 1912, Durkheim was fifty-four and at the apex of his career. Following the hostility provoked by his appointment to the Sorbonne nearly a decade earlier, he had devoted his teaching to social solidarity, through the transmission of a lay morality his enemies derided as dogmatic secular religion. A 600 page treatise on the religious practices of Australian aborigines by this devoted servant of the secular State was therefore received with as much consternation as praise,[26] despite the fact that the 'recovery of the sacred'[27] had been a unique feature of sociology since its inception as a discipline in the early nineteenth century. Irrespective of the sociologist's lack of personal belief, the religio-sacred was enlisted to examine such ostensibly non-religious matters as community, authority, status and personality. In Durkheim's last writings, however, the concept gains exceptional prominence: 'His use of the sacred to explain the cohesive nature of society, the constraint that society exercises upon man, the origins of culture and even of human thought must surely rank as one of the boldest contributions of a positivist non-believer.'[28] The polemics generated by *Elementary Forms* have not abated among scholars compelled to address its specific issues as well as its relation to his work as a whole. Most provocatively, the question remains, 'Why did this highly rational, secular, positivistic Frenchman decide sometime after 1895 to devote nearly fifteen of the most productive years of his life to the exotic cults, dancing and blood-letting of a primitive people?'[29]

In the response to follow, I place special emphasis on those passages of *Elementary Forms* which punctuate Durkheim's scholarly exposition with outbursts of poetic enthusiasm, in a pattern mimetic of the alternation between profane dispersion and sacred concentration organizing aboriginal social life. In them he celebrates the transformative effects of effervescent gatherings as the epitome of the sacred and argues that civilization's origins are ultimately collective. Often restricted to the religious domain narrowly conceived, or avoided because of its alleged resemblance to the crowd, collective effervescence must now be appreciated in terms of the sense of otherness it induces. While consistent with Durkheim's earliest contention that the collective holds out possibilities otherwise inaccessible to the individual, as well as providing the basis for social cohesion, in *Elementary Forms* it is viewed as the matrix from which all social forms emerge. The idea of religion itself evolves from such assemblies. In the course of rituals, the moral sense is heightened and collective representations generated. Conventionally termed ideal, this plane of reality is nonetheless credited with stimulating new and unforeseeable actions. Thus, whereas the Australian aboriginal ceremonies may provide the exotic trappings of cultural alterity – frenetic dancing, loud music, bizarre cults – the most exhilarating and radical sense of otherness is encountered when individual subjects are modified by the effects of collective assemblies.

The sacred's quality of otherness appears in Durkheim's earliest characterizations, even though he is quick to point out that the distinction does not imply any intrinsic property or transcendental quality, since it is 'added on' to persons, places and things and sustained by collective belief and ritual. By the time of *Elementary Forms* the difference between the sacred and the profane is declared *absolute*: 'In all the history of human thought there exists no other example of two categories of things so profoundly differentiated or so radically opposed to one another.'[30] Mauss had already demonstrated in his study of seasonal variations among the Eskimos that the sacred/profane duality corresponds to a universal distinction formalized by every culture between the need for moments of production and expenditure, taboo and transgression, euphoria and dysphoria.[31] The Eskimos offer what is undoubtedly one of the most elaborate versions, since virtually every detail of material, religious, mental, sexual, individual as well as collective life is affected: names are changed, laws are modified, houses are switched, spouses are swapped, kinship is restructured. Families dispersed into small groups of hunters and gatherers loosely allied by clan affiliations during one phase of the cycle are forged into a community of frenzied activity during the other. The long winter months, with everyone housed in common and personalities fused in sexual communion, immerse the Eskimos in sacred festivities rarely sustained in other cultures for such a duration.

Reinforcing Durkheim's conviction that the sacred exhibits *sui generis* qualities, Mauss notes that during congregations and festivities, individuals are not merely assembled in greater physical density and spatial proximity: a qualitative transformation occurs among those gathered to celebrate their sense of belonging to a whole greater than the sum of its parts. Confirmation of the sacred nature of the group in archaic cultures reinforced what was already a fundamental tenet of sociology in France: that the group, rather than the individual, constitutes the basic unit of social analysis. The infusion of ethnographic data nonetheless helped to deflect the conceptualization of modern social formations away from de Bonald's reactionary tradition, whose opposition to the principles of 1789 was marked by a total subordination of the individual to the group reinvested with absolute authority. But even as Durkheim tried to reconcile the sociological primacy of the group with republican and democratic ideals, the extreme valorization of the collective placed him at odds with the dominant economic and political individualism of liberal theory. While historically necessary for the liberation of individual subjectivity from the tutelage of tradition, liberalism had exhausted its social viability by the end of the nineteenth century.

From the outset of his intellectual activities, Durkheim sought to address the nature of the social crises plaguing *fin-de-siècle* France in terms of the dialectic between individual consciousness and social formations. Just as individual identity is inseparable from life in society, so the evolution of inner consciousness parallels social conditioning. But one of the paradoxes of modernity is that the increasing fragmentation of social and professional life has undermined the production of collective sentiments of a social nature, precisely at a time when they are most needed: 'It is, indeed, remarkable that the only collective sentiments that have become more intense are those which have for their object, not social affairs, but the individual.'[32] While Durkheim approves the emancipation of the individual from the 'mechanical' forms of social cohesion, he nonetheless was increasingly preoccupied with the nature of alternative means to appreciate one's 'dependence' on, or relation to, the social whole. For even if sociological doctrine asserts the existence of social facts and forces external to and independent of the individual; or, assuming that it can demonstrate that the individual is always already part of a social group from which he or she evolves a personal sense of identity, such assertions are relatively ineffectual against the stronger reality of daily life as experienced in individual, and in modern times, individualistic, terms. Attributing the imbalance to the weakness of current social representations and practices, Durkheim notes: 'With the exception of extraordinary moments, society exists within us in a state of abstract representation, whereas individual forces can be felt.'[33]

The exceptional moments referred to are those rare instances of spontaneous effervescence or ritualized gatherings which reinforce the duality of human nature, of the fact of being both self and other, individual as well as social. Faced with the exaggerated intensity of the communal months among the Eskimos, Mauss had concluded that the extreme polarization of social life imposes such a 'violence' on the participants that they must necessarily slow down and withdraw. Durkheim retains from this observation that the violence of the opposition was a necessary mechanism to dramatize the difference, just as it may have even stimulated the initial sensation of the sacred. This realization of otherness, marked by violence in the conventional sense as well as in the connotation of extreme intensity, becomes internalized when sacred and profane things form within consciousness two distinct and separate mental states.

The lesson Durkheim derives from Mauss can be compared with his interpretative strategy when confronted with the alterity of sacred rituals. At the point of general paroxysm in the fire ceremony cited above, Durkheim temporarily defers to his source, Spencer and Gillen, who equate the authenticity of the 'genuinely wild and savage scene' with their inability to convey it adequately in words.[34] But he rapidly counters the distancing effect by plunging into his own commentary with an emphatic as well as empathic 'One readily conceives how' or 'He naturally has the impression' etc. in order to underscore the extraordinary transformative capacity of such gatherings to project participants into another – superior – dimension of social and moral being.

This line of heuristic revaluation is especially evident in Durkheim's explanation of his shift away from modern social problems to the religious practices of one of the most 'primitive' societies on ethnographic record. He argues that however bizarre or seemingly barbarian the ceremony, or strange the myth, each translates some 'human need' which the sociologist, unlike the anthropologist responsible for gathering the data, must interpret from the perspective of a contemporary social issue. In the case of the Australian Arramunga, the fire ceremonies and snake worshipping rites dramatized religion's function as *'a system of ideas with which the individuals represent to themselves the society of which they are members, and the obscure but intimate relations which they have with it. This is its primary function'.*[35] Without some representation of the part to the whole, individuals are threatened by anomie and the collectivity risks dissolution.

Recourse to religious practices, however, also entails a basic contradiction. Whereas the transformative effects of effervescence may be undeniable, the propensity of the group immersed in their disorienting alterity is to project the collective forces their contact has generated onto an external object or even transcendent deity. Restricted neither to so-called primitive societies nor to archaic modes of thought, this delusion occurs in modern political life as well, because individuals feel themselves 'acted upon' by forces whose origins they cannot discern and the path of social action is too 'circuitous' for the average citizen to perceive. The process of displacement is most evident in the sacralization of persons who have no other claim to veneration than the powers invested in them through social consensus. And even the enigma of sacred things can be demystified as the projection of collective ideals onto material objects.

The triumph of a critical, 'de-fetishizing' sociology does not obviate Durkheim's impassioned call for a revival of feasts and festivals, so that modern society may overcome its crisis of moral mediocrity through social regeneration. One could argue that by enlisting the religio-sacred approach to the crisis of social cohesion and solidarity, Durkheim thus circumvented the dominant ideological biases of Le Bon's crowd psychology and embedded his own sociological argument in favour of collective experiences, especially the controversial notion of effervescence, within the more acceptable religious frame. While even the benefits of hindsight cannot fully elucidate the complexity of such manoeuvres, it is nonetheless now possible to consider the legacy of the Durkheimian re-reading of the sacred for the generation of Bataille and his affiliates at the Collège de sociologie.

In explaining the impulse to create a group brought together by sociology, Caillois compares their activities to the Surrealist 'fermentation'.[36] While united through their common explorations of the unconscious, with its rich dream material and innovative forms of 'le merveilleux', the Surrealists were less cohesive and effective at transmuting their esoteric experiments into political action. Caillois discerns their failure in the discrepancy between intimate preoccupations and collective causes, a gap better bridged by the research derived from developments in the social sciences over the last half-century: 'Just as there exists a primitive, irreducible experience of *self* constituting the basic dynamic of anarchic individualism, the same sort of existential, inalienable basis of collective effort must be brought to light.'[37] Moreover, the urgency for a Collège forged from 'moral sentiments' other than those to which scholars usually respond, is heightened by the general anxiety induced by the prospect of imminent war. The closing years of the decade were characterized by a sense of war's inevitability, at odds with the pacifying official discourse. But the political pressures exerted by the debacle of parliamentary democracy coupled with a domestic as well as foreign Fascist menace, did not deter the Collège from an appreciation of the crisis in terms of the horror looming ahead and the sentiments it provoked within.

Finally, conveners of the Collège acknowledge their debt to the French school's basic premises that the whole is indeed greater than the sum of its parts, that the collectivity induces transformations within its participants and that this transformation is only accessible and sustainable within a *mouvement d'ensemble*. For these reasons, the group becomes the privileged locus for explorations otherwise capable of inducing madness or suicide in the individual who pursues them in isolation. With his explicit repudiation of the individualistic mythologizing of romantic figures of the last century, intractably pitted against the forces of law and order represented by the bourgeois majority and in sympathy only with marginals, Caillois heralds the inauguration of a new era of relations between creators and consumers. However designated or enlisted, whether through elective affinities or otherwise, the group is necessary because writers and artists can experience the full deployment of their creative potential only within a communal situation. Both Caillois and Bataille allude to 'secret' societies, a qualifier that connotes a unifying basis in feelings and sentiments occulted in most social settings, rather than a conspiratorial plot against the establishment. The particular notion of the group at stake here resides in the interplay between oppositions its con-ceptualization set in motion, such as static versus dynamic, part versus whole and mutilated versus virile. 'Secret' touches on a reality which is constitutive and seductive, and comparable to myth: 'Myth is born in ritual acts concealed from the static vulgarity of a disintegrated society, but the violent dynamic belonging to it has no other object than the return to a lost totality.'[38] The group in question here is ascribed the status of a heterogeneous force of potential disruption, even destruction, within the homogeneous whole. Correlatively, it is also conceived as the 'foyer d'énergie' or kernel of 'violent silence' responsible for transmuting the forces of the left sacred into those of the right. In this way, members of the Collège, students of Mauss and second-generation Durkheimians to have survived the ravages of the First World War, draw on the distinction made by Robert Hertz regarding a deviant, virulent and threatening left sacred associated with death and malevolent forces, versus a consecrated right sacred aligned with power and order, albeit equally forbidding and forbidden to common contact.

Central to the experience of the group is the attainment of a *prise de conscience* which stands in a homologous relation to the vulgar consciousness as the secondary, elective community does to the primary one of origin. The status of 'person' is credited to individuals who initiate a rupture with identity acquired through birth. Liberation from the unexamined life presupposes recognition of the deluded nature of primary modes of consciousness, those restricted to an individualized, internal sense of presence: 'In any case, nothing allows us to content ourselves with the unique importance that the human consciousness of the lone individual assigns to itself.'[39] Bataille's deconstruction does not lead him to espouse the Durkheimian notion of a *conscience collective* either, for as he defies the reader, 'Why not bluntly acknowledge that we are here in the most obscure domain of knowledge?'[40] What he does assert, and will reiterate in subsequent works, is that a human being exists only in society, and that the ties which render communication possible also effect some type of psychic modification. Following the break with primary social affiliation, community is the term employed to designate the regrouping of individuals on a new plane.

For Durkheim, the ultimate instantiation of the transformative process was the added moral sustenance imparted by collective energies, allowing the individual to confront adversities with heightened courage and determination. But Bataille's *prise de conscience* underscores the paradoxes of the historical conjuncture designated modernity. With the realization that the sacred communal movement responsible for attraction as well as repulsion is generated by the negativity of death, individuals in a post-sacred society appear condemned to a 'negativity without a cause' ('négativité sans emploi'). Bataille salvages it from the compromised 'impotent negativity' ('négativité impuissante') of art and religion by embracing the task of giving its due to that part of human existence liberated from utilitarian considerations – 'to satisfy the portion of existence that is freed from doing: It is all about using free time'.[41] In 1911, Durkheim circumvented the impasse of the sacred's marginalization as superfluous or antithetical to action by redefining human telos in relation to expenditure.[42] And no more crucial form of recognition exists, according to Bataille, than for human nature to acknowledge itself agitated by what it holds in greatest horror: the possibility for modes of expenditure so extreme that annihilation appears the only outcome.

Historically, the rare expressions of such sentiments free of social censure were tragedy and religion. With their relative demise in the modern world, one must refer to the social sciences, especially the ethnographic representations emanating from the French school of sociology's research into non-Western cultures, for intimations of what sacred experiences can reveal: 'In this way science, to the extent that its object is human negativity – especially the sacred left – becomes the middle term of what is only a process of awareness.'[43] From its inception, the Collège declared that participants must draw upon the exotic representations derived from French anthropology, but without fear of their potentially contagious effects.

In the final reunions of the Collège, Bataille addressed the internal divisions contributing to its demise, including Leiris's reproach that he had betrayed the principles of the Durkheimian method by accentuating manifestations of the left sacred to the detriment of its more conventional forms. Ironically, unlike Durkheim's recourse to Australian aborigines, Bataille's most sustained illustration of the sacred as a transformative process leads to the antipodes of the exotic, since he refers the reader to the cemetery behind the church located at the heart of every typical French village. The entire complex comprised of building and burial ground forms the essential 'kernel' necessary for the transformative process of the negative forces unleashed by the proximity of death into the sacred 'right' of religious order and consecration. The process is symbolically represented by the passage from the church to the underground crypts and vaults preserving the purified bones of saints and holy persons now denuded of putrefying flesh. However devoid of traditionally religious sentiments one may be, it is possible to recognize that the sacred locus is shrouded in the aura of 'violent silence' respected as a necessary mediation in the face of death and destruction. Tears and laughter, common reactions to such forces, may add depth to communication, but cannot impart the same humanizing dimension as the kernel – 'the structure of the sacred center that is necessary to collective human emotion'.[44] For it is precisely within this rarefied experience that the movement traversing the group can be transmuted from one emotive extreme to another. Bataille's position is indisputably sociological in that it requires social forms to render possible what would otherwise be dissipated in random acts of violence or terror: a mediating 'silence laden with tragic horror weighs down on life' to make it profoundly human.[45]

Similarly, Durkheim viewed the group as the source of effervescence: one of the striking revelations of the Australian ceremonies is that the very process of gathering together induces the unusual intensity of sensations: 'When they are once come together, a sort of electricity is formed by their collecting which quickly transports them to an extraordinary degree of exaltation.'[46] Thus it was Durkheim who effected a courageous leap of cultural faith when he perceived the consecration of the group itself, and therefore the foundations of civilization, in assemblies that Evans-Pritchard, for one, had derided this way: 'No amount of juggling with words like "intensity" and "effervescence" can hide the fact that he derives the totemic religion of the Black Fellows from the emotional excitement of individuals brought together in a small crowd, from what is a sort of crowd hysteria.'[47] Conversely, Bataille, though focusing on the violently disruptive elements associated with the left sacred, was able to detect its traces within the banal landscape of the local village. He even argues that the social equilibrium the church provides by mediating the forces of attraction and repulsion associated with death, or when it organizes the festivals alternating sacred festivities with the realm of the profane, should shield it from any threat of destruction from secular opposition.

Representing the sacred

Acknowledging that his approach to the sacred may have transgressed disciplinary conventions, Bataille offers an eloquent defence of his unconditional endorsement of sociology as the only domain in which the 'capital decisions' of life are researched and appreciated. In this presentation, I have attempted to demonstrate that a re-reading of Durkheim in large part inspired by the concerns of the Collège could validate Bataille's claim to have resituated the realm of sociology within the profoundly serious perspective Durkheim had also staked for it. Moreover, in representing society as an ensemble of forces external to individual volition, Bataille assented to the Durkheimian view of society as a field of possibilities promoting transformations which the early crowd psychologies sought to discredit as primarily, if not exclusively, conducive to violence and irrationality.

By affixing 'sacred' to its general conceptualization of sociology, the Collège underscored the active, dynamic and transformative characteristics of the Durkheimian concept of the group. Contrary to the view that his extreme focus on the social hypostatized a process, one must appreciate that for Durkheim society connotes a totality that is always already divided, just as there exist neither natural groups nor superior social forms to be maintained and reproduced. At his most radical, he reaffirms the need for collective life and its transformative consequences because the very possibility of society is contingent upon individuals consolidated through the symbolic system and representations it produces. In a similar vein, Bataille concluded that the sacred was indeed discerned in the communication it engenders and, by extension, in the formation of new beings.

Given the particular resistance the sacred poses to representation – 'Initially it was very hard for me to represent convincingly the fundamental and vital animation, which the sacred engenders through shock as it were'[48] – the favoured images allowing Bataille to inscribe sacred violence without betraying its negativity revolve around wounds, and venture to the extremes of sacrifice and crime. For Durkheim, the advent of sociology as a 'new science of man' heralded at the conclusion of *Elementary Forms*, signals the need for a mediating discourse between the scientific demystification of social life and the religious function as safeguard of the sacred forces it has historically transmitted through rituals and representations. His unmasking of projections which occult the social must therefore be distinguished from his recognition of the value of the equally arbitrary, but necessary, symbols and representations in which every group concentrates the experience of effervescence as a communicative device. What distinguishes one social group from another is the *form* through which the collectivity sustains and transmits its relation to a distinct, separate and extraordinary domain designated as sacred. This explains the intensified focus on symbolic systems and modes of representation in Durkheim's later writings, since the basis for social solidarity is located primarily in the *conscience* the individual possesses of it by means of collective representations.

Ever sceptical of the distorting effects of language and the *mise en discours*, Bataille explored alternatives to the conventions of written discourse. In *L'expérience intérieure* subsequent to the Collège, he placed increasing emphasis on dramatization, and inscribed into his texts a visual representation of moments of violent silence through recourse to aphorisms, 'mots glissants' and ellipses. Already at the time of the Collège, its parallel 'secret' society, known through the brief publication *Acéphale*, contemplated stagings or re-enactments of (in)famous crimes. This literal resuscitation of the 'tragic spirit' was ultimately less significant than the political gesture of examining the nature of the group refracted through the prism of cultural difference. By means of the common reference to Durkheim, especially evident in Caillois and Bataille, the texts of the Collège impart something of the effervescent quality he had daringly proclaimed to be of continued relevance to modern society. Thus, without reducing the distance separating Durkheim from the Collège, it is possible to respond to critics who view their Durkheimian reference as distorted, or as an opportunistic appropriation of his scientific cachet. In this study I have skewed the terms of the debate by showing how the perspective of the Collège allows one to modify the standard reading of Durkheim. The ideological stakes of such a revision affect judgements relating to Bataille, the Collège and the very foundations of social being.

Notes

I am grateful to Gwendolyn Wells of the graduate programme in French at the University of Pennsylvania for generously sharing her admirable use of *le mot juste* during preparation of this essay.

1   This scepticism was expressed from the outset of the Collège by Alexandre Kojève, according to Hollier's notes to 'The sorcerer's apprentice' in *The College of Sociology*. Denis Hollier, trans. Betsy Wing, Minneapolis, University of Minnesota Press, 1988, 398.
2   See Bernard-Henri Lévy, *L'Idéologie française*, Paris, Grasset, 1981.
3   This is the title of Loubet del Bayle's study of such groups, Paris, Editions du Seuil, 1969.
4   Daniel Lindenberg, *Les années souterraines*, Paris, La Découverte, 1990, 59.
5   In the expanded version of his 1987 biography of Bataille, Michel Surya has added several strong statements attesting to Bataille's anti-Fascist sentiments as well as philosemitism. See Michel Surya, *Georges Bataille: La mort à l'oeuvre*, Paris, Gallimard, 1992, 437–48.
6   Lindenberg, *Les années souterraines*, 58.
7   Robert Nisbet, *The Social Group in French Thought*, New York, Arno Press, [1940] 1980, i.
8   Ibid., iv–v.
9   Elisabeth Roudinesco, *La Bataille de cent ans: Histoire de la psychanalyse en France*, Paris, Editions Ramsay, 1982, I, 181.
10   For a well-documented account of the use of violence on the side of 'law and order' rather than on that of the alleged 'crowd' (in reality, political demonstrations), see Susanna Barrows, *Distorting Mirrors: Visions of the crowd in late nineteenth-century France*, New Haven and London, Yale University Press, 1981.
11   See Erika Apfelbaum and Gregory R. McGuire, 'Models of suggestive influence and the disqualification of the social crowd' in *Changing Conceptions of Crowd Mind and Behavior*, ed. Carl F. Graumann and Serge Moscovici, New York, Springer-Verlag, 27–50.
12   Noteworthy exceptions can be found in Edward Tiryakian's 'Emile Durkheim' in *A History of Sociological Analysis*, ed. Tom Bottomore and Robert Nisbet, New York, Basic Books, 1978, 187–236, and in Mark Traugott's 'Durkheim and social movements' in *Emile Durkheim: Critical assessments*, ed. Peter Hamilton, London and New York, Routledge, 1990, II, 198–206.
13   Sigmund Freud, *Group Psychology and the Analysis of the Ego*, trans. James Strachey, New York, Bantam Books, [1921] 1960, 6.
14   See his response to Svend Ranulf, author of 'Scholarly forerunners of

Fascism' (1939) in *Emile Durkheim*, I, 23–37.

15   This is basically the position taken by Denis Hollier in his introduction to *Le Collège de sociologie* (Paris, Gallimard, 1979): 'Quant au choix de terme de "sociologie", il marque une pseudo-valorisation de la science invitée, comme troisième larron, à geler le conflit de la politique et de l'art, du communisme et du surréalisme' (p. 15).

16   Apfelbaum and McGuire, 'Models of suggestive influence', 47, emphasis added.

17   See André Akoun, Introduction to Gustave Le Bon, *La psychologie des foules*, Paris, Presses Universitaires de France, 1975, 10–11, my translation.

18   Roudinesco, *La Bataille de cent ans*, 181.

19   Le Bon, *La psychologie des foules*, 59, my translation.

20   Emile Durkheim, *Sociology and Philosophy*, trans. D. F. Pocock, New York, The Free Press, Macmillan, 1974, 94–5, emphasis added.

21   See Jean-Claude Chamboredon, 'Emile Durkheim: Le social objet de science', in *Critique*, 445–6, 1984, 460–97.

22   Emile Durkheim, *The Elementary Forms of the Religious Life*, trans. J. W. Swain, New York, The Free Press, Macmillan, 1915, 241.

23   Roger Caillois in *The College of Sociology*, 10.

24   Durkheim, *Elementary Forms*, 250.

25   Ibid.

26   For a summary of the reception to *Elementary Forms* see W. S. F. Pickering, *Durkheim's Sociology of Religion: Themes and theories*, London, Routledge & Kegan Paul, 1984, 86–9.

27   Robert Nisbet, *The Sociological Tradition*, New York, Basic Books, 1966, 221.

28   Ibid., 243.

29   Robert Bellah, introduction to *Emile Durkheim on Morality and Society: Selected writings*, Chicago, University of Chicago Press, 1973, xliii.

30   Durkheim, *Elementary Forms*, 53.

31   See Marcel Mauss, 'Essai sur les variations saisonnières des sociétés Eskimos' in *Sociologie et anthropologie*, Paris, Presses Universitaires de France, [1904–5] 1973, 389–475.

32   Emile Durkheim, *The Division of Labor in Society*, trans. George Simpson, New York, The Free Press, Macmillan, 1933, 167.

33   Emile Durkheim, *Textes 2: Religion, morale, anomie*, Paris, Editions de Minuit, 1975, 16, my translation.

34   Durkheim, *Elementary Forms*, 249.

35   Ibid., 257, emphasis added.

36   *College of Sociology*, 9.

37   Ibid., 37.

38   Ibid., 23.

39   Ibid., 80.

40   Ibid.

41   Ibid., 92. In his important study, Jean-Luc Nancy underscores how the Bataillian premise that all community is rendered possible by an expenditure or *dépense*, traditionally in the form of a sacrifice, breaks with the usual telos of community united through a work or collective goal. Whence Nancy's title 'La communauté désoeuvrée'. It is also significant that he

underscores the active sense of *dés-oeuvrée*, consistent with the citation from Bataille to the effect that the rehabilitation of non-utilitarian expenditure in the modern world will be his only form of 'activity'. See Jean-Luc Nancy, 'La communauté désoeuvrée', *Aléa*, 4, 1983, 11–49.

42   See Emile Durkheim, *Sociology and Philosophy*, 86.
43   Alexandre Kojève, in *College of Sociology*, 91.
44   Ibid., 112.
45   Ibid.
46   Durkheim, *Elementary Forms*, 247.
47   Cited in Pickering, *Durkheim's Sociology of Religion*, 396.
48   *College of Sociology*, 128.

6 Recognition in *Madame Edwarda*

Allan Stoekl

I

Georges Bataille always made clear his debt to Alexandre Kojève's reading of Hegel; in fact, as is well known, he considered himself a 'Kojèvian' as much as a Nietzschean – and perhaps more.[1] But one aspect of Bataille's Hegelianism has been largely overlooked: the fact that Bataille, while affirming the importance of a destructive negativity, and of an end of history which will 'liberate' that negativity for other purposes, rarely affirms the centrality of recognition in and as the genesis of human experience.

Kojève, in his *Introduction à la lecture de Hegel*, writes:

> in the final analysis ... the value that I am or that I 'represent' is the value desired by this other: I want him to 'recognize' my value as his value, I want him to 'recognize' me as an autonomous value. In other words, all human Desire, that which is anthropogenic, and which generates self-Consciousness, is, finally, a function of the desire for 'recognition'. ... To speak of the 'origin' of self-Consciousness is thus necessarily to speak of a death-struggle for 'recognition'.[2]

For Bataille, however – at least in what we think of as his 'theory' – recognition plays little if any part. In essays like 'The notion of expenditure' Bataille gives pride of place to sheer destruction, the 'death drive' of expenditure: he is quite explicit in stating that social recognition – 'glory' – is only the incidental after-effect of the 'tendency to expend'.[3] The chief in the potlatch ceremony expends in order to expend, not in order to achieve or retain social status. In other essays, such as 'Hegel, death, and sacrifice', he makes clear the centrality of death, and again avoids the question, or the problem, of recognition in social experience.[4]

Yet one cannot help but conclude that the absence of a problematic of recognition causes difficulties: if expenditure has nothing to do in its essence with recognition, how can we say it is a social experience at all? The automutilating madmen and women of the early essay 'Sacrificial mutilation and the severed ear of Vincent Van Gogh'[5] perform their horrible acts in secret, or before the befuddled gaze of the crowd: the most basic element of ceremony, Bataille tells us, is the sacrificial act of mutilation itself, and not its social appropriation. It is the same whether performed by a high priest before a crowd of dignitaries, or by a madman in the solitude of a cell. But if this is the case, how can we say that the experience (for want of a better word) is central to human society? Couldn't it just as easily be an aberration, a tendency that leads in the direction of a simple destruction of society and that should therefore be extirpated?

Perhaps part of the problem is that in thinking of recognition we usually think of it as involving personal achievement: if I am recognized, it is something that boosts my status within the community, makes me feel proud, etc. I am validated as an autonomous individual, with needs, rights, dignity. This is certainly the way Kojève saw recognition in modern society.[6] But with Bataille it's a different story. Perhaps in what is commonly called his 'fiction' there is another kind of recognition, one not simply of the sort one finds between autonomous agents in a 'bourgeois' drama, but between substituting and mutating terms situated in ritual. Bataille, in other words, may displace the problem of recognition by resituating it in religious ceremony, which always tends to operate through the play of substitution. Such recognition, however, will serve not to validate a conventional religion (in this case Christianity, and more specifically Roman Catholicism), but will accompany the opening out of religion to the very death it hypocritically tends to deny (promising us, as it does, a deliverance from anguish, sexuality and death: 'eternal life'). By reorienting recognition, in other words, Bataille may also be reorienting the way we conceive of religious experience. Ritual substitution and recognition, as I will argue in my reading of *Madame Edwarda*, are inseparable.

II

The preface to *Madame Edwarda* (9–10; 137–9)[7] informs us of the tragic nature of sexual experience and death, and thus of their gravity: Bataille argues they are both due a respect, a recognition, that death alone commonly receives in ceremony (sexual experience or expression, on the other hand, is usually the object only of contemptuous laughter). The preface does not, however, stress very strongly the fact that tragedy as sacrificial ceremony is inseparable from ritual. As we will see, the basic 'events' of *Madame Edwarda* can be viewed as the carrying out of a tragic ritual that involves the divinization and even the martyrdom of the central character, but a martyrdom accomplished through sexual experience rather than death (although the two are, so the preface argues, inseparable).

Now at first ritual almost by definition would seem to exclude that which cannot be taken seriously: the death of the hero/victim in tragedy or in religious sacrifice is the highest, most grave outcome imaginable of any ceremony. It is certainly not laughable. But if ritual is solemn there is also very often something ridiculous about it, something that calls into question the very seriousness on which it depends. Substitution always seems to undermine the very process it makes possible: the king who tears out his eyes in a Greek tragedy, after all, is not a real king, put a paid actor. The victim 'himself', at least in many religious rituals, is not human at all, but a wretched and not at all heroic animal (typically a chicken, sheep or pig). Catholicism carries out its most sacred ritual, the mass, under the grotesque and shameful representation of a nearly nude and gruesomely mutilated man hanging from an execution device reserved for the lowest orders of society. What could be more ridiculous than substituting a sheep for a man, and then taking the killing seriously? Or worshipping under a softcore-porn-style image of ignominious death? Bataille himself, in 'Hegel, death, and sacrifice', notes the 'comedy' of sacrifice, in which a mere vicarious experience of death, and hence only death's representation, is substituted for the real thing – one's own death – which by definition cannot be *experienced*.[8]

Central to tragic and sacrificial ritual, then, is substitution – of images and of persons. The latter can be ridiculous, comical or horrifying as well as grave. Bataille himself in the late 1920s noted the tendency of the sacrificer to identify with the victim: in 'Sacrificial mutilation and the severed ear of Vincent Van Gogh' he posited the self-mutilator as a figure who conflates, in his or her own person, the functions of both ritual priest and squirming victim, of mortal man and vengeful, all-powerful god.[9]

Perhaps Catholicism has pushed this representational–substitutional logic further than any other system of ritual activity. The priest, after all, is a stand-in for Jesus, via the pope. In the consecration he carries out literally the same actions performed by Jesus at the Last Supper. But the host is the Body of Christ as well, despite the fact that it is also merely a piece of unleavened bread. Divinity, materiality, the animate (the body of the priest), the inanimate (the host), all come to be associated in the very act of dissociation (the carrying out of the sacrifice), for the priest re-enacts the sacrifice of the mass, and also of God (through the host's transubstantiation–consumption), but all the same he is *not* God. He is a substitute for God doing what God does (carrying out the sacrifice) to God in His real presence (the host), which in turn does not act like God at all, at least before He is ritually consumed (He is, after all, only a piece of bread).[10]

I mention all this not only to set the stage for a discussion of some of the Catholic resonances of *Madame Edwarda* – and they are crucial – but also to note the almost surreal tendency toward substitution in tragic drama and sacrificial ritual. Roles are shared or reversed, the laughed-at and spat-upon become the exalted, the inanimate becomes the divine, and so on, with little respect paid to the boundaries of the respectable and the grave. Nothing is ever quite what it seems, and one is hard pressed to assign a stable role – social, sexual, divine, mortal, physical, spiritual – to any one figure or element. And yet the most important thing may be, when considering the question of the recognition of the desire of the other in a story such as that of *Madame Edwarda*, to note the ways in which figures are substituted for each other, and the significance of those substitutions – for in a sacrificial context of the sort elaborated by Bataille mutual recognition occurs through mutual ritual substitution.

Madame Edwarda, as we know, is, among other things, God, and for Bataille God was never far from the Catholic Church he both execrated and affirmed. One need think only of the priests (and their fates) in *Histoire de l'oeil* and *L'Abbé C.* to grasp the importance of transgression in the context of established religion in Bataille.[11] The priest is himself an erotic figure, to be sure, but beyond his (sometimes ambiguous) sexuality and mortality he represents the institution of the Church and even the institutionalization of God Himself. When Bataille's priests are tortured or murdered, and when they in turn self-mutilate and betray their 'friends' to authorities who themselves torture and murder, we see the simultaneous undermining and maintaining of a figure of supreme authority. Bataille makes volatile the sacredness of the priest, opening his function to the 'left-handed' sacred of eroticism, decomposition and laughter.[12] But it is important to remember that the priest in Roman Catholicism is already a volatile figure in that he is always on the move: as the celebrant of the mass, he is constantly walking, bringing things forward, putting things away. John Coventry, SJ has noted the tripartite nature of the mass and a 'recurring pattern' within it:

The Entrance [of the mass], a procession, is accompanied by a psalmody (the Introit) and concludes with a formal prayer (the Collect). In such a formal prayer (*oratio*) the priest speaks to God in the name of the whole people present: he prays to God 'through Christ our Lord,' a formula which forms the conclusion of the prayer: the whole people (originally – now only the server) answer *Amen*, the prayer is preceded by a greeting (*Dominus vobiscum*) answered by the people (*Et cum spiritu tuo*), and by a call to prayer (*Oremus*). Thus the prayer forms the climax of the Entrance Rite, a conclusion to which the rest has led up. Now this pattern – a procession of some sort, accompanied by singing and concluded by a formal *oratio* – occurs at two other places in the Mass, and each time the prayer is the climax of a clearly definable section of the Mass. The second time this pattern occurs is at the Offertory: the procession is that of the faithful bringing up their gifts to the altar, accompanied by the Offertory chant, the whole Offertory concluding with the *oratio super oblata*, now called the Secret. The third time the pattern occurs is at the Communion: the procession is that of the faithful coming to receive Communion, while the choir sing the Communion chant, and the whole rite of Communion is concluded by a formal prayer, the Post-Communion.[13]

While *Madame Edwarda* contains no singing (at least not until a film version is made), it does have three sections, each of which contains a sort of procession and entails, if not a formal prayer, then at least a conclusion, a denouement, that gives the section a rough narrative coherence – but a conclusion which is, nevertheless, questioned within the narrative itself. In fact the second of the three sections explicitly poses the problem of the narratability of Mme Edwarda's divinity.

The first section, then, corresponds roughly to the Entrance Rite in the mass. Catholics (lapsed or otherwise) will recall that this first section is called the 'Mass of the Catechumens' because it originally was open to the non-converted (those undergoing instruction). The faithful are called, the priest enters in a procession, welcoming prayers are offered, instruction is given. It is a 'gathering' (*Synaxis*) in the most straightforward sense of the term. In *Madame Edwarda*, the procession occurs already on the first page: the narrator, wandering from bar to bar in the area of the rue St Denis, takes his pants off:

The night was nude in the deserted streets and I wanted to denude myself like it: I took off my pants and put them over my arm; I would have liked to catch the coolness of the night in my legs, a stunning freedom carried me along. I felt bigger. I held my stiff member in my hand.

(19; 148)

This procession clearly marks the narrator as a kind of celebrant, albeit a lonely one in darkness: instead of vestments he wears his nudity, carrying his genitals instead of a chalice.

In fact his congregation only emerges when he enters into a bordello (called 'les Glaces' – 'Mirrors') where he immediately chooses God. Yet as the two sit and indulge in a 'sick kiss' (20; 149), they are circled by a crowd: 'I sensed laughter through the tumult of voices, lights and smoke.' The mocking unbelievers are the only congregation for the introductory ceremony in which the celebrant and the deity are united in sadness and anguish:

> I became sad and felt abandoned as one is in the presence of GOD. It was worse and crazier than drunkenness. And first I felt sad at the thought that this grandeur, which was descending on me, detracted from the pleasures I had hoped to enjoy with Edwarda.
>
> (20; 149)

Surrounded by the profane, by mockers, the narrator disappears momentarily into 'the night'.

But there is a sudden substitution, a transference of roles: the Catechumens are not in the surrounding crowd: the initiate is now the narrator himself. Edwarda declares herself God through the display of *her* genitals, which she then commands the narrator to kiss. The narrator must look at the 'living wound' which in turn 'looks at' him: the 'rags' (*guenilles*), as Mme Edwarda calls them, are specifically what is divine ('You see', she says when she shows them, 'I am GOD'). This rite is a *monstration*, a showing, in which the sacred or divine object stares back: it is as if monstrance and host were identified and then endowed with an all-seeing eye. In this case the divinity of the genitals, through a metonymy, comes to be associated with the person who displays them (just as the faithful are often elevated in sanctity metonymically through the display of divine wounds – St Francis's stigmata, etc.); they in turn are the lowest of the low, the most wretched things imaginable (*guenilles* are defined by the *Petit Robert* dictionary as, in addition to rags, 'contemptible things, of no importance whatsoever [*d'importance nulle*]'). But the rite is also a Communion: the narrator first puts his lips on the *guenilles*, on GOD, and then, a little later, engages in another ritual with Mme Edwarda, one in which the traditional mirrors of the bedroom 'multiply the animal image of a coupling' (22; 151).

If Bataille were simply rewriting the mass in a transgressive register, it would seem that he is getting ahead of himself: the first rite, the Entrance, has fast-forwarded to the Communion. But one must stress that the coupling so far is only animal: the laughter and the 'tumultuous indifference' of the crowd serves to put in its place the 'royal consecration and vibrant [*fleuri* – literally, "flowering"] festival' (22; 151) of the procession as it ascends to the privacy of the reflecting and reflexive room. The narrator as celebrant is still a mere client, preceded by a ferocious and uncompromising God; he is initiated, dazzled, but humbled ('I am crazy') and timid ('But ... I protested, in front of the others?'). He too is an indifferent catechumen, hesitant, doubting: he is separate from God, at a safe distance, following, narrating. He has not yet given, or offered, anything; no exchange has taken place. Nor has his position in narration, in presentation and observation, been challenged. Like the room itself, and the bordello ('Mirrors'), he merely reflects.

If the first section is a Mass of the Catechumens, with the narrator himself as principle catechumen, the second should correspond to the Offertory. The procession this time leads up to the offering of gifts – a kind of Christian potlatch in which the goods of the community are recklessly dropped at the foot of the altar (at least they were at one time). *Madame Edwarda*'s Offertory on the other hand entails the offering up of the narrator himself as a mediation between the animal and the divine: by the end of this section, he is no longer the stable, human (and male), principle that would make sense of Edwarda's madness, reflect on it, write a coherent story about it, etc. – he is no longer playing Breton, in other words, to Edwarda's Nadja.

The narrator ('Pierre Angélique')[14] follows Edwarda as far as the Porte St Denis: at the opening of the second section, she is standing under the arch. Her aspect has changed radically: instead of the lively, beautiful and vivacious figure of the previous section, she is now emptiness, and it is this that convinces 'Pierre' that she indeed is God.

> Edwarda waited under the doorway, in the middle of the arch. She was entirely and simply black, as anguish-provoking as a hole: I understood that she was not laughing and that even, precisely, under the clothes that veiled her, she was now absent. I knew then ... that She had not lied, that She was GOD.
>
> (24; 152)

There is literally nothing under the *domino* (a cape with cowl) and *loup* (a velvet mask with a lace fringe) that she has put on. These two pieces of clothing, whose very names convey the divine (*domino*) and the animal (*loup*, 'wolf') by themselves indicate the nature of Edwarda's radical absence: it is not a contemptible one, a degrading one, but simply one that is not human, that is not a function of interiority or knowledge. It is instead both beyond and beneath any possible understanding.

And yet that is what the narrator wants to do: he wants to follow her, track her down, know: 'And, moreover, I wanted to know [*savoir*]: this woman, just now so nude, who gaily called me "fifi" . . . I crossed, my anguish told me to stop, but I went forward' (24; 153). Is this desire to go forward a desire for loss, for the void, that Mme Edwarda seems to incarnate, or is it merely a desire to make sense of things, to bring back a story? At the border, the edge that the 'door' of St Denis marks, the narrator stops. His quarry is gone, he is alone in the silent night. Will he go forward, into the space of the border, the space of the god Dianus, Janus, Denis, Dionysus, a space that is neither inside nor outside, but the demarcation between life and death, sanity and madness, the space of a 'death agony', a moment comprising both life and death?

> Without having thought of it for a moment, I 'knew' [*je 'savais'*] that a time of death-agony [*un temps d'agonie*] had started. I accepted, I wanted to suffer, to go further, to go, even if I had to be struck down, all the way to the very 'void' [*jusqu'au 'vide' même*]. I knew [*je connaissais*], I wanted to know [*connaître*], avid for her secret, without doubting for an instant that death reigned in her.
>
> (25; 153)

Like St Denis the beheaded martyr, 'Pierre' is willing to risk all for his God: but that God now is only the promise of an infinite emptiness, a beheading without reason.

He is afraid to lose her: 'trembling' with the idea that she could 'disappear for ever', he throws himself into the space of the archway, and careens around the right-side pillar. Eventually he catches sight of her *domino* disappearing into the darkness, on the other side of the boulevard. When he finally catches up to her, she seems to be losing consciousness, but then wakes up; she asks him, 'Where am I?' (25; 154). His answer, a mere gesture of the hand indicating the empty sky, apparently sets off in her an insane rage: after being supported by him for a brief moment and thrashing about madly, she pushes him away, insulting him with an obscene gesture. She then strikes his face 'in a rage, with closed fists', as if she were in a fight (26; 154). Finally, having pushed him down onto his knees, she screams, 'I am suffocating, but you, you dirty priest [*peau de curé*], I SHIT ON YOU [*JE T'EM-MERDE*]' (26; 154).

A naturalistic reading here might argue that this is the only way a prostitute can get the upper hand in a relationship with a client: instead of being abandoned by him, with a derisive payment, she tries to abandon him, fleeing into the darkness. That he rediscovers her and attempts to 'help' her only underscores the bitterness of her defeat and her aversion for the one who sees himself, in a literal sense, as her follower. Another reading, one perhaps more attentive to Bataille's concerns in general, may not be all that different. 'Pierre' would exert his control not through money but through the power of knowledge and narration itself: what he brings to the altar of St Denis, and what he wants to carry through it, is not a monetary offering that would assure status or control within a couple or a congregation (as the case may be), but instead a sense, a meaning, that would serve to orient and explain. Mme Edwarda, after all, explodes when he attempts to show her where she is. True, her location is only the empty sky, the void, but even this is a direction, an orientation, and worse, an attempt at conveying sensibly, visibly, what defies all sense and visibility: the utter emptiness of the void. And, no matter how minimally, it is a way of taming the *angoisse* of the nothing, the *rien*.

She pointedly calls him a priest – literally a 'priest's skin' – and it is clear why: his offering, the gift that he has brought to the door of the tabernacle before which God's sacrifice is performed, is a gift only to himself. It is an offering that in this case returns to the very person who has given it: the narrator–priest. The celebrant receives from himself the contribution of a narration that promises knowledge, that offers a sense of where he is and where he is going: before a void, into the empty night of the city's sky.

Mme Edwarda, on the other hand, remains 'locked in silence' (26; 155), and in the absence of all possible communication. Perhaps the final offering of this section is again on the part of the narrator, but this time he offers himself up, without concern for knowledge, coherence or summation: he tells us that 'I was lost [literally "I absorbed myself" – *je m'absorbai*] in this lack of a way out [*cette absence d'issue*] – in this night of the heart that was neither less deserted nor less hostile than the empty sky'. The offering now, it would seem, is of himself, a strangely sexual-sounding release of his 'self' into the body of absence. But there is a ceremony yet to be performed: the re-establishment of the link between celebrant and sacred victim not so much in mutual respect as in a narration that returns the divinity to animality, or vice versa, through the substitutions of ritual roles. This narration itself is not so much one of the attribution of sense and direction – what we have seen in this second section – as it is the elaboration of a ritual interchange, a communion.

In the third section the narrator steels himself for a torture when he sees Mme Edwarda 'twisting on the ground'. Like the condemned person who sees the preparations for his own execution, 'Pierre's' world suddenly shrinks to the few objects which come to take on a heightened meaning. And yet another procession now starts: after lying down on the ground next to Edwarda, the narrator picks her up:

> Exhausted, for a short moment I lay down on the street alongside her. I covered her with my clothing [*vêtement*]. She was not heavy and I decided to carry her: on the boulevard the taxi stand was nearby. She remained inert in my arms. The journey took some time, I had to stop three times; nevertheless she came back to life and, when we arrived, she wanted to stand up: she took a step and faltered. I supported her and she got into the car.
>
> (28; 156)

The passive narrator, whose power, we are told on the previous page, depends on his own self-hatred, now seems to be playing the active role. But it is much more complicated than this. First, 'Pierre' is associable with St Denis, the beheaded bishop who, according to legend, picked up his head and walked with it; 'Pierre' walks down the street that bears the saint's name (the rue St Denis, one of the centres of Parisian prostitution). As St Denis, he is the *acéphale*, the headless god, the incarnation of a divinity *not* grounded in Spirit, Reason or Grace. But his burden, his severed head, is Edwarda herself, the God whose torn-apart genitals (her 'rags') are the visible proof of her divinity. Edwarda, at least in this mythic configuration, is (as the head) both the reason of religion, its principle of order and religious leadership, and, at the same time, since she is a dead head, the decapitated head of a martyr, the principle of the *loss* of reason and sense. Thus, through metonymic transformation, she is both sacred direction *and* the void of her divine 'rags'/genitals. Then, of course, the narrator is also Christ himself, carrying the Cross, having to stop three times; in this version, Edwarda is now a piece of wood, an inanimate but menacing torture implement, of the very sort that threatened the torture victim with whom 'Pierre' compared himself earlier. But as the cross, she is also the symbol of life, the tree whose wood, in the form of relics, guarantees the sacredness of altars, and, in stained-glass church windows, represents the renewal of growth (the phallic 'Tree of Jesse', to which the Cross was linked). Finally, she too is Christ himself, for she 'comes back to life', before she ascends not to heaven but to the interior of the taxi.

In this series of ritual metamorphoses we can see a kind of exchange taking place between a number of substitutable terms: between the divine and the human, certainly, but also between the active and the passive; the alive and the inanimate; the male and the female. The narrator, both active (the carrier) and passive (the decapitated), carries the other (Edwarda) as both other (the Cross, the dead Christ) and as himself (his own head). Edwarda, both passive (the carried) and active (the self-resurrected, St Denis's head as principle of direction, and Christ), is carried as both the female God (which is what we are told she is) and as the male God (the Cross as the model of phallic patrilineal descent [the Tree of Jesse], and as the about-to-be resurrected Christ).[15] Each 'person' – Edwarda and the narrator – splits into a number of subsidiary persons, forms, entities and principles, each of which can enter into relations of exchange and substitution.

The substitutability of active and passive (and, by implication, male and female) can be seen above all in the problem of 'leading'. At one point, writing of his efforts to write about Edwarda, the narrator states: 'I myself would like to lead [*je voudrais conduire*] to the point at which I arrived when led by her [*conduit par elle*]' (28; 156). He sees himself as the possible substitute for Edwarda, then, in the realm of language; but beyond this there is a larger question: who, at the end of the story, will do the leading, the driving (for *conduire* in French can mean 'drive' as well as 'lead')? The human, presumably will drive, or lead, the other, the non-human. But is it that simple? Is there ever a non-human? Isn't the non-human itself a joining of the animal and the divine?

There is a final driving in the story, a final procession, a final consecration and Communion. After getting into the cab, Mme Edwarda and the narrator go to the Halles, the old Parisian central market, site of butchers and the hacking apart of meat. There Edwarda stops the cab, displays herself nude to the driver, orders him into the back seat, and, without saying anything, mounts him (29; 157). Now the interesting thing in this Communion, if we can call it that, is not so much the 'angoisse' of the 'blind slide into death', but rather the exchange between Edwarda and the narrator that takes place over the mute and sprawling body of the 'worker' (as the narrator calls him). The one who works, who produces, who drives, the *chauffeur*, becomes the driven, but he is inert, a cipher. Neither 'Pierre' nor Edwarda is driving. As Lucette Finas points out in her reading of the story, Edwarda at this point is both a kind of parodic Jeanne d'Arc, *à cheval*, riding the driver like a horse, and she is also a giant erection, ejaculating by means of the *crue*, the overflow, of the tears spurting from her eyes.[16] But if she is an erection, she is also Christ on the Cross, his/her body in its death-agony emitting water instead of blood. And if she is the Most-High, the principle of divinity, worthy of reverence and respect, at this moment of crisis she is also the most laughable or most grotesque, an enormous male sex-organ discharging into the void. Whatever she is, though, she is not the human, but a kind of amalgam of the divine and the animal.[17] The narrator, in turn, is not the human either, but a kind of reader, a blind repeater of death or absence ('Love in [her] eyes was dead, the cold of dawn emanated from them, a transparency in which I read death'). He is also a comically passive, inanimate, but phallic Cross (a sterile version of the Tree of Jesse), supporting but also doubling the Jesus–erection in his/her orgasmic agony.

Neither Edwarda nor the narrator 'leads' or 'drives'; that is the function of the human, the *chauffeur*, the worker. But he is absent, a mere body to be mounted like a horse. Across the gap of the human, the space of its impossibility, Edwarda and 'Pierre' communicate; their transfer, substitution, Communion, is one of animality and divinity, reading and death, the comic and the divine. There is no mediation; the final ceremony also implies an exchange of roles, one in which Edwarda's *leading* is replaced, if only momentarily, by the narrator's purposeless *reading* – a reading that does not attempt a sufficient writing or authoritative narration (in fact at this point the 'story' is abruptly cut off; all the rest, we are told, is 'irony, the long wait for death' [31; 159]). And that, if anything, is the moment of recognition offered by the story; it is certainly not one of the mutual recognition of talents or qualities by two opponents. Rather recognition here appears in the form of exchange between unstable terms – between divinity and animality, activity and passivity, the female and the male. The recognition of the other – be it another person, another myth, another gender, another mode of being – is now not so much a way of solidifying a society through the identification of respect with the 'human' (and the identification of the 'human' *as* respect). Instead the 'human' is entirely short-circuited: recognition between terms is that, finally, between celebrants in a ceremony that entails the transfer of roles, often within a single 'person'. Recognition, in other words, is ceremonial rather than existential. My being, such as it is, is constructed and dismantled through its ritual substitutability with the other.

At the end of the story, when Edwarda is *à cheval* the driver, 'Pierre' holds up her head (29; 157). He sees the tears, reads the death in her eyes. He recognizes the gravity of those tears, that death; that recognition, though, is also an exchange, because her head is his head, and vice versa; both are St Denis, after all, and both are Christ. The recognition is an empty one, an 'impossible' one: they recognize each other not as autonomous and comfortable humans, but as dead or animal or divine. They recognize, in other words, that which cannot be recognized, that which is most missing, that which missing is. 'God,' the narrator informs us at the end, 'if he "knew", would be a pig' (30–1; 159). The ritual and tragic recognition of the other is an offering and a consecration of the other: 'God' recognizes herself or himself as that which is most disgustingly different – not only an animal, but a contemptible animal – but also as that which, as him or her, will be sacrificed (the pig as the victim of a sacrificial slaughter). At the end, self-recognition and other-recognition are the same: God, impossibly, 'knows' herself, recognizes herself, in a kind of post-dialectical knowledge as infinitely worthy of veneration, but also as definitively unworthy of it. Recognition in respect, even reverence, can be substituted for misrecognition in contempt: recognition defines itself through the appropriation of that misrecognition; recognition recognizes itself as its own misrecognition. The laughter of contempt, with its object, is now on a different if not a higher level: laughter is *recognized* as ritually substitutable for reverential and silent homage.

Notes

1 Bataille, on first meeting Lionel Abel, declared himself to be a 'disciple' of Kojève. See Abel, *The Intellectual Follies: A memoir of the literary venture in New York and Paris*, New York, W. W. Norton, 1984, 174.

2 Kojève, *Introduction à la lecture de Hegel*, Paris, Gallimard, collection 'Tel', 1980, 14. My translation.

3 See Georges Bataille, *Visions of Excess; Selected writings, 1927–39*, ed. and trans. Allan Stoekl, with Carl R. Lovitt and Donald M. Leslie Jr, Minneapolis, University of Minnesota Press, 1985, 122–3.

4 Georges Bataille, 'Hegel, death, and sacrifice', trans. Jonathan Strauss, in *On Bataille, Yale French Studies* 78, ed. Allan Stoekl, New Haven, Yale University Press, 1990, 9–28.

5 In Bataille, *Visions of Excess*, 61–72.

6 See Alexandre Kojève, 'Tyranny and wisdom' in Leo Strauss, *On Tyranny*, ed. Victor Gourevitch and Michael S. Roth, New York, The Free Press, 1991, 162, esp. note 6.

7 All references to *Madame Edwarda* and its preface will be to the final version of the story, as republished in vol. III of Bataille's *Oeuvres complètes* (*OC*), Paris, Gallimard, 1973. All translations are my own. Additional page numbers (immediately following those of the French edition) refer to the Austryn Wainhouse translation (London, New York, Marion Boyers, 1989). The Wainhouse translation, while fluent, is not terribly faithful.

8 Bataille, 'Hegel, death, and sacrifice', 19.

9 See Bataille, *Visions of Excess*, 70.

10 The interplay between symbolism and the real transformation of bread and wine into the Body and Blood of Christ in the consecration is an extremely

difficult one that has given rise to much theological speculation. See on this question above all Canon Eugène Masure's *Le sacrifice du corps mystique, sacramentum-et-res*, Paris, Desclée de Brouwer, 1950.

11   See also the willfully mocking and shocking 'Discussion sur le péché' of 1943 (*OC*, VI, 315–59), as well as the very early, still devout piece 'Notre Dame de Rheims' (*OC*, I, 611–16).

12   For a consideration of the 'left-hand sacred', see Bataille's lecture of 5 February 1938 in *The College of Sociology*, ed. Denis Hollier, trans. Betsy Wing, Minneapolis, University of Minnesota Press, 1988, esp. 123.

13   *The Breaking of the Bread: A short history of the Mass*, by John Coventry, SJ, London, Harvill Press, 1960, 20–1. Of course this is a pre-Vatican II description.

14   This name, meaning 'angelic stone' – and which conveys the impossible joining of the most dead and the most holy – was used by Bataille both as a pseudonym when *Madame Edwarda* was first (clandestinely) published, and then, later, as the name of the narrator in writings meant as sequels (or prequels) to *Madame Edwarda* (such as *Ma mère*).

15   Mme Edwarda's name certainly suggests this gender-bending identity of male and female. In addition it calls forth the traditional aristocratic English hero of French pornography (caricatured in *Histoire de l'oeil*'s 'Sir Edmund'), only now as a woman.

16   Lucette Finas, *La crue, une lecture de Bataille: Madame Edwarda*, Paris, Gallimard, 1972, 409–11.

17   The divine monster–woman is a familiar enough figure, displayed in the nineteenth century by such authors as Baudelaire and the decadents. Whether Bataille should be condemned out of hand because he recycles this *idéologème* and uses it for his own purposes remains an open question. For an excellent discussion of this problem, and the larger question of the role of women in Bataille's 'pornographic' fiction, see Susan Rubin Suleiman, 'Pornography, transgression, and the avant-garde: Bataille's *Story of the Eve*' in *The Poetics of Gender*, ed. Nancy K. Miller, New York, Columbia University Press, 1986, 117–36.

7 Sacrifice and violence in Bataille's erotic fiction

Reflections from/upon the *mise en abîme*

Leslie Anne Boldt-Irons

> The sacrifice that we consummate is distinguished from others in this way: the one who sacrifices is himself affected by the blow which he strikes – he succumbs and loses himself with his victim.
>
> (*L'expérience intérieure*)

In both *L'expérience intérieure* and *L'érotisme* Bataille declares that his view of sacrifice is to be distinguished from that of others: his view entails the loss of the sacrificer and witness *along with* the victim, whereas, traditionally, the former are *not* lost along with the victim, for they profit from the latter's loss and return to continuity. It is this *mutual* loss of witness and victim in sacrifice that Bataille hopes to realize in his erotic fiction, but to effect a loss in both reader (witness) and fictional character (victim), he must avoid transforming this loss into a gain for the reader.

At the same time, however, Bataille's fiction cannot aim to provoke a loss in the reader that is so radical that the experience of sacrifice is 'lost' altogether. In other words, the sacrifice depicted in his fiction would in itself be 'lost' or would not properly constitute sacrifice if this loss were too radical to be recognized as such by the reader. Bataille's objective in representing sacrifice in his erotic fiction must therefore be to effect a loss in the reader that is neither fully lost (unrecognized) nor gained as a profitable experience. I argue in this chapter that he maintains this precarious balance between loss and gain in sacrifice through the idiosyncratic use of the *mise en abîme* in his fiction.

One will notice my deliberate alteration of the spelling of the word *abîme*, which usually appears as *abyme* in the phrase *mise en abyme*. This expression is used to describe, within a literary text, the repetition or doubling, in miniature, of structural or representational elements appearing in the larger context of the work itself.[1] An example of this technique might be the description, in a novel, of a painting which depicts, in miniature, events taking place within the larger framework of the novel itself. Similarly, the *mise en abyme* technique would be used if a character were to read a novel in which the events of its own fictional existence were to be depicted.

In using the phrase *mise en abîme*, I have deliberately altered the spelling of the word *abyme*, in order to reflect Bataille's particular use of this technique, for his use of it denotes both the well-known structural technique of framing or replication within a larger frame (usually identified as a *mise en abyme*) *and* the capacity of his images to deliver notions and fictional characters to loss in continuity, a *mise en abîme*, understood as a 'putting into the abyss'. The complexity of Bataille's idiosyncratic use of the technique becomes apparent when one observes that the *mise en abîme* of characters and notions sets off a second *mise en abîme* in the reader or witness. There is, then, a structural *mise en abyme* of an initial *mise en abîme*, the difference in spelling separating the two operations and their different functions in Bataille's text. As will become clear, the function of this *mise en abîme* in Bataille's texts is to initiate in the reader a loss that is neither fully lost nor gained, but caught, rather, in the paradox of a simultaneous and impossible loss *and* gain.

This precarious balance between profit and loss becomes more apparent if one examines more closely the status of the self and its relative loss in the sacrifice depicted in Bataille's literary texts. In *La littérature et le mal*, for example, Bataille writes that one can only recognize or love oneself completely if one is the object of a condemnation: 'man is of necessity pitted against himself and ... can recognize himself ... [or] ... love himself completely only if he is the object of a condemnation'.[2] This act of self-condemnation implies the loss of discontinuous and limited selfhood. It implies the violation of a limit, a limit that facilitates the creation and contemplation of the discontinuous self, for, if François Wahl is correct, conscious knowledge, itself limited, is knowledge of the discontinuous and the limited.[3] When the limits of the self are violated, however, one is able, writes Bataille, to recognize oneself completely [*jusqu'au bout*] in what he describes as a profound 'accord with one's self'. Given that Bataille often situates this 'recognition' of self in a continuity always already at the basis of discontinuous being, it is clear that the 'recognition' and the 'accord' of which he writes elude the simple and strictly discontinuous contemplation of self that necessarily remains this side of an intact limit. This 'accord with one's self', this 'recognition' – situated as they are, then, beyond the limits of conscious contemplation – can perhaps be best designated by what Klossowski has termed a 'simulacrum of death'. Klossowski's term 'simulacrum of death' is, I believe, an appropriate designation of the impossible sacrifice to which Bataille aspires in his erotic fiction, for it is caught between the two extremes of radical loss (death beyond the simulacrum) and profit (consciousness of death, this side of the simulacrum). The 'accord with one's self', the 'simulacrum of death', are able to designate, at the limit of notional language, that loss of self that is neither fully lost nor gained in an experience of the *impossible*.

Such an accord, passing as it does through condemnation and sacrifice to a 'sort of death', requires and assumes violence in various forms and degrees of intensity. As in all sacrifice, there is violence in the brutal release of energy which accompanies the violation of the limit of the self, and in Bataille's erotic fiction there is also violence in the wounding and mutilation of self and other. Indeed, in this fiction, violence as the operative force of sacrifice generally falls into two categories: one associated with a radical release of energy, and the other arising from cruelty and injury inflicted upon an other. For the remainder of this chapter, I will be concerned primarily with the first category of violence, as it appears in the representation of sacrifice in Bataille's erotic fiction.

A consideration of this type of violence reveals that its brutal force promises both the potential for destruction, and an enormous release of energy in action. Bataille himself associated the words force and violence, for he viewed the latter as the unleashing of heterogeneous force which had been contained (in a gesture of violence) by the structures ensuring the stability of the homogeneous:

> Violence, excess ... characterize heterogeneous elements to varying degrees ... *Heterogeneous* reality is that of a force or a shock. It presents itself as a charge, as a value, passing from one object to another.[4]

This association of violence with disruptive force leads me to propose a model for the operation of violence in Bataille's erotic fiction: this model suggests that it is necessary to stress two moments – the moment of *destructive potential* and that of the *radical release of energy*. The question arises, then, of the role of the limit *vis-à-vis* this brutal force and its two moments. In other words, does the limit not oppose this force in order for it to be recognized as such? In physical terms, force is present when a static body is compelled to change its speed or direction. From this definition of force, one might extrapolate the following: in a first moment, there would be within the acting body a potential to effect change, a store of energy which, when released in a second moment, would cause this change in the body acted upon. A limit would serve in the first moment to contain this energy within the acting body while another limit would serve in the second moment to provide a point of resistance – the surface of the body acted upon – against which the force of energy might be directed.

This model which I am proposing for the violent passage of energy between bodies or entities is complemented by another put forward by Bataille in *La part maudite* and in 'La notion de dépense'. In those texts, Bataille situates such movements of exchange within a general economy, stating that an inevitable excess of energy within each discontinuous being exerts pressure upon its limits until it is unprofitably spent in either a glorious or a catastrophic fashion. If there is no relief for the pressure of this surplus energy, conflict and destruction may result, for outlets must be sought within the confines of limited space. Both this model and my own are useful in determining the extent to which Bataille's fiction, through its representation of sacrifice, initiates a loss in the reader that is neither fully recuperated as a gain, nor left unrecognized and therefore lost altogether.

My model suggests that violent energy is circumscribed in the first moment by Bataille's image itself; the parameters of this image may be thus seen to contain the potential force of poetic violence. The limit against which this brutal force is directed (in the second moment) is formed by the boundaries delimiting received notions,[5] be they those of God, of mother, of the eye or of any other signified; what is altered is the integrity of these notions as the energy of Bataille's image – the acting body – exceeds the confines of its discursive parameters and collides against the parameters of the received notion, opening it and releasing its energy as body acted upon. In *Méthode de méditation* Bataille describes poetry as a sacrifice or hecatomb of words:

> [Poetry] ... is the power words have to evoke effusion, the unlimited dépense of its own forces; thus, to an already determined effusion (comic or tragic), sovereignty adds not only the rhythm and overflow of the verses, but the *special capacity of the disorder of words to annul the ensemble of signs which constitutes the realm of activity.*[6]

Yet despite Bataille's reference to a hecatomb of words, to an 'annulment' of signs, to 'the unlimited dépense' of energy, other questions inevitably arise, namely: once the limits of notions have been ruptured to permit a release of energy, what remains of this destructive force? What becomes of this energy once released, and what is the status both of Bataille's image and the sacrificed notion after the act of poetic violence? Do they both submit to unlimited loss, a loss precluding the possibility of profit? Or does one figure gain from the other's loss? The answers to these questions may be found in several passages of *L'erotisme* in which the violence of sacrifice is described:

> The [sacred] is the revelation of continuity through the death of a discontinuous being to those who watch it as a solemn rite. A violent death disrupts the creature's continuity: what remains, what the tense onlookers experience in the succeeding silence, is the continuity of all existence with which the victim is now one.[7]

While this passage suggests the acquisition of an *experience* on the part of onlookers whose lives are not lost in the sacrifice, the quotation at the beginning of this chapter specifies that Bataille views the sacrificer and the onlookers as not only *witnessing* the victim's return to continuity, but as returning to continuity along with their victims. In the context of the sacrifice of *notions* outlined above, the victim of sacrifice within the text is the discontinuous notion which is ruptured and returned to continuity. Bataille's *image* transgresses, in opening the notion to continuity, in committing the act of sacrifice.[8] The energy which is released from the notion reverberates within the reader as a simulacrum of death, and what reverberates is a sense of transgression, in the return to continuity, in the fading of the notion. The limit of the notion does not, therefore, disappear altogether, for, as Foucault writes in his 'Preface to transgression', the limit is not annihilated in transgression, but remains to heighten the sense of transgression. Similarly, during the sacrificial act, the witness, who identifies with the victim, retains, despite the victim's rupture and return to continuity, a sense of its former integrity, in order that the sacrificial moment be heightened in transgression. The retention of the sense of the victim's limit or former integrity during sacrificial loss ensures that this loss not be lost, but suggests at the same time that this loss is ultimately gained *as such*. Bataille tries in his erotic fiction to approach the 'impossible' of a loss that is neither fully lost nor gained in sacrifice by engaging the reader in a *mise en abîme*. For the reader who witnesses the *mise en abîme* of a notion or a character through the representation of sacrifice, the experience of continuity, as it is triggered by poetic violence, appears as a *simulacrum* of death. Caught in this simulacrum of death, the reader and writer absorb the energy released from the initial sacrifice of a notion or a character, only to be later absorbed themselves in a subsequent *mise en abîme* of which *they* are the sacrificial victims, this second *mise en abîme* preventing the energy lost in the initial sacrifice of the notion from being transferred into a gain by the reader. Klossowski characterizes the moment of 'communication', which I would locate in this second *mise en abîme*, as one of complicity, which he distinguishes from the act of comprehension or grasping:

> The simulacrum has an object entirely other from that of the intelligible communication of the notion: it is complicity ... the simulacrum, aiming at complicity, arouses in one who experiences it a movement which can immediately disappear; and to speak of it will not in any way account for what has thus happened.[9]

Klossowski's discussion of the simulacrum 'aiming at complicity' can, then, be linked to Bataille's idiosyncratic use of the *mise en abîme* in his erotic fiction. The initial *mise en abîme* of a notion or a character sets off a second *mise en abîme* in the reader, who attains 'complicity' without either grasping, *or* failing to recognize, the representation of a sacrifice permitting a *mise en abyme* of a *mise en abîme*. Indeed, the reader both meditates upon the sacrifice of the discontinuous notion (a reflection *upon* its initial *mise en abîme*) and 'experiences' it as his or her own return to continuity (a second *mise en abîme* which affords reflection *from* the initial *mise en abîme*, since conscious reflection *upon* the latter is now problematic). It is this intentionally curious paradox of reflections (and their *mise en abîme*) that is the characteristic effect of Bataille's imagery. The latter entails a structural *mise en abyme* of an experienced and perceived *mise en abîme*, in which the fading of the notion and the self is both elusive *and* recognized.[10]

In the following passage from 'Hegel, la mort et le sacrifice', Bataille describes this paradox of reflections characterizing the *mise en abîme* of the witness *as* victim, a *mise en abîme* that neither sacrifices consciousness nor preserves its integrity:

> The privileged manifestation of Negativity is death, but death in fact reveals nothing ... for man ultimately to reveal himself to himself, he would have to die, but he would have to do it while living – by watching himself cease to be. In other words, death itself would have to be consciousness (of itself) at the very moment that it destroys conscious being.[11]

Consciousness of the fading of consciousness without however bracketing this for consciousness – this is the 'accord with one's self' that escapes notional language, for notional language can only represent loss as a gain.

A further examination of the poetic hecatomb, or release of 'notional' energy described earlier, shows that it operates on several levels in Bataille's texts. It may be practised between signs, when one sign mutilates another. In *Story of the Eye*, an obvious example of the assault which Bataille's images practise upon the integrity of the notion occurs when the holy chalice becomes a receptacle for priestly urine:

> After barricading the door, Sir Edmund rummaged through the closets until he finally lit upon a large chalice . . .
>
> 'Look', he explained to Simone, 'the eucharistic hosts in the ciborium, and here the chalice where they put white wine.'
>
> 'They smell like come', said Simone, sniffing the unleavened wafers.
>
> 'Precisely', continued Sir Edmund. 'The hosts, as you see, are nothing other than Christ's sperm in the form of small white biscuits. And as for the wine they put in the chalice, the ecclesiastics say it is the *blood* of Christ, but they are obviously mistaken. If they really thought that it was the blood, they would use *red* wine, but since they employ only *white* wine, they are showing that at the bottom of their hearts they are quite aware that this is *urine*.'[12]

In this passage, Bataille invites the reader to imagine a rite in which Christ's sperm and urine are ceremoniously swallowed; the images of sperm and urine are used to violate the received notions of the host and Christ's blood respectively; one sign violates another without, however, permitting either one to dominate the other. The value (or energy) of the received notions, once released, continue to reverberate in a loss that is not entirely subverted to the profit of the image inflicting sacrifice.

However, the mutilation and sacrifice effected by Bataille's imagery does not always operate *between* signs. It may also be directed from signifier to signified within the boundaries of a single sign. There it is a question of Bataille setting a destructive reverberation in motion, a slippage by which the normally static objects of signifier and signified are disturbed into a movement upsetting their discursive equilibrium. This is the case of the slipping word, whose capacity for self-destruction or auto-mutilation (sacrifice) had been silenced by the straightjacket of discourse. The slipping word, the sign in reverberation, becomes, therefore, the site of a mutual antagonism, an antagonism between signifier and signified, which discursive language had silenced for the purposes and profit of project, and which Bataille sets off in a gesture of poetic violence.

It is at this juncture that Bataille's own model for the exchange of energy is useful as well, for in his description of the conservation and expenditure of energy, conflict arises from the pressure of energy straining against imposed limits. It is as if Bataille, in violating the limit protecting the signified from the energy of the signifier, opens the latter to destructive expenditure, thus freeing it from the pressure incurred by its restricted use in the designation and preservation of meaning. As my model suggests, this force of energy, no longer limited within the signifier, is directed against the limit of the signified, opening it in turn to release in an expenditure that is neither radically dissipated into loss, nor recuperated into gain.

The words *silence* and *God* are privileged examples of slipping words, whose reverberating signifiers rupture the limits of their corresponding signifieds, in order that their energy be released. In both cases, it is the integrity of the signified that is mutilated, it is its store of energy that is sacrificed: in other words, the intact image of the signified provides the limit against which the energy of the signifier is released in a movement of force:

> I will give only one example of a 'slipping' *word* ... [Silence] is already, as I have said, the abolition of the sound which the word is; among all words it is the most perverse or the most poetic: it is the token of its own death.
>
> (*IE*, 16)

> The word *God*, to have used it in order to reach the depth of solitude, but to no longer know, hear his voice. To know nothing of him. God final word meaning that all words will fail further on.
>
> (*IE*, 36)

As the sign reverberates in automutilation, the reader is aware of the fading of the signified (its sacrifice) which entails the fading of its corresponding signifier (the sacrificer is affected by the blow that it strikes). What remains of this energy? Derrida writes of the sovereign operation as a reduction *of*, not *to*, meaning. Like Klossowski, he has recourse to the term 'simulacrum':

> This sliding is risky ... It risks making sense ... In order to run this risk within language, in order to save that which does not want to be saved – the possibility of play and of absolute risk – we must redouble language and have recourse to ruses, to stratagems, to simulacra.
>
> (*WD*, 263)

To save play and risk as that which does not want to be saved and to lose the identity of non-meaning as that which wants to be saved from the sovereign operation – one risks all the more a slippage between these two possibilities if one considers that the presence of reader and writer are put in question, in play, for what is also mutilated in poetic violence is the integrity of the writing and reading self. Bataille's objective is to target these entities as those to be emptied in communication, engaged as they will be in a *mise en abîme* that pre-figures a loss neither gained (which would mean saving the identity of non-meaning) nor lost (which would mean losing play and risk as that which does not want to be saved). As author, Bataille presides over the sacrifice of notions, but this is a sacrifice to which he as poet/executioner risks succumbing, since he bears these notions within and becomes the site for their *mise à mort*:

> I rely on God to deny himself, to loathe himself, to throw what he dares, what he is, into absence, into death. When I am God, I negate him right to the depths of negation.
>
> (*IE*, 131)

> The world, the shadow of God, which ... [the] poet ... himself is, can suddenly seem to him to be marked for ruin. So that the impossible, the unknown which they are in the end, are revealed.
>
> (*IE*, 155)

> For *me* the words 'I will die' are suffocating ...[13] But when, how will I die? Something that others, no doubt, will know one day and that I will never know.
>
> (*LC*, 342)

The reader is invited, through the violence of Bataille's imagery, to witness sacrifice – in the first case, that of the notion of God and ultimately of the poet himself; in the second, that of Bataille as he imagines his death. These are sacrifices which risk condemning the reader as well who, as guilty observer, or *voyeur*, becomes the executioner, in imagining the poet's succumbing to sacrifice. As guilty observer, the reader or *voyeur* becomes, in turn, a victim whose identification with the poet as victim lost in continuity provokes his or her own loss in continuity. As victim, the reader risks falling from the precipice of the page's edge into a *mise en abîme*:

> I write for one, who, entering into my book, would fall into it as into a hole, who would never again get out ... poetic existence in me addresses itself to poetic existence in others ... I cannot myself be *ipse* without having cast this cry to them. Only by this cry do I have the power to annihilate in me the 'I' as they will annihilate it in them if they hear me.
>
> (*IE*, 116)

It is this very construction of the text as 'hole' or '*abîme*' that allows Bataille to pull the reader into the textual space of his writing, where the former joins him, lost with him in continuity.[14] Pulled into the abyss, the reader's loss is neither lost (forgotten) nor transmuted into profit, but inhabits the impossible space where the experience of sacrifice is neither recuperated nor left unrecognized.

Given the energy required to effect this sacrifice or loss in the reader, it is not surprising that the theoretical texts of *La somme athéologique* should, at various breaking points of the text, expose a writing in the first person in order to lay bare the cry capable of initiating this loss:

> The third, the companion, the reader who acts upon me ... it is he who speaks in me, who maintains in me the discourse intended for him ... even more than [project, discourse] ... is that *other*, the reader, who loves me and who already forgets me (kills me), without whose present insistence I could do nothing, would have no inner experience ... I tolerate in me the action of project in that it is a link with this obscure *other* sharing my anguish, my torment, desiring my torment as much as I desire his.
>
> (*IE*, 61)

In cases such as these in which Bataille seems to address his reader in a reverberating *mise en abîme*, it is the limit of the poet's 'I' that is violated; the energy that is thereby released is a force that encounters the limit of the body acted upon, the reading self: as this second limit surrounding the reading self is violated, as the reader succumbs to the pull into the 'hole' of the text, the energy contained within the reading self is released. An emptied notion, the reader's violated self is no longer able to take its bearings *vis-à-vis* its own intact limit. It is therefore no longer 'pitted against itself' in an inner division that had previously ensured the self's integrity, be this a superficial and fallacious integrity which is ruptured in this accord with the self. Through the contagion of poetic violence, then, the self risks loss in continuity – 'a sort of death' – that, since it permits profound recognition while eluding conscious contemplation, constitutes a loss that is both elusive and recognized. This complex and multi-faceted, multi-layered *mise en abîme* operates, therefore, on both an intra- and extra-textual level: there is the reverberation within the boundaries of the sign or slipping word which Bataille had set in motion in a gesture of poetic violence. There is the violence which the image inflicts upon the sacrificed notion. The energy, the vibrations released from the sacrifice of notions and signifieds, from the opening of images, signifiers and characters, are not entirely dissipated or lost, for they are now echoed and enclosed in a reverberating *mise en abîme* moving from writer to reader and back again in an ever-deepening cycle. The author/executioner sacrifices notions and characters, a *mise en abîme* that returns to sacrifice him. The reader/*voyeur*/witness becomes an accomplice in the sacrifice – identifying with an initial *mise en abîme* which returns, in a *mise en abîme* of a *mise en abîme*, to sacrifice him or her. This intentional sacrifice of reader having been achieved, the author re-emerges as sacrificer. This reverberation and loss between and in signs, between and in writer and reader renders the position of the critic problematic at the very least, for as witness to this *mise en abîme* of a *mise en abîme*, he or she is also subject to risk: that of succumbing in turn to the contagion of sacrifice reflected and multiplied in the Bataillian text.

The problem for the critic becomes that of maintaining critical distance, there where the *mise en abîme* of Bataille's texts suggests succumbing to its reverberation. If this distance, necessary for critical activity, is maintained, does the critic necessarily finish by writing *of* this writing and by being restricted to a reflection *upon* it? Does the critic, in other words, betray the sense of (and refuse the invitation to) Bataillian sacrifice by using notional language (which always translates loss into gain) in order to describe and react to the ramifications of an experience in reading: that of a loss which, 'ideally', is simultaneously and paradoxically a loss and a gain, Bataille having tried to privilege neither in his own texts? In *L'expérience intérieure*, Bataille writes of the 'absurdity of reading what should tear one apart to the point of dying and, to begin with, of preparing one's lamp, a drink, one's bed, of winding one's watch' (*IE*, 37). In this case it is Bataille's reflection *upon* the possibility of a *mise en abîme* (the possibility of the impossible) that almost renders the impossible impossible:

> And ecstasy is the way out! ... The way out? It suffices that I look for it: I fall back again, inert, pitiful: the way out from project, from a will for a way out! For project is the prison from which I wish to escape (project, discursive experience): I formed the project to escape from project! And I know that it suffices to break discourse in me; from that moment on, ecstasy is there, from which only discourse distances me – the ecstasy which discursive thought betrays by proposing it as absence of a way out.
>
> (*IE*, 59)

In lieu of a response to the question of the critical distance to be maintained in the face of Bataille's invitation to sacrifice (for this response can, in the end, only be determined individually and personally in the space of the precipice pre-figuring the '(w)hole' of Bataille's text) I will simply refer to Bataille's own practices when confronted with the difficulty of writing about the *impossible*. He himself had several ways of escaping from the prison of discourse in order to allow the contagion of violent energy to reverberate in a *profound mise en abîme*. There are the repeated attempts to undermine his own discourse in his more theoretical books (Bataille sacrifices his own notions and presides over their loss in continuity, echoing the strategy put forward in *L'abbé C.* by Charles in his reflection *upon* the *mise en abîme* of Robert's writing – 'The only way to compensate for the fault of writing is to wipe out that which is written'). It is as if Bataille occupies the positions of Robert and Charles in his situation both inside and outside of the *mise en abîme* housed by his theoretical texts.

It is true that Bataille's own *mise à nu* in his theoretical texts also allows him to set off the mechanism of the *mise en abîme* in his readers and critics, for he aimed repeatedly to engage them in a *mise en abîme* of his own *mise en abîme*. If one absorbs the energy released by his imagery, one's reading and writing may reverberate in a movement in and between the various *mises en abîme* of his texts. Despite the attempt to maintain critical distance, one then risks losing the possibility of effecting solely a reflection *upon* texts which have incessantly aimed to engage the reader and critic in a reflection *from* a *mise en abîme*. In the end, it is perhaps the curious paradox of reflections *from* and *upon* the *mises en abîme* of Bataille's text that would solicit a different kind of critical writing, one that would no longer diminish the heterogeneous force of Bataille's writing by subverting it to the strictures of *discursive* writing, but that would allow the latter to surpass itself, to put its own notional language into question through a response to the various *mises en abîme* and *mises à nu* of Bataille's erotic fiction and philosophical texts.

Notes

1   For a good study of the technique of the *mise en abyme* see Bruce Morrissette's 'Un héritage d'André Gide: La duplication intérieure', *Comparative Literature Studies*, June 1971, 125–42. See also Lucien Dallenbach's book-length study of the subject, *Le récit spéculaire: Essai sur la mise en abyme*, Paris, Seuil, 1977.

2   Bataille, *La littérature et le mal, Oeuvres complètes (OC)*, V, Paris, Gallimard, 1979, 193. All translations mine throughout the chapter, unless otherwise specified.

3   François Wahl, 'Nu, ou les impasses d'une sortie radicale', *Bataille*. Direction: Philippe Sollers. *Colloque du 29 juin au 9 juillet 1972 à Cerisy-la-Salle: Vers une révolution culturelle: Artaud, Bataille*. Coll. 10/18, no. 805. Paris, Union générale d'éditions, 1973, 218.

4   Bataille, 'The psychological structure of fascism' in *Visions of Excess: Selected writings, 1927–39*, ed. and trans. Allan Stoekl, with Carl R. Lovitt and Donald M. Leslie Jr, Minneapolis, University of Minnesota Press, 1985, 142, 143.

5   In this discussion, I have chosen to use the term 'notion' to occupy the position of body acted upon and 'image' to represent the sacrificial agent or acting body. This distinction is supported by dictionary definitions which define 'image' as 'a representation to the mind by speech or writing'. This relative lack of qualification suggests that an image is not tied to established connotations and has the potential to transgress limits through poetry and unconventional language uses. The word 'notion', on the other hand, is defined as 'a general concept under which a particular thing or person is comprehended or classed' (suggesting relative stasis, adherence to established connotation and the strictures of predetermined language use). In his 'Discussion sur le péché', Bataille uses the term 'notion' as something whose limits he aims to open: 'I set out from notions which normally enclose certain beings around me and I played with them … Language fails, because language is made up of propositions which cause identities to intervene … one is forced to open notions beyond themselves' ('Discussion sur le péché', *OC*, VI, 349, 350). Finally, Klossowski's distinction between the simulacrum and the notion is revelatory here: 'The simulacrum is all we know of an experience; the notion is only its residue calling forth other residues … The notion and notional language presupposes what Bataille calls closed beings … it is evident … that, dependent on the notion of identity … the opening of beings or the attack on the integrity of beings … are developed like a simulacrum of a notion' ('A propos du simulacre dans la communication de Georges Bataille', *La Ressemblance*, Marseille, Editions ryôan-je, 1984, 24, 25, 26 (article referred to hereafter as *AP*)).

6   Bataille, *Méthode de méditation*, quoted in Michèle Richman's *Reading Georges Bataille: Beyond the Gift*, Baltimore, Johns Hopkins University Press, 1982, 70. Translation and emphasis Richman's.

7   Bataille, *Eroticism*, trans M. Dalwood, San Francisco, City Lights Books, 1986, 82.

8   Derrida describes the sacrifice of notions occurring in Bataille's text as the mutation of the meaning of concepts: 'the same concepts, apparently unchanged in themselves, will be subject to a mutation of meaning, or rather will be struck by (even though they are apparently indifferent), the loss of sense towards which they slide, thereby ruining themselves immeasurably. To blind oneself to this rigorous precipitation, this pitiless sacrifice of philosophical concepts, and to continue to read, interrogate and judge Bataille's text from within "significant discourse" … is assuredly not to read it' (*Writing and Difference*, trans. Allan A. Bass, Chicago, University of Chicago Press, 267 (text referred to hereafter as *WD*)).

9   Klossowski, *AP*, 24.

10 It would be very difficult, and no doubt distortive, to try and establish a temporal schema for the paradox of reflections *from* and *upon* the *mise en abîme*. In *Inner Experience*, Bataille writes of a cycle of reversals or slippages from points of knowledge to non-knowledge:

NON-KNOWLEDGE LAYS BARE.
This proposition is the summit, but must be understood in this way: lays bare, therefore I see what knowledge was hiding up to that point, but if I see, *I know*. Indeed, I know, but non-knowledge again lays bare what I have

> known. If nonsense is sense, the sense which is nonsense is lost, becomes nonsense once again (without possible end).
>
>   (*Inner Experience*, trans. L.A. Boldt, Albany, State University of New York Press, 52: text referred to hereafter as *IE*)

Derrida writes of the instant which 'slides and eludes us between two presences; it is difference as the affirmative elusion of presence' (*WD*, 263). Libertson prefers to maintain that there is tension between two conditions, a tension which he qualifies as impossible, the impossible. This defines an ipseity 'whose closure is both absolute and uncertain'. The paradox stems from the fact that discontinuity always 'contains more than it can contain'; it 'must escape its limits', but 'cannot escape its limits'. For Libertson, transgression is both an activity, a *dépense*, and a form of cognition (J. Libertson, 'Bataille and Communication: *savoir, non-savoir, glissement, rire*', *Sub-stance*, 10, 1974, 50).

11   Bataille, 'Hegel, la mort et le sacrifice', *OC*, XII, 336.
12   Bataille, *Story of the Eye*, trans. J. Neugroschel, London, Marion Boyers, 1979, 61, 66.
13   Bataille, *Le coupable*, *OC*, V, 365 (text referred to hereafter as *LC*).
14   The mutual loss of reader and writer in continuity and their respective power to precipitate the other into a common *mise en abîme* implies, for Bataille, their shared strength and vulnerability. This union of writer and reader is, of course, ideal and corresponds to what Bataille had hoped would occur through his literature. For an excellent commentary on feminist responses to Bataille's imagery, see Susan Rubin Suleiman's chapter 'Pornography, transgression, and the avant-garde: Bataille's *Histoire de l'oeil*' in *Subversive Intent*, Cambridge, Harvard University Press, 1990.

8 The hatred of poetry in Georges Bataille's writing and thought

Marie-Christine Lala

Haine de la poésie in Georges Bataille's work refers primarily to the text published in 1947, and republished in 1962 with its definitive title, *L'impossible*. In his preface to the second edition, Bataille says:

> Hardly anybody understood the meaning of the original title, which is why I now prefer to talk in terms of *L'impossible*. I admit that this new title is no easier to understand. But one day it might be.[1]

I should like to rise to this challenge offered by Bataille to the potential future interpreter. And, after looking initially at what the text of *Haine de la poésie* represents in terms of writing, I shall reflect on the significance and implications for Georges Bataille's thought.

From the moment of its annunciation in *Haine de la poésie*, the concept of the impossible is deployed as a challenge, a provocation or even a term of abuse. I shall take the risk of accepting that challenge, even if it leads me to transgress the frontier separating logic from non-sense in order to show that 'the category of the impossible' finally operates as the theme of the void in the works of Georges Bataille.[2]

Furthermore, in this chapter I shall develop an investigation into the nature and the existential status of the impossible object of exchange in the thought and writing of Georges Bataille. Understanding the meaning of the hatred of poetry entails considering the role played by the impossible in the circuit of communication. For it is in the hatred of poetry that Georges Bataille discovers that *'part maudite'* – that doomed part – of exchange, whose use value he generalizes through the concept of the impossible not only in terms of textual poetics but in terms of logic, economics and religion.

Nonsense and the irreducible object of absence

L'impossible (or *Haine de la poésie*) strikes us as an original and exemplary text in so far as it deploys in its language certain strategic mechanisms which exploit the resources of poetry in order to present a textual configuration whereby *the truth of the impossible and of death* may be translated without losing its originality. In order to sustain the violence and the excess of this truth, Bataille's writing espouses an experience lived out as emotional ecstasy. If it is difficult in the first instance to interpret *Haine de la poésie*, it is because interpretation keeps disappearing, as each attempt returns us to the terrain of language: we slide 'as in quicksand' through its unstable, fugitive meanings. The text astonishes, but Bataille himself underlines its disturbing nature:

> As to the reason for publishing in a single book both poetry and a subversion of poetry, a dead man's diary and notes written by an ecclesiastical friend of mine, I would be hard pressed to explain. Yet this kind of caprice is not without precedent, and I would like to state here that, in my experience, it is also capable of translating the inevitable.[3]

The second edition of the text entitled *L'impossible*, reverses the order of the three sections: the two narratives, 'Histoire de rats' and 'Dianus', become the first two panels of the triptych, leaving the poetry and the subversion of poetry to close the text in 'L'Orestie'. If Bataille chooses to ground his thought initially in the narrative mode, it is in order to push to its limits the trajectory traced out by fiction, because only this will allow him to grasp 'the category of the impossible' and use it to 'translate the inevitable'.

The narrative and the death of narrative fuel a dramatic alternation where the disappearance of the object is at stake. The constant possibility that the narrative may vanish threatens the discourse with the prospect of non-sense, while the loss of the desired object endangers the subject. If the narrative vanishes, his discourse collapses. Similarly, in the place of the missing object there looms *a lack* which is the mark of its absence. In thus dramatizing the disappearance of the object, Bataille lays bare the subjectivity which is a problematic feature of man as he confronts his own death and faces it naked. As the narrative fades, the *nothingness* that was masked by the repetition of the story is clearly revealed to consciousness as *a void*, and the story is unable to assuage the terror of lack which is unleashed by the loss of the object: '"what had I done", I thought, "to deserve to be so thoroughly expelled into the realm of the impossible?"'[4]

The narrative constantly repeats the same process, playing with the object-as-lack, and the problem of death, once situated in this way within language and the speech-act, throws into high relief an unbridgeable distance. However hard it is, this tension must be maintained, because it keeps man moving in the right direction:

> What do we know of the fact that we live, if the death of a beloved being does not introduce the horror (the void) to such an extent that we cannot bear it to intrude: but then we know we know which door the key will open.[5]

There is in this experience of the void such a trial that the experience of writing cannot be dissociated from the experience of loss, for without the dramatization of existence such experience would remain inaccessible. This moment of excess is often communicated through sovereign modes of behaviour such as drunkenness or eroticism, but the narrative displays it as its impossible limit: at that point of intensity where 'being is given to us in an intolerable transcendence of being', suffering becoming transfigured into the exuberance of desire.

The impossible uses the object-as-lack as a medium to translate something irreducible, which makes it impossible to render it directly accessible. That is why the configuration of the text of *Haine de la poésie* struggles to dramatize it, to expose it. For it is indeed in the text that the rationality of discourse is finally overcome by the irrational, which springs out of danger or ecstasy. Everything connives at the deconstruction of meaning, the prospect of madness as much as ecstasy. It is always an experience which is communicated in negative terms, of tearing, of extreme anxiety, and which is expressed through illness or suffering, grounded now in love, now in radical solitude, now in echoes of warfare, now in violent destruction and now in writing. The malaise arising from the disappearance of meaning, from the trials imposed by the loss of self-identity and the love-object, induce a state of crisis which is aggravated by intensive efforts to decompose all constituted forms. Language, the body and the subject reach their own limits in this trial imposed by the impossible and by death.

Death in the narrative throws into relief the loss of the object and the loss of the subject, whose coincidence reveals a moment of emptiness, of suspension of meaning. When the narrative finishes, exhausted, it becomes possible to recompose the coherence of the text in terms of poetry, for non-sense can arise as the product of the dice-throw of the signifier falling onto the page. Non-sense is a 'sudden splinter of bone', the heterogeneous remains and sloughed skin of meaning, clearly revealing the operation of a *remainder* within language. Meaning escapes, its formulation ever impossible, but the poetic function of language ultimately shows itself naked in ravishing ecstasy and in 'rich', dazzling 'madness':

the trumpets of joy
ring insanely
and burst with the whiteness of heaven[6]

From the first to the third panel of *L'impossible*, the trial imposed by the impossible and by death fosters the emergence of a subject divided. The signifier manipulates him as fictional subject, and at the same time he recovers in the symbolic order in order to recompose himself differently and communicate the implications of the experience which produced him. He intervenes as witness – in so far as he accepts loss of self and agrees to become 'the prophet announcing what is lost in the moment of absence'. He is that sovereign subject who comes to regenerate meaning around him, for his loss is the sign of what may be generated by radical absence, from the position of absence that is death. He is the subject of fiction, but also the subject of critique, and he is thereby enabled to speak 'the subversion of poetry'. The workings of death in the text of *Haine de la poésie* designate the place where the subject of the speech-act comes to die, to dissolve and be born again, or, more precisely, to lose himself in order to recompose himself differently, since loss is the enabling condition of symbolic enactment. Obeying the principle of loss, that is of 'unconditional expenditure', the sovereign subject is renewed as he goes through the motions of dying, and, recovering immediately afterwards, he formulates the meaning which is generated by non-sense through the principle of subversion.

The meaning of the hatred of poetry

The gesture of subversion rejects 'the beauty of poetry' (lyric poetry) in order to ground the meaning of poetry in its opposite, 'the hatred of poetry'. Bataille points out that if there is no subversion, poetry stays trapped in the realm of everyday activity, which reduces it to the status of merely 'beautiful poetry', that is, pure rhetoric, or poetic verbiage.

In the hatred of poetry it is *the hatred* which makes the poetry authentic, by maintaining the dynamism of the force to hate as a force for infinite renewal and resurgence: 'How could there be any way of assuming, without inner violence, this negation, which bears us towards the utmost limits of the possible?'[7] This is what Bataille means by 'adding to poetry the explosive glitter of failure', for 'poetry which fails to rise to the level of the non-sense of poetry is only the void of poetry, only beautiful poetry'.[8] The explosive glitter of failure lies in the refusal to repress hatred, the refusal to repress the violence and the vital energy of truth that are *hatred*. It also lies in the refusal to amalgamate and reconcile everything irreconcilable 'in a blind, inner brilliance'. It lies in choosing Artaud against Breton.[9]

Such a refusal is part of an ethical decision to oppose the repression of hatred, knowing that the repressed will always find a way to express itself in the end. The act of subversion (which is an affirmation of sovereignty) is a decision to express and sustain the vital energy of truth that is hatred, without avoiding its violence and preventing it from finding expression as negative destruction. Thus, when poetry becomes 'the hatred of poetry' and attains self-subversion, it becomes an affirmation of sovereignty intended to defuse the lethal effects contained within hatred. The truth effect of the impossible which manages to resurface through the hatred of poetry is not lethal. On the contrary, it liberates life through its glittering explosion, liberating the spark through which life is renewed.

As it becomes 'the hatred of poetry', a sovereign mode of behaviour, poetry takes on a special status, because it alone can at once maintain non-sense in the midst of poetic ecstasy, and also generate a commentary on its absence of meaning in the very act of subversion.

In this way the subject of writing, in so far as he is a sovereign subject, reaches the peaks at the moment when he falls and collapses: his position of collapse becomes *authoritative* by opening up within the symbolic order an entirely different field of recomposition. What is at stake is a process of transformation, and the 'term of poetry may be considered to be synonymous with expenditure: it indicates creation by means of loss. Its meaning is therefore close to that of sacrifice.'[10]

The 'hatred of poetry' maintains the place of the void as enactment of a negative but enabling force. Its exact tenor may be understood as a function of the workings of death and of the impossible. For in fact there is in Bataille's writing a process of negation, which may be seen at work from its origins in the suspension of meaning to its culmination in the zero degree of oblivion:

> I have sought to speak a language equivalent to zero, a language amounting to nothing, a language returning to silence.[11]

Through this practice of writing, Bataille proceeds towards discovering and laying bare the power of negativity which is at work within language.

In language there is a point of junction and separation where meaning is suspended and broken. At this point the signified is perceived as non-sense, since any understanding which thinks metaphysically can only repress it, or conceive it by conceptualizing it as 'nothingness'. Hegel, according to Bataille, 'took up the concept of sovereignty only as a burden immediately to be dropped'. In the language of the theologians, the signifier to which his referent corresponds is the word 'God' and Bataille derisively grants it the status of the impossible in order to maintain it in the guise of the theme of the void and, in so doing, to regenerate its vital force of renewal, replacing God with the impossible.

Left hanging in the balance, the signified's name is not a rose's, but 'O-restes', meaning 'No rest'-itution, a zero remainder, the journey's-end dregs or detritus whose trace none the less marks the place where the irreducible object-as-lack is obtainable.

There is considerable difficulty in conceptualizing this 'lack', grounded as it is in the process of becoming and in the status of the object. Its ungraspable, irreducible reality may be compared to 'a hard, alien fingertip pressing into the small of the back'. It is the moment of the strongest contradiction between life and death, the moment when the force of hatred maintains its activity within the work. Because of its irreducible nature, thematized by Bataille as 'le supplice',[12] the contradiction never relaxes, dissolving as soon as it is formed, but with no possibility of any solution or resolution.

The moment of stasis is only a pivotal point of transformation: the void is not nothingness, it is an unmarked term, the *nothing* where the passage from one term to another comes to pass, the slippage from meaning to non-sense:

> Whatever given meaning I start from, I exhaust it ... or I finally fall into non-sense.
>   But how can we remain, dissolved, in non-sense? It cannot be done. Any non-sense must inevitably open up onto some kind of meaning ... leaving an after-taste of ashes and madness.[13]

In order to escape from this moment of black, destructive negation, bordering on insane hatred or apathetic inertia, we must keep fingering the open wound of the contradictory moment, exposing its energetic, vital core.

The wound formed by this lack will have served merely to dramatize the mark of a trajectory where the power of the negative articulates that blinding, explosive far horizon where life and death cease to be perceived in terms of contradiction, where a radiant flash, in a timeless instant, reveals them as being nothing but contradiction, where they erupt in a blaze of beauty which is 'impossible, and yet present'.

This version of 'the hatred of poetry', thus interpreted in terms of a poetics of the text and of logic, reveals the incidence of the vacant moment of the impossible relation between the subject and the object. The status of the object, at once unobtainable and irreducible, assuming the function of a *remainder*, of a *heterogeneous residue*, does in fact allow us to understand the meaning of poetry as it turns into its opposite, into the hatred of poetry. Authentic poetry, conceived in terms of expenditure, takes as its issue the function of the remainder in poetic language. Its meaning is close to that of sacrifice, rather than merely being a symbolic representation of tragic loss. It may even 'cease to be symbolic in its consequences', since the impossible object, assuming the function of a remainder which is both doomed and sacred, thereby attains a lethal limit. This 'doomed part' is the incarnation of a sort of demoniac schism; this doomed remainder, adopted by the 'victim', is a source of ill, perhaps even of *Evil* . . . it therefore obstructs communication, becoming a source of suffering in the pain of separation. However, it is also sacred and encourages the mode of communication authorized by sovereign types of behaviour: communication through excess, the exuberance of the activity of *unproductive expenditure*. Paradoxically, it becomes the catalyst which reveals the divine part in man . . . and this irreducible part, which is communicated through art, eroticism and religious sacrifice, remains inscribed within man as something secret and sacred. 'The hatred of poetry' thus holds open the urgent need to respond to an *effusion*, since its sacrificial site is a part of our most intimate existence.

The impossible, the fatal dimension and sin

'The hatred of poetry', or the impossible, stands for an a-logical difference, which Bataille's thought reveals as a stark coincidence of contradictory terms, while refusing to reduce it to the identity of opposites. The a-logical principle of a live contradiction (the reservoir of vital hatred) prevents a fusion which would entail self-enclosure: through this process the subject constantly moves between loss and recovery, between speech and silent play. Fusion is already dissolution, projected towards the effusion of sovereign behaviour. Starting out from this logical condition, Bataille develops its consequences in the field of economics, making an explicit formulation of the themes of unproductive expenditure and of sovereignty.

The effusion of sovereign behaviour introduces disorder, it causes the modification of an existing order (the order of hierarchized objects, the order of discourse, the order of utilitarian work) in favour of the liberation of a doomed part. A considerable part of the originality of

Bataille's thought consists in its tendency to grant this doomed part, this feature of exchange that is superfluous and therefore disruptive, a dignity and an impact in the order of knowledge. For Bataille, it is expenditure which is the primary object, whereas production is only a function of expenditure. This reversal of traditional perspectives betrays Bataille's concern to found a 'general economics', a science relating the objects of thought to moments of sovereignty, and erecting the doomed part as the generator of social relations and value. Unproductive expenditure primes the circuit of exchange, and sacrifice (or the wasteful consumption of wealth) constitutes the foundation of this operation, whereby the principle of subversion (which is at once revolt and affirmation of sovereignty) is grounded in the principle of loss. The impossible both designates and preserves the site of this doomed part.[14]

For the impossible, seen in terms of the theme of the void, is indeed a conceptual simulacrum which designates the site of a vacancy. Instead of the name of God, 'guarantor of the individual self', its heterogeneous residue constantly acts out that loss of identity which constitutes sin. What is more the *hatred* which constitutes authentic poetry creates excess energy, in so far as 'the sum of energy produced is always superior to the sum necessary for production'. In this way the unconditional expenditure sustains the impossible object of the exchange, the doomed and sacred remainder that simultaneously hinders and fosters communication:

> this continual, bubbling superfluity of energy – leading us ever upwards towards the peaks – which constitutes the malevolent part that we attempt (to no great avail) to spend for the benefit of all.[15]

We see that this *impossibility*, whose virtual presence we have discovered in writing – springing from the process of death and 'the hatred of poetry' – has repercussions in terms of its doomed part. Not only does the impossible put the poetics and the aesthetics of the text to the test, but it also raises the crucial question of the relations obtaining between crime and communication, between sin and action . . .

The poetics of the text of *Haine de la poésie* has allowed us to disentangle the logical functioning of *hatred* conceived as 'a-logical difference', then to grasp the *doomed part*. Gradually we have been led to seek the articulation of this economic phenomenon in the domains of ethics and religion. According to Bataille, man bears within himself, despite himself, a question which acts as an explosive charge:

> What can be achieved in this world by a lucid man? A man whose urgent inner demands brook no concessions?[16]

The search for the foundations of an ethics where neither hatred nor the doomed part are eluded, and which takes into account 'the dynamics of evil', is a difficult and paradoxical search in which Bataille's thought is enriched by its contact with Nietzsche's.

This experience of his limits leads man 'from the ebb of pain to the flow of joy', it is inseparable from eroticism, from drunkenness, from sobbing (half laughing, half crying) and it releases 'a tiny fragment of blinding life'. All these forms of unproductive expenditure unleash the dynamics of exuberance whose life and liberty are inseparable from death and the unbounded void.

The effusion which they presuppose had been able to find a limit in institutionalized forms: those of 'beautiful poetry', of philosophy, or of religion. But Bataille, through the practice of sovereign behaviour, removes the barrier which this limit imposes, in order to recover the authentic meaning of the sacred, and the true meaning of poetry returning as its opposite. *L'érotisme* shows how the system works in the realms of biology, psychology and anthropology, with all its implications for philosophy, morality and religion. And *Les larmes d'Eros* sums up the tragedy and the comedy of the drama acted out within the ethical and aesthetic fields that are at stake in eroticism, at the interface between love, laughter and death.

The secret springs of eroticism and religion are revealed at the same time, being based on an understanding of the vital necessity of hatred and the doomed, impossible and superfluous dimensions of exchange:

> It requires a great effort to perceive the link between the promise of life, which is what eroticism signifies, and the luxurious aspect of death. Humankind has agreed to ignore the fact that death is also the youth of the world. With blindfold eyes we refuse to see that death alone secures the constant resurgence without which life would decline. We refuse to see that life is a booby trap opening up beneath our feet as we stand on it, that it is nothing more than a pit of instability and vertigo into which we are plunged. It is a tumultuous process which constantly leads to explosion. But since the ceaseless explosions constantly exhaust it, it can only continue on one condition: that among the beings which it engenders, those whose explosive force is exhausted should leave room for new beings, joining the game with new vigour.[17]

An obscure but meaningful contradiction sustains the enigma of existence, for it simultaneously affirms and withdraws the truth of life: 'the wind of truth is a violent wind'. In order to keep his eyes open in this face of what he is founded on, man must sustain this definitive contradiction of life and death 'making clear distinctions between different possibilities' and 'using his ability to reach out to the utmost extremities'.

Eroticism gives access to a part of thought that philosophical reflection is unable to communicate, and which finds a framework in *Théorie de la réligion* and *La somme athéologique*. A violent interruption (the disruptive moment of wounding, of pain, of abandonment) is necessary for communication, for life. This is why we must seek out the sacrificial site and become 'guilty', keep the marks of the sinner to 'win interest against God'. The confrontation between man and the void leads to a confrontation between man and God, 'the limit of the Limitless'. We must no longer delay examining the void which indicates his name and 'puncturing it with our laughter'. In order to reach out to the utmost limits of the mystical (secret and doomed) part, we must destroy all hope of salvation, exhaust all mysticism, thus destroying all refuge for religion. Through eroticism and sacrifice, Bataille's thought recovers its sense of the sacred, which answers the need that used to be satisfied by religion while it jettisons its beliefs. Atheology pursues the fundamental goal of reaching that pitch of exuberance where 'we leave Christianity behind'. Bataille treats the concept of sin as a conceptual simulacrum, on a par with the impossible, in order to emphasize the principle of loss and inaugurate the need to 'open concepts up to what overflows them'. To be without guilt is tantamount to avoiding expenditure, whereas being guilty is making expenditure our first concern. Sin remains the pivotal point of the subversive offensive which pits man against God. It only stages its failure to communicate (its doomed part of repressed *hatred*) the better to grant access to lucidity and a state of consciousness turned towards its own capacity for action. It is formulated in the following terms in *La littérature et le mal*, which formulates the problem of the conditions which would enable the accomplishment of a 'hyper-ethics':

> The tumult is radical ... But it is time to attain lucidity of consciousness.[18]

> The need to lose oneself fills the whole of life with suffering, but in this need being escapes from closure.[19]

It is a paradox of the human condition and existence that man can only escape the finitude of his being if he accepts losing himself. Only the impossible can provide an answer ... because it is both centre and derision of any centre. In terms of the theme of the void, it serves to designate the site where expenditure and sovereignty are articulated, for it preserves, through 'the hatred of poetry' and the doomed part, the vacancy enabling the formulation of a thought where the consciousness of foundering subsists. In his preface to *L'érotisme*, Bataille underlines the exigency which presides over his work:

> I have sacrificed everything to the search for a viewpoint able to disclose the unity of the human spirit.[20]

This viewpoint, which is provided by the impossible, in relation to the process of death, to a vital hatred, to a doomed part, is mobile enough to offer a perspective which will ultimately yield the diverse possibilities of mankind.

At this moment of absolute silence, with its doomed and sacred part, the charm of nudity counterbalances the 'miraculous element' contained within death. The impossible offers the possibility of a sudden and magical reversal, in a burst of wonder, with a new upsurge of life and the triumph of laughter charged with exuberance.

The search for an impossible object, which is the essential, leads man beyond accepted limits. This experience of a point of limitation remains inseparable from eroticism and writing. It is in fact the experience of the impossible, grounded in the body and in language, and it affirms the specificity of literature, with its 'intense communication through the knowledge of evil'.

The poetics of the text of *L'impossible* (or *Haine de la poésie*) opens up an investigation of ontological implications, since the aesthetic part of literature, put on trial by the impossible and by death, finds itself confronted with the limits of being. This investigation measures beauty (the aesthetic) in the light of evil, and thus raises the crucial question of ethical exigencies. Using new bases for aesthetics and for knowledge, Bataille's thought takes an experience of writing driven by the impossible and by the hatred of poetry, and develops the substance of an anthropology.

Translated by Peter Collier

Notes

1 Bataille, *L'impossible*, Paris, Editions de Minuit, 1962, 10.
2 I have examined this question, following the theme through from literature to the concept of a general economy in a seminar entitled 'L'impossible, le don et la dette', which I gave at the Collège International de Philosophie. See *Le Cahier du Collège International de Philosophie*, 7, Paris, Osiris, 1989, 174–7.
3 Bataille, *Oeuvres complètes* (*OC*), III, Paris, Gallimard, 1971, 509.
4 Bataille, *L'impossible*, 97.

5   Ibid., 79.
6   Ibid., 171.
7   Bataille, *OC*, III, 509–44.
8   Bataille, *L'impossible*, 184.
9   Bataille, *OC*, II, 51–109.
10 Bataille, 'La notion de dépense' in *La part maudite*, Paris, Editions de Minuit, 1967, 29.
11 Bataille, *OC*, V, 25ff.
12 Ibid., 43.
13 Bataille, *L'impossible*, 129.
14 Bataille, *La part maudite*.
15 Bataille, *OC*, VI, 60.
16 Ibid.
17 Bataille, *L'impossible*, 136 and *Sur Nietzsche*, *OC*, VI.
18 Bataille, *La littérature et le mal*, *OC*, IX, 171.
19 Bataille, *L'impossible*.
20 Bataille, *L'érotisme*, *OC*, X, 12.

9 Surrealism and the practice of writing, or The 'case' of Bataille

John Lechte

Preface

This is a work in progress.[1] And it will remain so if this notion can refer us to a writing which resists closure. Indeed, Julia Kristeva has proposed that the subject now has to be seen as an open work rather than as an entity closed in upon itself.[2] As such the subject is always open to modification because of its potentially dynamic encounter with the real. Georges Bataille's *oeuvre* is also a work in progress, I suggest, in as far as it puts all static forms of thought (forms which would claim to resolve the opposition between thought and the real) on trial. And this, by refusing closure, by fictionalizing, by entering into contact with the impossible, with 'non-knowledge', and, most importantly, with chance.[3]

This chapter discusses the relationship between Surrealism (as represented by Breton) and Bataille. It examines the Surrealism–Bataille relation with respect to writing (poetry), the image and metaphor.

My aim, in part, is to show that Surrealism resists the practice of writing understood as an engagement with the semiotic in Julia Kristeva's sense of the word.[4] As Breton labelled Bataille a psychiatric case in the *Second Surrealist Manifesto*, I also think it important to consider Surrealism in terms of the 'madness' which it (through Breton) considered to be outside writing.

Breton and the 'case' of Bataille

None of Bataille's prewar literary writings appeared in a conventional format before the publication of *Le bleu du ciel* in 1945. In fact, as Denis Hollier points out, Bataille had not published a book before *L'ex-périence intérieure* in 1943.[5] *Histoire de l'oeil*, *L'anus solaire* and

Sacrifices, Hollier claims, were not printed in sufficient numbers to be considered truly 'published'.[6] However, *Histoire de l'oeil* did appear in a limited edition of 134 copies in 1928, under the pseudonym of Lord Auch.[7] Although Breton himself may have read Bataille at an early stage, when the *Second Surrealist Manifesto* was first published in December 1929, Bataille was not widely known. Yet Breton still engaged in a polemic against him at the end of the *Manifesto*. There, Bataille is deemed to be a 'case' largely because he is obsessed with manure and, more generally, with impurity and defilement. Indeed, Breton could point out that Bataille was the editor of the prestigious art/ ethnography journal *Documents*, where he (Bataille) had published (in June 1929) an article called 'The language of flowers' on plant genitalia, an article containing an image of Sade throwing rose petals into a heap of manure. No beauty without defilement, is Bataille's dictum. For the Breton of the late 1920s, this is too much. He writes:

> What is paradoxical and embarrassing about M. Bataille's *case* is that his phobia about 'the idea', as soon as he attempts to communicate it, can only take an ideological turn. A state of conscious deficiency, in a form tending to become generalized, the doctors would say. Here, in fact, is someone who propounds as a principle that 'horror does not lead to any pathological complaisance and only plays the role of manure in the growth of plant life, manure whose odor is stifling no doubt but salutary for the plant.' Beneath its appearance of infinite banality, this idea is in itself dishonest or pathological.[8]

The significance of this passage, as several commentators have noted, is that Breton plays psychiatrist to Bataille the patient. In short, for Breton, Bataille is not like Nadja, the mysterious heroine of Breton's text of the same name. Indeed, while Breton sees Nadja's madness as a kind of hyper-lucidity, and her incarceration in an asylum as the true madness, Bataille's behaviour is seen as being 'pathological'. Moreover, whereas Breton acknowledges that Nadja puts him in question by leading him to doubt the very nature of his own experience, he refuses to see anything comparable in his encounter with Bataille.

Here, it is the form of Breton's stance that must be grasped: in order to make a judgement about Bataille, Breton must objectify his quarry; that is, he must clearly separate himself from him in order to represent him: he must assume a position of transcendence *vis-à-vis* the 'patient'.

Breton's 'objectification' of Bataille is evoked in Elisabeth Roudinesco's acclaimed history of psychoanalysis in France.[9] There, the author discusses Breton's relationship to clinical psychology and to psychoanalysis. On the one hand, Roudinesco indicates, the

Surrealists, with Breton in the van, staked their very identity on cocking a snook at orthodox psychiatry and psychoanalysis, which tended to see all art as a form of madness. During the 1920s, the orthodox view 'gave rise to *psychobiography*, which restricts itself to the study of classics and treats writers' lives as though they were case histories, making writing the expression of a neurosis or mental illness'.[10] Psychobiography 'thought of creation as a kind of pathology and made of the creator a "superior abnormal individual". In that perspective the artist was a "case", like other neurotics, but he was a "pathological case" since he possessed a hereditary "defect" which others did not'.[11] Seemingly wedded to his psychiatric training, Breton, the Surrealist scourge of Pierre Janet and orthodox psychiatry, suddenly seems to fall back on the very psychiatric view he, as a Surrealist, had rejected. Again, Breton and other Surrealists broke out and began to talk quite openly of their own sexuality in 1928 (cf. 'Recherches sur la sexualité' in *La révolution surréaliste*, 11, March 1928) while the institution of psychoanalysis frowned on such apparent frankness. Yet, Roudinesco recalls, Breton's attempted openness on sexuality needs to be seen in relation to his inhibition regarding homosexuality. Under Breton's guidance, Roudinesco points out, Surrealism was still caught within the medicalizing framework of a psychobiography which used literature, and art in general, as a means of distinguishing between the normal and the pathological. Here, the medical gaze puts the literary work in question, the reverse being seen as impossible. Put another way, in the passage of the *Second Manifesto* where he refers to Bataille as a case, Breton assumes a position on what we shall come to describe as the vertical axis, while, for his part, Bataille is located on what we shall describe as the horizontal axis. It is thus that Breton will mark out the parameters of our enquiry into Georges Bataille's relation to Surrealism.

The vertical and the horizontal

Bataille, in fact, speaks of the vertical and the horizontal as the 'two axes of terrestrial' life in his essay, 'The pineal eye'. More specifically, we see that vegetation occupies a position more or less exclusively on the vertical axis, whereas animals, although they do strive to raise themselves up to the vertical position, tend to be situated along the horizontal axis.[12] Complete verticality is never attained, even by humans.

These two axes illuminate Bataille's own work in a number of different but related ways. For instance, verticality can refer to the axis of transcendence, where transcendence refers to objectification, conceptualization, representation, distanciation, homogeneity, knowledge, history (as written or as narrative) and, more generally, to the domain of theory, especially in the sense of *theoria*: to see.[13] Horizontality, on the other hand, refers to immanence, and thus, secondarily, to ritual, difference, horror, silence, heterogeneity, abjection (in Kristeva's sense) and, more generally, to the domain of the non-discursive, or practice (also to history as practice, or to fate). Societies organized through a State apparatus (Western democracies) provide instances of social life dominated by transcendence, while non-State societies (cf. Australian aboriginal society) are organized through ritual practices and kinship alliances of tradition. Needless to say, there are immanent features in State societies (especially at the more private level of kinship alliances and affections), just as there are transcendent features in non-State societies – if only because of language. The point is that although transcendence and immanence can be considered to be two modes of integration, they are not at all compatible with one another. Immanence is a threat to transcendence, and transcendence works to eliminate immanence.

In her essay on abjection Julia Kristeva has shown, with reference to India, how horror (of the mother's body) can constitute a crucial element in social cohesion.[14] And in her earlier work, Kristeva has shown how the thetic phase – or the positing of the subject–object dualism – privileged by Phenomenology, assumes that the subject, *qua* subject, is always already in language, and thus already fully in the symbolic.[15] Lacan, for his part, did not radically depart from Phenomenology on this point when he set the mirror stage at the origin of the child's entry into language and the symbolic. The mirror stage would constitute the most elementary form of the subject–object relation. Bataille, by contrast, speaks about the 'inner experience' as being 'objectless' and a break with all objectification. The inner experience as ecstasy, Bataille says, means that the subject is a 'non-knowledge' (*non-savoir*), and thereby sovereign. Thus does the inner experience come to 'embody' the horizontal axis in its capacity to shake (cf. '*solicitation*' and '*moirer*')[16] the transcendent thetic. Seen in this way, the horizontal axis is a threat to the vertical axis. But it can also prove to be a source of rejuvenation for a flagging transcendence – as, for example, when different cultural practices pose a clear challenge to the existing mode of representation and the symbolic order that produces it.

For Bataille, writing itself constitutes a challenge to existing modes of integration in that it places the idea of a homogeneous subject under pressure. More generally, in Bataille, horizontality ceaselessly challenges verticality. One version, in particular, of the clash between these two axes distinguishes Bataille from the Surrealists, and notably from Breton. It concerns the difference between metaphor, the privileged trope for Surrealism, and metonymy, which, I shall argue, comes closest to a general figure that allows us an insight into Bataille's writing. Metaphor evokes the vertical, paradigmatic axis; metonymy, the horizontal, syntagmatic axis. Thus do we find a basis for interpreting the relationship between Bataille and Surrealism.

Dream, image

In the first *Manifesto of Surrealism* (1924) Breton places the Surrealist project beyond the positivist realism of common sense which, he claims, has dominated intellectual and cultural life from Aquinas to Anatole France. Positivist realism has, he says, become banal, a way of putting the mind to sleep, and of maintaining stifling conformity. Breton had met Freud in Vienna in 1921, and although the founder of psycho-analysis had not exactly treated him with the *obsequium* he craved, Freud ostensibly remained, for Breton, the spiritual father of Surrealism. The Surrealist realm, in light of Freud, would thus be the realm of the unconscious, an unconscious revealed in automatic writing, dreams, everyday objects juxtaposed in unpremeditated ways (cf. Lautréamont's sewing machine and umbrella on a dissecting table), and in artistic endeavour (especially poetry). Rather than creating a new world, Surrealism proposed combining dream and reality through the imagina-tion, thereby creating a new form of absolute reality: *surreality*.[17] Indeed, one could do worse than claim that Surrealism, as a new form of consciousness, is an imaginary seeing that valorizes chance and also provides access to the unconscious. For Breton, the way to tap into the unconscious and see the world anew is through the 'psychic automat-ism' explained in the first manifesto by the famous definition of the word 'Surrealism'.[18] Psychic automatism, it is said, will give access to the real workings of thought, beyond any aesthetic, moral or rational considerations. In Freudian terms, Surrealist practice would bypass the mechanisms of repression and so allow direct access to repressed psychic material. This material would form the basis of the marvellous, enchanted and totally fascinating Surrealist world, a world of 'superior reality'.

If the poet is the key figure in producing Surrealist effects, this is because seeing, and the associations tied to it (sight, vision, image, light, sun, etc.), is privileged in poetry. Indeed, Surrealist poetry begins to erase the gap between word and image. Consequently, the Surrealist object, according to Breton, emerges when one comes to 'compose a poem in which visual elements take their place between the words without ever duplicating them'.[19] Moreover, through the image the poet can protect the freedom of the imagination; for the image deepens the rift between poetry as image and freedom, and what threatens it: prose.[20] Through a fusion of inner (poetry) and outer (image), poetry and painting unite with one another. Painting becomes poetic, and poetry uses painting's image to create '*the image present to the mind*'.[21] To exclude the external object, and to consider 'nature only in its relationship with the inner world of consciousness' is the 'poetic step par excellence'.[22]

Significantly, Breton confirms that poetry's privileged form is metaphor, metaphor borne by the image. To acknowledge this is now a commonplace. As Breton clearly states, the poet must make the trench between poetry and prose ever deeper, and for this he or she 'has one tool and one tool only, capable of boring deeper and deeper, and that is the *image*, and among all types of images, *metaphor*.'[23] From this it is to be understood that poetry is to prose as the enchanted world of dream and metaphor is to banal, everyday reality – a reality which receives its symbolic inscription in our culture through metonymy. Just one qualification needs to be made here: everyday reality gives dreams their raw material. Dream and reality are thus united. Such would be the result of the seduction of Breton by the romantic Hegelian thesis of the unity of contraries.

If not in their practice, at least in their theory, Breton and the Surrealists, as a number of commentators, including Denis Hollier, have pointed out, are pre-Freudian. Bataille, on the other hand, leads us closer to the Freudian problematic. In this regard we note that the Surrealist privileging of metaphor is challenged by Bataille's writing. This writing, invoking horror, ecstasy and obscenity, brings the metaphorizing process to a halt. But what kind of presence does metaphor have in language if it may be brought to a halt? What precisely is metaphor?

Metaphor

Metaphor is located on the vertical, paradigmatic axis of substitutions. Lacan pushed this further by saying, in light of the work of Jakobson, that metaphor is the substitution of one word for another, the fact of this substitution being tied to an evocation of what is absent. Thus, in the line from Victor Hugo's *Booz Endormi*, 'His sheaf was neither miserly nor spiteful . . .', cited by Lacan, 'his sheaf' refers to the absent Booz; Booz thus has a kind of presence in the text in the very absence of his name.

Against the Surrealist belief in the possibility of the realization of the juxtaposition of two disparate signifiers 'equally actualised', Lacan argues instead that the principle of substitution, as described above, more accurately explains what is at stake.[24]

Perhaps, in retrospect, we can now reflect more carefully on this Lacanian shibboleth of substitution. For in his desire to give a linguistic turn to psychoanalysis, Lacan neglected to give a psychoanalytic explanation of language as a whole. At least he failed to push it much beyond references to the *metaphor* of the Name-of-the-(dead)-Father. This metaphor signals a very important conceptual distinction between language as metaphor (where the dead, thus absent, father would be the founding metaphor of language) and metaphor in language.

To explain this point more fully, I refer to Julia Kristeva's theory of the subject in depression and melancholia. For Kristeva, the separation of the child from the mother takes place through both the semiotic (i.e. musical, affective) aspect of language, as well as through Lacan's mirror stage. The semiotic dimension would provide the drive energy necessary for language to have an emotional charge at the same time as this energy, as the basis of this emotional charge, is an evocation of difference, materiality and death. As Kristeva says in *Black Sun*, separation from the mother is exchanged for an eroticized object.[25] The erotic object offers a way of escaping social censorship; it is *metonymic* (and not metaphoric) in structure. In other words, it is linked to desire.

But desire here is paradoxical: it is caught between the desire for the original object (the mother, who, structurally speaking, occupies the position of death), or for satisfaction, and the desire for desire (that is, for life). In the formation of the subject, and against satisfaction, separation is a vital necessity. Yet the struggle against separation also constitutes the subject as formed in and through language as metaphor. From this it follows that if the body is in language, it is only there through metaphor (which is not to say that the body is a metaphor). Similarly, if difference, otherness or death are in language, they are so only through metaphor. As a result, we recognize that language is linked to its other (call it reality, materiality, externality, etc.) only via the leap of metaphor. Metaphor here is to be understood as the potentially endless process of translating the unnameable other.

The force of affect, however, weighs heavily on the process of translation. For while affect can be the source of new and startling metaphors, it can also cause the process of translation to falter – as happens in depression and even more so in melancholia. For the depressed person, translation becomes submerged in tears and silence. As Kristeva puts it: 'If I am no longer capable of translating or metaphorizing, I become silent and die'.[26]

Kristeva's perspective, it could be said, is one that tries to grasp the outside of language from the inside. More pertinently, though, Kristeva begins the arduous process of theorizing the place of the real in language by focusing on features of human experience – such as tears, cries, silence. Tears, cries, silence can threaten language as such, but they also hold out the prospect of its renewal and revitalization through 'strange concatenations, ideolects, poetics'.[27]

Once we focus on the 'interior' of language, however – that is, once our focus overlaps with a linguistic perspective – we are no longer grapling with what threatens the working of language, but are concerned with a restricted definition of metaphor, one that situates it in relation to other tropes. Although lacking a technical, linguistic interest in the matter, Surrealism's focus with regard to metaphor is exclusively linguistic in the sense just mentioned. Metaphor becomes a figure that can be objectified and used by the poet; it is not grasped as being part of the very precondition of language, as psychoanalysis understands it. The sun in Batailles's text provides further insight here.

The sun

In a certain sense, Bataille writes in order to put out the light of the sun. That is, he writes in order to bring metaphor to an end – just the opposite of the Surrealist enterprise. Death in Bataille's writing is the death of metaphor – a death premised on the birth of obscenity and horror. In this regard, Bataille's version of Rimbaud's 'je est un autre' (meaning 'I am not an identity, but am other, difference, body and waste'), is 'I am the dead one / the blind one / the shadow without air / like the rivers in the sea / in me noise and light / endlessly lose themselves.'[28]

Before pursuing further this specifically Bataillian approach to death, we need to ask: Why the sun? Why is the sun in a sense the metaphor of all metaphors? The question is a thorny one. For it implies that an answer free of metaphor can be given, that somehow we can escape language within language. Nevertheless, one should also recognize that this is what language *qua* symbolic system allows us to do. Here we touch on what Kristeva has called the *dénégation* of language. That is, although every user of words knows that words are only words, words also have the power to make their users forget this truth, and so act as though words were transparent. Metaphor, too, is a *dénégation*. The sun gives life. Light gives life. But like the father in the reproductive process, the sun, as light, is not directly present in this process. The word 'sun', in invoking a real sun, is a *dénégation*. With illumination, brightness and light, the sun disappears as such, and metaphor appears, although it would seem that without a real sun somewhere metaphor would be impossible.

Surrealism and Bataille's vertical and horizontal sun

The sun is both a way of pointing to something fundamental to Bataille's project, and a way of distinguishing the latter from the logic of Surrealism. As may be gathered, Surrealism – in its use of dream, in its associating together image, metaphor, poetry and reality – assumes that metaphor is the passage to the real. Freud, by contrast, said that dream is the royal road to the unconscious. He also said that a dream is a psychosis,[29] with a hallucinatory aspect where words become things, where language thus becomes opaque, and where, consequently, the metaphoric function of language, the function which would render language transparent, ceases to work. Because Surrealism assumes a continuity between dream and reality, it thus assumes that a dream, like everyday reality, can be objectified, that is, translated into ordinary language and images, as opposed to being interpreted, as Freud proposed. Breton even says that the dreamer can be conscious of the dream as a dream within the dream.[30] The Surrealist other, then, tends to be the other as represented in the symbolic, while Bataille's other is the other of the symbolic itself, the other which begins to bring metaphor to a halt. In transcribing this onto our two axes, we see that Surrealism tends to remain tied to the vertical axis which generates a hypothetically endless play of substitutions through similarity, while Bataille, whose preference for metonymy is clearly marked, valorizes the horizontal axis and all that this entails regarding horror.

Given the privileging of metaphor within language by Surrealism and given, paradoxical as this may seem, that it thereby objectifies without end, it follows that Bataille's writing will also come within the Bretonian purview of the drive to objectify. 'Pathological' is the category used in Breton's judgement of Bataille's work. The objectifier would indeed claim to give the truth about the object *in* the objectification. In effect, the objectifier claims the transparency of language in the (act of) objectification.

By contrast, Bataille wants to render language opaque. This follows, in part, from his valorization of horizontality. The sun, in these circumstances, becomes a series of transpositions: from egg to eye to testicle. The streams of light become streams of liquid: urine, tears, sperm, sweat. Although initially within a structure of metaphor, the metonymic chains proliferate in the *Histoire de l'oeil*, as Barthes noted.[31] Both anagrammatically, and by homophony, the series of terms endlessly expand. The poems by Bataille set the scene for what will proliferate in the fictional writings. I have analysed this in more detail elsewhere,[32] while Lucette Finas has provided a similar demonstration of the process of double inscription of sounds and meanings in her study of Bataille's *Madame Edwarda*.[33] All of these poetic strategies experienced in Bataille's text render it still more opaque precisely because the semiotic aspect begins to stand out against the symbolic function.

Bataille's writing

As Bataille's writing is a writing of limits (it moves to the edge of the abyss and confronts death), it threatens metaphor (though it does not fail to make limited use of it) and makes metonymy its instrument for exploring horizontality. Metonymy, which exemplifies contiguity, is thus spatial in that the link between elements tends to be the result of proximity rather than similarity or equivalence. Lacan of course said that desire is a metonymy because the object of desire is always lost, never immediately present. Desire, constituted by the 'original' metaphor of separation, takes a horizontal trajectory and only comes to an end when the drive energy necessary to sustain it comes to an end. My argument is that Bataille's writing, *qua* writing, is the outcome of the tension between the metonymy of desire which produces writing, and the themes of this writing which, in effect, repeat the dream of bringing writing to an end in the maelstrom of horror, *jouissance* and death. Bataille's unadorned style (which Marguerite Duras once described as an absence of style) approaches horror and becomes a symptom of the effects of horror. Horror and abjection continually drain desire of the drive energy needed to sustain it. This, then, is indeed a writing to the point of exhaustion and loss. Death thus haunts Bataille's writing, not simply as a theme of his fiction, but as a reality embodied in a writing practice. As my title suggests, it is this practice that the Surrealists could not fathom, so concerned were they with the *themes* of Bataille's fiction, in contrast to the *practice* of his writing.

From a thematic perspective, death in Bataille's universe figures as the synthesis of joy – ecstasy – and horror. Or rather, just as the sun (as metaphor) provides illumination but is also blinding if really looked at directly at noon, so joy, when pushed to the limit, topples over into horror – like the priest's orgasm at the point of death in *Histoire de l'oeil*. There, the narrator is paralysed before the reality of the juxtaposition of orgasm – provoked by Simone – and death – a totally explosive combination: 'all I could do was squeeze her in my arms and kiss her mouth, because of a strange inward paralysis ultimately caused by my love for the girl and the death of the unspeakable creature.'[34] Exhaustion, anguish, loss are not just emblematic, but are the reality of a meeting of opposites in what would be the realization of contradiction if death did not intervene. The first 'sign' (mark) of death is the exhaustion of the writing practice itself. No doubt this means that writing for Bataille is locked into the logic of *dépense* rather than the logic of the restricted economy. Anguish (*angoisse*) is the mark of the tension that generates, and at the same time threatens, the text. Light, knowledge, self, the gaze, pleasure, joy never exist in Bataille's writing without evoking anguish, horror and loss. Unlike the Hegelian turn of Surrealism as outlined by Breton, contraries do not merge into one another, but remain in a relationship of extreme tension. Bataille's writing embodies this tension. It is a writing of anguish (*angoisse*), a writing of the self (*moi*) almost at the point of destruction. Even to see, to know, to understand, opens up a tension in which blindness, non-knowledge (*non-savoir*) and incomprehension are immediately on the horizon.

Thus, when, in *Le bleu du ciel*, the narrator and Dorothea finally come together, without anguish, and walk in the mountains near the Moselle river, they look into each other's eyes, 'not without dread',[35] and without hope. And then, as they are walking down into the valley in the darkness, at a turn in the path, a void opens up before them. 'Curiously, this void, at our feet, was no less infinite than a starry sky over our heads.'[36] Here is an image in which stars of the vertical axis reflect the void of the horizontal. The stars, in fact, look like candles on coffins and, as such, become a reminder of the death inscribed in the void. The latter fascinates the novel's protagonists – so much so, that they become sexually excited and have sex in the cold, slippery mud on the mountain. It is like 'making love over a starry graveyard' (death is always in the background). So slippery is the mud, that at the height of passion, the lovers begin to slide towards the void: 'If I hadn't stopped our slide with my foot, we would have fallen into the night, and I might have wondered if we weren't falling into the void of the sky.'[37] The slide renews the anguish, the tension, deriving from the very reality of the abyss. The abyss is the joy *before* death; it is not at all the joy *of* death. In a discarded passage from *Le coupable*, Bataille relates how, when visiting Laure's grave, he remembers walking with her up to the crater of Mount Etna. Suddenly, Laure was seized by a violent anguish before the void of Etna's crater.[38] This experience of anguish (psycho-analytically, an experience of castration), an experience repeated throughout Bataille's fiction, becomes an intimation of the impossible as a premonition of death, in the sense that the impossible is the impossibility of persevering in desire, in eroticism. The 'impossible as a void', we read in *L'impossible*.[39] All erotic energy goes into this void, for no return. 'Erotic licentiousness results in depression, disgust, and the impossibility to continue. Unsatisfied sexual need completes suffering. Eroticism's too heavy a burden for human strength.'[40] Anguish, however, is inseparable from the cry (*cri*) of anguish, a cry that often tips over into laughter (*rire*) and horror. Laughter – especially the laughter of women – is always a cutting, lascerating (cf. *déchirer*) laughter that often provokes a cry. To write (*écrire*), therefore, is, as Mark Taylor has pointed out, to evoke laughter and the cry (*cri*) which in turn open out onto anguish, the void and death.[41] In one sense, then, to write at all is to maintain desire, thereby invoking the anguish of the cry – and the laughter – before death. Again, nudity and death are linked because to see nudity is to see erotically and so expend without return – even though seeing might dissimulate this effect through the clinical gaze.

The problem for the clinical gaze (for the more clinical psycho-biographical version of psychoanalysis as employed by Breton in the *Second Manifesto*) is that it is always ready to go to excesses in its circumspection, in its sanitized vocabulary and in its euphemisms. This very excess may confront it at any moment as a kind of madness that puts it on the trail of the sources of the fear and horror that it tries to repress so totally. 'Not that horror is ever to be confounded with attraction', we read in the preface to *Madame Edwarda*, 'but if it cannot inhibit it, destroy it, *horror reinforces attraction!*'[42] The eagle, like Icarus, flies high. It can see over a vast area. However, if it flies too high, it risks being blinded, as Icarus was blinded when the sun melted his wax. The sun, as we know, is an ambiguous object; it is both life and death. The Hegelian urge of the modern era can lead reason and knowledge, exorbitantly situated in the vertical axis, towards the fall brought about by the reassertion of the horizontal axis.

The dream of the Hegelian edifice of a fundamental reconciliation between practical and theoretical knowledge in the Absolute Idea, I am not the first to say, is, for Bataille, destined to turn, without knowing it (because fate, or rather, chance, is always obscure), into the excesses of reason the modern world has witnessed only too often. The Hegelian system constitutes such a delirium of metaphoricity and verticality that it has no outside. Such a system is closed. As such, it ceases to be a work in progress. For Bataille, by contrast, the void, the erotic, excrement and the sources of all kinds of horror, coming from an exorbitant outside, put the subject in question to the point of death – to the point, quite clearly, where writing and the symbolic order itself are put in question.

If Breton poeticizes through image and metaphor, Bataille shows that any writing that expands symbolic capacities is one that takes place in the wake of its very impossibility. For Breton, writing as poetry is always possible; metaphor is always possible – that was the point of poetry inspired by automatic writing. For Bataille, writing is also impossible, dogged by its blindness: it is the cry and laughter, desire and horror, the erotic and anguish, day *and* night. In short, writing is also the excrement that cannot 'be'.

Blindness and objectification

For many, the *raison d'être* of psychoanalysis is to illuminate the enigmas of psychic life through interpretation. Certainly, in some of its versions, it has acquired a sensitivity to the dynamics of inter-subjectivity that are unheard-of in other discourses. The question none the less remains as to the nature of the objectifying urge in this interpretative endeavour. To objectify is to invoke the light of the sun in order to see into even the darkest of recesses. Recall here Freud's statement that woman is a 'dark continent'. Being illumination itself (like other discourses in the Humanities and Social Sciences), psycho-analysis has to bring woman into the light. She must be objectified. The question is: can psychoanalysis celebrate its capacity to see without denying the inevitable blindness implicit in this very capacity? Such is Breton's blindness with regard to Bataille when he sees him as a 'case'.

My thesis is that Bataille's writing is a form of blindness – an excess – that, paradoxically, would illuminate the blindness of every exclu-sively objectifying discourse – not simply in the manner referred to by Shoshana Felman when she notes that psychoanalysis has taken some of its terminology and its concepts from literature,[43] nor perhaps simply in the manner of Denis Hollier when he points out that theory (seeing) cannot grasp its other,[44] but rather in the sense that the obstacle of the impossible reveals seeing as a will to see. In effect, seeing is not a simple reflection of the world in the eye. Rather, it entails a component that links it to drive energy. In this sense, psychoanalysis and seeing take on the characteristics of Lévi-Strauss's version of myth. Myths survive, says Lévi-Strauss, for as long as there is intellectual energy available to sustain them.[45] No doubt, for Bataille, the notion of will can be translated into that of an expenditure without return. At one level at least, Bataille's writing is an expenditure without return: its meaning is contained in its practice because to write becomes a will to write. Ironically, like Nietzsche, from whom the notion of will has been taken, the act of writing is by no means to be taken for granted. The exhaustion and fatigue to which Bataille's texts constantly refer is also manifest in the relatively fragmentary nature of the *oeuvre*, in the bursts of poetry and in the cost incurred in producing a sustained text.[46]

With Bataille, it is as though the will to write were fragile and about to collapse, although this writing also constitutes an insight into the nature of what sustains it. In contrast, the text capable of a sustained expenditure, and marked by an excess of the will to see, or to objectify, often exhibits a blindness as to what sustains it. So let us now bring theory out of the sun and into the cooler recesses of the cave where, Bataille tells us, art may have begun.

Notes

1 Since I presented this paper at the May 1991 Bataille conference, the ideas in it have already undergone modification, thus confirming its 'work-in-progress' status. I am, however, unable to include the modification here. I will simply say that, now, I believe it important to focus much more on the Surrealist *principle* of automatic writing (rather than the result) and the chance which is inseparable from it.

2 See Julia Kristeva, 'Joyce, le retour d'Orphée', *L'Infini*, 8, autumn, 1984, 5.

3 I say 'most importantly' now, while re-writing this piece for publication, because I have come to suspect that chance might be the element which in the end *links* Bataille to, rather than separates him from, Surrealism.

4 Kristeva defines the semiotic in the Greek sense as follows: 'distinctive mark, trace, index, precursory sign, proof, engraved or written sign, imprint, trace figuration'. The semiotic is also a 'modality' which harbours the drives, or the affective dimension of psychic life, in contrast to the symbolic, which is the 'rational' principle of articulation and signification in language. See Julia Kristeva, *Revolution in Poetic Language*, trans. Margaret Waller, New York, Columbia University Press, 1984, 25.

5 Denis Hollier, *Against Architecture: The writings of George Bataille*, trans. Betsy Wing, Cambridge, Mass., MIT Press, 1989, 118.

6 Ibid.

7 As is known, Bataille refers in the preface to an earlier manuscript, *W.C.* (Michel Leiris was one of its few readers), that was burned.

8 André Breton, *Second Surrealist Manifesto* in *Manifestos of Surrealism*, trans. Richard Seaver and Helen R. Lane, Ann Arbor, University of Michigan Press, 1972, 184. Emphasis added.

9 Elisabeth Roudinesco, *Jacques Lacan & Co.: A history of psychoanalysis in France, 1925–1985*, trans. Jeffrey Mehlman, Chicago, Chicago University Press, 1990, Pt 1, ch. 1.

10 Ibid., 6.

11 Ibid.

12 Georges Bataille, 'The pineal eye' in *Visions of Excess: Selected writings, 1927–39*, ed. and trans. Allan Stoekl, with Carl R. Lovitt and Donald M.

Leslie Jr, Minneapolis, University of Minnesota Press, 1985, 83.
13 On this point see Gregory Ulmer, 'Theoria' in *Applied Grammatology: Post(e)-pedagogy from Jacques Derrida to Joseph Beuys*, Baltimore and London, Johns Hopkins University Press, 1985, 30–67.
14 See Julia Kristeva, *Powers of Horror: An essay on abjection*, trans. Leon S. Roudiez, New York, Columbia University Press, 1982, 74–5.
15 See Kristeva, *Revolution in Poetic Language*, 43–5.
16 See Ulmer, *Applied Grammatology*, 38.
17 Cf. Breton, *Manifesto of Surrealism* in *Manifestos of Surrealism*, 14.
18 Ibid., 26.
19 Breton, 'Surrealist situation of the object . . .' in *Manifestos of Surrealism*, 263.
20 Ibid., 268.
21 Ibid., 260. Breton's emphasis.
22 Ibid.
23 Ibid., 268. Breton's emphasis.
24 Jacques Lacan, *Ecrits, A Selection*, trans. Alan Sheridan, London, Tavistock, 1977, 157.
25 Julia Kristeva, *Black Sun: Depression and melancholia*, trans. Leon S. Roudiez, New York, Columbia University Press, 1989, 27–30.
26 Ibid., 42.
27 Ibid.
28 Bataille, 'Le Tombeau', *Oeuvres complètes* (*OC*), Paris, Gallimard, 1971, III, 77.
29 Freud's exact words are: 'A dream . . . is a psychosis, with all the absurdities, delusions and illusions of a psychosis. A psychosis of short duration, no doubt harmless, even entrusted with a useful function, introduced with the subject's consent and terminated by an act of his will. None the less it is a psychosis' (*An Outline of Psycho-Analysis*, trans. James Strachey, London, The Hogarth Press and The Institute of Psycho-Analysis, revised edition, 1969, 29). As a psychosis, a dream is not a metaphor, but is closer to a hallucination.
30 See André Breton, *Les vases communicants*, *Oeuvres complètes*, Paris, Gallimard, 'Bibliothèque de la Pléiade', 1992, 145.
31 Roland Barthes, 'The metaphor of the eye' in Bataille, *Story of the Eye by Lord Auch*, trans. Joachim Neugroschal, Harmondsworth, Penguin Books, 1986, 125.
32 See John Lechte, 'An introduction to Bataille: the impossible as (a practice of) writing', *Textual Practice*, summer, 1993, 173–94.
33 Lucette Finas, *La crue: une lecture de Bataille: Madame Edwarda*, Paris, Gallimard, 1972.
34 Bataille, *Story of the Eye by Lord Auch*, 65.
35 Bataille, *Blue of Noon*, trans. Harry Mathews, London and New York, Marion Boyars, 1991, 143.
36 Ibid. Translation modified.
37 Ibid., 145.
38 Bataille, *OC*, V, 500. See also, for a weaker evocation of this image, Bataille *Guilty*, trans. Bruce Boone, Venice, The Lapis Press, 1988, 47, 118–19.
39 Bataille, *L'impossible*, Paris, Editions de Minuit, 1962, 22.

40 Bataille, *Guilty*, 13. Cf. also: 'eroticism ... demands ruinous outlays' (ibid., 22).

41 Mark Taylor, *Alterity*, Chicago, Chicago University Press, 1987, 148.

42 Bataille, preface to *Madame Edwarda* in *OC*, III, 11.

43 See Shoshana Felman, 'To open the question' in S. Felman (ed.), *Literature and Psychoanalysis: The question of reading otherwise*, Baltimore and London, Johns Hopkins University Press, 1982, 9.

44 See Hollier, *Against Architecture*, 87.

45 Claude Lévi-Strauss, 'The structural study of myth' in *Structural Anthropology*, trans. Claire Jacobson and Brook Grudfest Schoepf, Harmondsworth, Penguin Books, 1972, 229.

46 Cf. Bataille's *Eroticism*, trans. Mary Dalwood, London and New York, Marion Boyars, 1990, where the attempted full-length book gives way to a series of occasional essays that make up nearly half the text. Cf., too, the following statement by Bataille from *Inner Experience*, trans. Leslie Anne Boldt, Albany, New York, State University of New York, 1988, 57: 'Almost every time, if I have tried to write a book, fatigue would come before the end. I slowly became a stranger to the project which I had formulated.'

10 The use-value of the impossible

Denis Hollier

Beauty shall be irretrievable, or not at all.

Documents

The story of *Documents*, spanning two years and fifteen issues, begins very far from the avant-garde, in the gallery of medals at the Bibliothèque Nationale. Georges Bataille and Pierre d'Espezel were colleagues there, d'Espezel editing several journals as well, very official and rather specialized ones: *Aréthuse*, in which Bataille's first notes appeared, when he was a numismatist; and *Cahiers de la république des lettres*, which published Bataille's first major article, 'L'Amérique disparue', in a special issue devoted to America before Christopher Columbus, in 1928. D'Espezel was also on the board of *Gazette des beaux-arts*, which was financed by Georges Wildenstein. He was to serve as intermediary. Wildenstein was to finance *Documents*.

Numismatics, according to the definition later given by one of the *Documents* contributors, is the science of 'coins that no longer have any currency except within scholarly speculations'.[1] It also includes medals, coins that have never had any currency. There is something of the miser in the numismatist's passion. He loves money but, like Molière's Harpagon, only to keep it and look at it. He cannot stand expenditure. He is possessed by a strange, disinterested love for money, a love for that which makes everything possible, but cut off from all that it permits; a love for that which is dead and forbidden, at once on display and in reserve. He demands of the carriers of exchange value that they themselves be out of service. Currency takes leave of the Stock Exchange in order to be recycled, two blocks away, on the rue de Richelieu, at the Bibliothèque Nationale.[2]

It was Bataille who suggested the title. It seems that, for the founders (Bataille, d'Espezel, Wildenstein), this title had the status of a programme, a contract almost. But, in the opinion of d'Espezel and Wildenstein, before the journal had really even begun, Bataille – who, as 'secretary-general', was to actually edit it – had already stopped respecting it.[3] As early as April 1929 (when the journal had published only one issue), d'Espezel sent Bataille a sarcastic and threatening note. 'The title you have chosen for this journal is hardly justified except in the sense that it gives us 'documents' on your state of mind. You really must return to the spirit which inspired our first plan for this journal, when you and I talked about it with Mr Wildenstein.'[4]

The word *document* had appeared in Bataille's presentation of *L'ordre de chevalerie*, his 1922 thesis for the Ecole des Chartes. The only value of this medieval text, he writes, is as a document. 'The poem, without any literary value, without any originality, has no interest aside from being an old, peculiar document about chivalric ideas and the rites of dubbing.'[5] Was the agreement, in accordance with the Chartist notion of documents, to publish in *Documents* only texts with no originality or literary value? If that is the case, one can well understand that d'Espezel would have been troubled: for, in *Documents*, Bataille published his own texts, as well as texts by Leiris and others, which, without even considering their literary aspects, are not without, as d'Espezel rightly suspected, a certain originality.

Ethnography

Among the headings listed in the subtitle of the journal, the most prominent position is occupied by the trinity 'Archeology Beaux-Arts Ethnography'.[6] Each refers to an independent domain: ethnography exceeds the auspices of the fine arts geographically, as archeology exceeds it historically. But this relativization of Western aesthetic values is aggravated by an even more radical relativization of aesthetic values as such. It is the latter that is signalled by the choice of the term 'ethnography' rather than the expression 'primitive arts'. It has the quality of a manifesto: it announces that *Documents* will not be another *Gazette des beaux-arts*, and even less a *Gazette des beaux-arts primitifs*.

Documents was to have as its platform a resistance to the aesthetic point of view, a resistance that is the title's first connotation.[7] A document is, by its very definition, an object devoid of artistic value. Devoid or even stripped of it, depending on whether or not it ever had any. But there are only two possibilities: it is either a document or a work of art. This binary opposition (which gives the term *document*, even when used alone, its anti-aesthetic connotations) is not a case of lexical daring. Leiris takes it for granted, in all innocence, without giving any impression of quoting or of playing on the word, in *Documents* itself, when discussing a collection of anthropological photographs. 'Until now', he writes, 'there was no book which presented the general public with a selection of purely ethnographic documents rather than just a series of works of art.'[8]

And Carl Einstein, without using the word *document* itself, alludes to the same opposition in the report he gives of one of the most important exhibitions of primitive art of the period, the exhibition of African and Oceanic art organized by Tristan Tzara and Charles Ratton at the Théâtre Pigalle gallery: 'this art must be treated historically, and no longer considered just from the point of view of taste or aesthetics'.[9]

Use-value

Aside from Bataille's contribution to the first issue, his article on Gaulish coins, 'Le cheval académique', the numismatist's perverse interest in the lackeys of exchange value was to leave no deep trace on *Documents*.[10] It was use-value that took the offensive right away, constituting the axis of reflection for the ethnographers gathered around Georges Rivière, the deputy director of the Museum of Ethnography at the Trocadéro.[11] But it is not simply on values themselves that ethnographers and numismatists disagreed. They also disagreed on what attitude to take toward their objective (or rather objectal) support: the ethnographers resisting the aesthetic exemplification of tools; the numismatists subscribing to just such an exemplification of coins out of circulation. The very shop windows that revive the fortune of the devalued coins devalue the obsolete tools.

Marx's name is not mentioned even once in *Documents*. But the considerations on the museum, which these ethnographers elaborate there, follows quite closely the opposition between use-value and exchange-value established by Marx at the beginning of *Capital*, in the chapters devoted to the analysis of the commodity. It was this critique of the commodity that was also to serve as the basis for the short-lived alliance between ethnographers and dissenting Surrealists that was to constitute the specificity of *Documents*. An important part of the avant-garde, during this period of resistance to modernist formalism, is actually animated by the desire for a return, indeed a regression, to what might be called the primitivism of use-value. And it is in effect in the name of use-value that each of these two trends critiqued in its own way the decontextualization performed by formalism.[12]

The description of this use-value given in the first pages of *Capital* is well known. 'The usefulness of a thing', Marx writes, 'makes of this thing a use-value.' This usefulness or use-value of the thing is therefore inseparable from its material support. It has no autonomous, independent existence. But it is at the same time a property of the thing that is only realized in the consumption, that is, the destruction, of the thing: use-value cannot outlast use; it vanishes at the moment it is realized. It is thus a value that the thing can only lose. Exchange-value, on the other hand, is not an intrinsic, exclusive property of any of the objects it allows us to exchange: by definition, it must be common to at least two of them. But above all, it is on account of a delaying of consumption that an object is endowed with an exchange-value and that this exchange-value is detached from the object it quantifies. It is use-value deferred. The commodity is an object whose consumption has been postponed, an object laid aside, an object taken out of circulation, in order to be put on the market and exchanged. The same diversion that defines the market holds for the museum as well: objects enter it only once abstracted from the context of their use-value. It was this diversion (the aesthetic, if not mercantile, surplus value of what is taken out of circulation) that was to be thematized in the *Documents* ethnographers' reflections on the museum.

A brief article by Marcel Griaule, 'Pottery', constitutes a good example of this refocusing of museographical thought around use-value. Griaule denounces 'the archeologists and aesthetes' for their formalism; they admire, he writes, 'the shape of a handle, but', he adds, 'they carefully refrain from studying the position of the man who drinks'.[13] By looking only at the form of objects (that is, by only looking at the objects), they no longer see how they were used, they no longer even see that they were used. Taking use-value into account implies, in other words, an equal footing with the object. Instead of being the man who looks at a vase, the spectator must enter into its space and place himself in the position of the man who drinks.

But it is in André Schaeffner's article on musical instruments ('On musical instruments in a museum of ethnography') that we find the best-developed critique of a museography in which the exhibition requires a scrapping of the object, a falling into obsolescence achieved by the decontextualization of the piece exhibited. In the museum he evokes, Griaule requires, next to the vase, the ghost of the man who drinks. For Schaeffner as well, an isolated musical instrument is an abstraction. It needs accompaniment. Photographic and phonographic documents must allow it to return to the concrete: that is, the position of the musician who plays it, the sound or sounds which it produces, etc.[14] Moreover, there is a whole range of performances that unfold with no more instrument than the (mortal) body of the musician, consisting of gestures which, Schaeffner says, 'would vanish if the photograph did not preserve their character'.[15] Use-value, according to Marx, always refers in the final analysis to the needs and organs of a living body. It is thus to be expected that, according to this logic, taking the use-value of the exhibited objects (their function instead of their mere form) into account should lead to the introduction of the body into the space of the museum (opening the space of the museum to the world of the body and its needs). The central concept of this museology is that of bodily techniques.

There is a certain agreement with regard to beauty: just as we do not discuss money at the dinner table, we must silence the laborious origins of the objects exhibited in the museum. Like money, beauty has no smell. All that is behind us. Aesthetic *arrivisme* demands it. No art lover will ever ask what these objects did before they cost so much money. No art lover will ever ask why they were never seen before they were put on exhibit.

The ethnographers of *Documents* challenge this agreement and the repression of use-value it implies. They want a museum that would not automatically reduce exhibited objects to their formal, aesthetic properties, an exhibition space from which use-value would not be excluded, but rather one in which it would not only be represented, but exhibited, demonstrated. They would like to undo the opposition which dictates that one uses a tool and looks at a painting. A tool's inclusion within a museum would not have the renunciation of its origins as condition. Instead of replacing it with an exchange- or exhibition-value, this space would preserve use-value, permitting it to survive decontextualization, cut off from its goal, but use-value all the same, a use-value on sabbatical. Useful and idle at the same time. It is the Utopia of a space where it would be possible to have one's cake and eat it too. These are not Sunday shoes, these are everyday shoes but on the day of rest.[16]

In 1937, seven years after the end of *Documents*, the Trocadéro was destroyed, replaced by the Palais de Chaillot. The next year, in the new premises, the Museum of Ethnography becomes the Museum of Man. Leiris presents the goals of this institution in *La nouvelle revue française*. The term *document* appears several times in this brief article. 'How should we proceed so that the documents (observations, objects, photographs), whose value is tied to the fact that they are things taken from life, may retain some freshness once confined within books or locked up in display windows?' he asks. 'An entire technique of presentation must intervene as a follow-up to the techniques of the collecting, if we want to keep the documents from becoming merely materials for a ponderous erudition.'[17]

On the spot

It is not entirely by accident that it was with respect to jazz that Sartre, returning from New York, formulated his aesthetic imperative: like bananas, cultural products should be consumed on the spot. The primitive arts (to which jazz belongs) are indeed subject (or rather they subject themselves) to what Proust called the tyranny of the Particular. They do not obey the laws of the market, recognizing only use-value; but that is also what allows them their particularity. It is inseparable from the fact that they cannot be displaced. One cannot expect them to make the first move. These immovable objects, inserted in the space of the social fabric so intimately that they would not survive being extracted, impose a law of consumption on the spot.

It is in connection with the church of Balbec that Proust evokes this tyranny of the Particular: Balbec being 'the only place in the world that possesses Balbec Church', this church, like Sartre's bananas, gives up its taste only on the spot.[18] The narrator of the *Remembrance* makes this remark in front of the church. But at the same time he remembers the casts of its statues that he saw in the Trocadéro Museum. During the Third Republic the Trocadéro sheltered, next to the Museum of Ethnography, that other 'invitation au voyage' – even if it was for shorter trips – the Museum of French Monuments. Without making an ethnographer of Proust, the conjunction is significant. More than a few trips must have been planned in the course of visiting the two museums in this now-vanished building, where every visitor was being told that the thing out of place is never the real thing. An identical resistance to the laws of exchange- and exhibition-value leads ethnography and aesthetic reflection to the same demand for the irreplaceable, to the same longing for a world subject to the tyranny of use-value. The 'particular' refers here to the inexchangeable heterogeneity of a real, to an irreducible kernel of resistance to any kind of transposition, of substitution, a real which does not yield to a metaphor.[19]

The same articulation of the tyranny of the Particular and of use-value is at the heart of one of the most important reflections of the time on the status of the work of art in the context of its commodification, Walter Benjamin's essay, 'The work of art in the age of mechanical reproduction', published in 1936. It is Benjamin himself who refers to use-value to explain the origin of the value that the original of a work of art is assigned by the mere fact of its uniqueness. 'The unique value of the "authentic" work of art', he writes, 'has its basis in ritual, the location of its original use-value.' Or, 'The uniqueness of a work of art is inseparable from its being imbedded in the fabric of tradition.'[20] The reference to tradition thus indicates the ritual, cultic (rather than economic or instrumental) nature of the use-value invoked here. In other words, the work of art is unique only because it is not detachable from its context, because it can only be consumed on the spot. Furthermore, its originality was corrupted by the museum well before photography threatened it (or, as Georges Duthuit has shown, the museum was 'imaginary' well before Malraux). Before the question of its reproduction, there was that of its displacement, or even of the possibility of its displacement. The depreciations to be ascribed to mechanical reproduction were, if not present, at least already implicit within the decontextualization which is the museum's programme. It follows, moreover, that strictly speaking no work of art in a museum would fit the concept of original in the Benjaminian sense of the term: in effect, aura is linked less to the original object as such than to its cultic articulation at a given place and time. The aura of the work of art comes down to its use-value; and Benjamin writes that the use-value of a work of art as cultic object is diametrically opposed to 'the absolute emphasis on its exhibition value'.[21]

The triple conjunction of use-value, ritual and the uniqueness of the place, which is the form that Proust's tyranny of the Particular takes in Benjamin's analysis, purifies the concept of use-value of any utilitarian connotation. Use-value has nothing to do with usefulness. Benjamin roots it not in factories but in churches. It does not connote the instrumentality of an object or the usefulness of a technique. Use-value implies only this: the thing takes place on the spot, and only there. It can be neither transposed nor transported. It resists displacement and reproduction. And the metamorphosis of the gods. Use-value (ritual) lies beyond the useful (it refers not to a profit, but to an expenditure). The tyranny of the Particular simply names an absolute dependence on 'jealous', irreplaceable objects. In the last analysis, then, use-value describes the anxious dependence of someone who cannot change objects, who, unable to do without, wastes away on the spot. In Proust, following the church of Balbec, it is the irreplaceable Albertine who exerts this tyranny.

Yet, with *Documents*, the nostalgia for use-value follows two different trajectories. For the ethnologists, it follows a profane axis, and for them use-value refers to the technical, social and economic use of the object (it is vases that Griaule discusses, and the man who uses them is not necessarily a priest). But it is not of this sort of material production that Leiris is thinking when he reproaches the aestheticism of the museum for transforming 'a mask or a statue constructed with a view to specific, complex ritual purposes into a vulgar piece of art'.[22]

As with Proust and Benjamin, here too use-value follows a sacred axis, use referring to the category that Bataille was to explore under the name of non-productive use. And it was around these two versions of use-value, one profane and the other sacred, that the two active branches of the *Documents* editorial board, the ethnographers and the avant-garde, were to diverge.

The strongest critique of exchange-value published in *Documents* came not from an ethnographer, but from Bataille. His target is the marketing of the avant-garde: in 1928 (referring to the publication of *Le Surréalisme et la peinture*), the productions of the avant-garde entered the market of exchange-values. Before this date, the avant-garde expended itself; now it allowed itself to be bought. Before, it had responded to unspeakable, untransposed obsessions; now it hung on display shelves ('One enters an art dealer's shop as one enters a pharmacist's, in search of nicely presented remedies for unspeakable ailments'). Having previously dispensed 'images which form or deform real desires', this movement is no longer anything more than a period in the history of art. 'I challenge any art lover', Bataille writes, 'to love a canvas as much as a fetishist loves a shoe.'[23] For the opposition is not between the expert and the collector, but rather between the collector and the fetishist, between the distance of the collector and the obsession of the fetishist. I challenge a lover of modern art to waste away for a canvas as a fetishist does for a shoe.[24]

The example Bataille chooses, though standard, is nevertheless interesting. This shoe actually serves to underscore the gap being drawn here between the two versions of use-value, Bataille's and the ethnographers'. For the shoe is in effect a useful object, an object that works (it is used for walking, etc.). But it is not for walking that the fetishist 'uses' the shoe. For him it has a use-value that begins, paradoxically (this is what Bataille will later call the 'paradox of absolute usefulness'), at the very moment it stops working, when it no longer serves locomotion. It is the use-value of a shoe out of service. One will recall that it was while discussing shoes painted by Van Gogh that Heidegger entrusted the work of art with the task of revealing the 'work-being'.[25] The use-value of the shoes let loose within the painting. But Bataille's fetishist will never stand free enough before this shoe to get anything out of the painting; without putting it back to work, he wants to shield the shoe from the idleness of the painting. And Bataille's Van Gogh is not Heidegger's. Not the Van Gogh of shoes without a subject, of the shoes unbound by painting, but that of another unbinding, the sacrificial catachresis which seized his body proper, the detaching of the ear which belongs to his body. An ear which might belong to someone who spits it out over the market, crying: this is my body, inexchangeable. An ear diverted from the exchange market. Bataille's Van Gogh rejects the logic of transposition: 'Vincent Van Gogh belongs not to art history, but to the bloody myth of our existence as humans.'[26]

Neither high nor low

The question of the anthropological document (its collection, its preservation) occupies a central place in *Documents*. Moreover, the journal quite closely followed the reorganization of the Museum of Ethnography, undertaken by Georges Henri Rivière under the direction of Paul Rivet, its director since 1927. In the first issue, Rivière summed up the project.[27] Two months later, it was Rivet himself who formulated the ideology governing this reorganization.[28]

Not for an instant did Rivière envision competing with the Louvre. On the contrary, he applauded Rivet for having placed the Trocadéro under the wing of the Musée National d'Histoire Naturelle, linking it 'with one of the foremost scholarly bodies in the country, while remaining faithful to his object: ethnography'. He even talks about protecting ethnography from the vogue enjoyed by the primitive arts within the avant-garde:

Following the example of our most recent poets, artists and musicians, the favour of the elite is shifting toward the art of peoples said to be primitive and savage ... This prompts strange forays into ethnography, increasing a confusion which we thought to diminish ... The remodelled Trocadéro could have been founded on this misconception, becoming a Museum of Fine Arts where the objects would be divided up under the aegis of aesthetics alone.[29]

It was actually the ethnographers who took up the first line of attack in the anti-aesthetic crusade.[30] Rivet:

It is essential that the ethnographer, like the archeologist, like the historian of prehistory, study everything which constitutes a civilization, that he neglect no element, however insignificant or banal it may seem ... Collectors have made the mistake of a man who wishes to judge contemporary French civilization by its luxury goods, which are encountered only in a very limited sector of the population.[31]

Griaule: ethnography must 'distrust the beautiful, which is quite often a rare, which is to say freakish, event in civilization'.[32] Schaeffner: 'No object with a resonant or musical purpose, however 'primitive' or formless it may appear, no musical instrument will be excluded from a methodological classification.'[33] Just as the psychoanalyst must give everything equal attention, just as the Surrealist, in automatic writing, must let everything come through, so must the anthropological collector keep everything. He must never privilege an object because it is 'beautiful', never exclude another because it seems insignificant, or repugnant, or formless.

Nothing will be excluded, Schaeffner says. No object, however formless it may be.

In the December 1929 issue, Leiris and Griaule each devoted a brief article to spitting. Is the article ethnographical or Surrealist? It is, according to James Clifford, at once one and the other: a piece of Surrealist ethnography. 'The ethnographer, like the Surrealist, is licensed to shock.' Clifford adds: 'Spitting indicates a fundamentally sacrilegious condition. According to this revised, corrected definition, speaking or thinking is also ejaculating.'[34]

This definition obviously demands that we be able to apply it to itself. The article on spitting, doing what it says, must itself become a sacrilegious ejaculation. When he talks about spit, the ethnologist must shock as much as he would if he were actually spitting. Hence the recourse to the right to shock. Furthermore, we are confronted here with an article (in all senses of the word) of a palpably different type than those with which we have been dealing until now.

Thirty years later, after Bataille's death, it was by this change of register that Leiris would characterize the turn taken by *Documents*: 'The irritating and the heteroclite, if not the disturbing, became, rather than objects of study, characteristics inherent to the publication itself.'[35] The collecting of anthropological documents is abandoned in favour of an intervention of a different sort. At the very moment that science, in the name of the neither-high-nor-low, claims to appropriate the low, something happens to it. Science gets dirtied by its object. Lets itself be contaminated by it. The object fails to keep its distance, abandons its reserve, overflows onto the page which describes it. I say 'flower' – and it appears. Things occur in the very place where they are narrated. On the spot. An article by Leiris, 'Metaphor', sets up the same irruption of the referent: the object of study becomes, as it were, a feature of the publication: 'This article itself', he concludes, 'is metaphorical.'[36] It is not yet the shadow of the bull's horn, but something bites into the very page that wanted to appropriate it, something that is not in its place, something heterogeneous. Like the fly on the lecturer's nose. Or like the ego in the metaphysical whole. The appearance of the ego, Bataille says, is utterly shocking. Certainly it was this ego which shocked d'Espezel. 'The title you have chosen for this journal is hardly justified except in the sense that it gives us "documents" on your state of mind.'

Licensed to shock

But, Clifford says, that is just it, the ethnographer, like the Surrealist, has the right to shock.

He knows only one rule. To show everything. To uncover everything. To say everything. The Museum of Man will be the museum of the whole of man. *Nihil humani alienum.* No object, however formless it may seem, will be excluded. Everything that exists deserves to be documented. There is a sort of compassion, a gesture of epistemological charity, in this bias toward the little things. Science consoles these lowly realities for the scorn they receive from the elitism of the aesthetes. Clifford concludes that ethnography 'has in common with Surrealism a renunciation of the distinction between high and low within culture'.[37] And, from the renunciation of this distinction, it follows that the low no longer shocks. D'Espezel does not share his opinion. He had not yet read the article on spitting.

There is something Nietzschean about this project of saying yes to everything. Of wanting what exists in its totality. Of saying yes without choosing, to what one has not chosen. Of reaffirming, one thing after another, the totality of what is in the ontological display of a museum without reserve. But this eternal return of everything has a price. No one affirms the whole innocently.

In the same issue in which Griaule's and Leiris's articles on spitting appear, Bataille published 'Formless', which echoes them: 'To assert that the universe does not resemble anything and is merely formless, amounts to saying that the universe is something like a spider or spit.'[38] Formless: it is the same word that Schaeffner uses, but here it has lost the humility it had in the hands of the ethnographer. It is no longer a question of showing what everything, including the formless, resembles; it is the whole which, because it is formless, takes on an unexhibitable monstrosity. It resembles nothing. It is a totality without example. The formless (too present to be presentable) no longer allows itself to be contained. Placed *en abyme*, it destabilizes the difference between object and world, between part and whole. And, once again, the common front between the avant-garde and ethnography is undone. The same words do not accomplish the same tasks everywhere. The use-value of the word *formless* is not the same whether it is Schaeffner or whether it is Bataille who uses it. Schaeffner wants to classify even the formless, while, for Bataille, the formless *declassifies* (*déclasse*), getting things out of order, depriving them of their proper status. On the one hand, the law of 'no exceptions'; on the other, that of an absolute exception, of that which is unique but without properties.

Ethnographer's licence

Clifford insists on the importance that Mauss's teaching had for *Documents*. But the Mauss he quotes is not that of the great texts (the gift, sacrifice, seasonal variations, etc.), but instead the author of the paper on bodily techniques (subsequent to *Documents*; it dates from 1934), a text that in many ways confirms (without confronting) the museographical problems that were so central for *Documents*.

It happens, moreover, that among the bodily techniques which Mauss mentions we find that of spitting. But it is a spitting that is not sacrilegious, but rather therapeutic (it figures under the heading of oral hygiene). It can thus be done and said in the most appropriate way. And, moreover, if ever there was a sin to be redeemed, the ethnographer is there, ready to pay. This pasteurized spit spares Mauss the necessity of invoking the ethnographer's right to shock.[39]

For Bataille and Leiris, however, hygiene excuses nothing. On the contrary, it is their *bête noire*. In their hands, the word *hygiene* has precisely the impact of spitting. Dirtiness is proper to man, from which it follows that the less a thing is clean (*propre*), the more human it is. And inversely, Leiris formulates the equation explicitly. Speaking of the nude as represented in conventional painting, he declares it to be 'clean and emptied, and somehow dehumanized'.[40] The same equation is implied in Bataille's definition of the big toe as 'the most *human* part of the human body': the most human, he explains, because the most dirty, that which is subject to 'the most nauseating filthiness'.[41]

It is no longer a question here, as with the ethnographers, of rehabilitating the lowly. Everything can be said. But throughout Bataille, there remains something unmentionable. To say it, one must expose the taboo and, in exposing it, expose oneself. By inducing an expenditure, communication shifts from the level of exchange-value to that of use-value. Or, to put it differently, the forbidden is reintroduced into science. Everything must be said, yes, but on the condition that not everything can be said. The categorical imperative is here caught in a revolving door where the barely formulated 'you must' gives way to a 'therefore you cannot'. The avant-garde has no use for the right to shock proffered by the ethnographers: where, if anyone takes offence, one simply shows one's permit. Ethnographer's licence? But what would a sacrilege be within the limits of mere reason?

Gaps, deviations

Griaule, Rivet and Schaeffner criticized the aesthetes for abandoning the average. In selecting the beautiful, they privileged the rare, and thereby the monstrous. Bataille's position is exactly the opposite. In 'The deviations of nature', beauty is to be found not in the exceptions, but in the statistical norm: 'Beauty', he writes, 'would be at the mercy of a definition as classical as that of the common measure.'[42] And this teratology (the deviations of nature) is at the core of his aesthetic. But such a teratology implies an inverting of the relationship between the freakish and the ugly: while the ethnologists reject the beautiful because they consider it statistically monstrous, Bataille privileges the monstrous because he considers it aesthetically ugly. His definition of the freakish is no longer statistical, but aesthetic. It is not rare. On the contrary, the monstrous is now the core of the definition of individuality (the impossible is everyday): given the 'common character of personal incongruity and of the monster', the individual as such is the site of all deviation.[43] Bataille is certainly against the common denominator, but it is not in the name of a romantic excess; rather it is in the name of something like a very common excess, a general absence of a common denominator. Further, in 'Human face', the species itself is described as a 'juxtaposition of monsters'.[44] In addition, deviation is the concept responsible for the greatest divergence between the two driving forces behind *Documents*, the ethnographers and the anti-aesthetes. The ethnographers wanted continuity; Bataille wanted a rupture. They wanted to reconstruct contexts so that everything would seem in its place, while he would have the document expose the radical incongruity of the concrete: suddenly, the most ordinary people do not resemble anything; they are no longer in their place. One wonders who was responsible for *Documents*'s publication of 'The crisis of causality', in which Hans Reichenbach denounces the 'false idealization' that underlies the belief in determinism: 'each event is a roll of the dice', he adds.[45]

This deviation (the *hiatus irrationalis*) is one of the decisive components of the aesthetic ideology of *Documents*. With modern painting, writes Carl Einstein, 'we are placed outside the normal . . . We have distanced ourselves from biological monotony'. The speed of Picasso's imagination 'exceeds biological conservatism'.[46] Modern art begins at the precise moment when the same causes cease to produce the same effects. It thwarts the reproduction of similarity, the engendering of the same by the same, the law of biologico-aesthetic homogeneity. In other words, beauty is always the result of a resemblance. Meanwhile, ugliness (like formlessness) resembles nothing. That is its definition. Its space is that of a failure. It never manages to raise itself to the level of the double, of the image, of reproduction (of the typical or characteristic). It remains a case. But the *Documents* aesthetic reverses the value judgements relative to these definitions. It is for want of that impossible copy of what is ugly that beauty emerges, a beauty that is nothing more than the result or the residue of the failure of the ugly to reproduce or be reproduced. For this aesthetic of disparity, which is above all an anti-aesthetic of the untransposable (a resistance to aesthetic translation), it is secondary that ugliness is a failure of reproduction; what matters is that the beautiful itself is a failure of non-reproduction. A reproduction that has not managed to fail. An expenditure that has not taken place without reserve. The use-value would not have been completely consumed on the spot. The failure of a failure.

Documents – I invent nothing

There is another feature of the document. A document is ready-made. Contrary to the products of the imagination, it is not endogenous. Like social acts in Durkheim, the document is transcendent. It is not up to me. I invent nothing. It has not yet been assimilated by an aesthetic metaphorization. Heterogeneous and foreign, it has an impact, it shocks (it has a shock-value) as a trauma would. X marks the spot, to quote the title of a collection of sensationalist photographs of the Chicago gang wars on which Bataille commented.[47]

This promotion of the ready-made document stands within the framework of a more general condemnation of the imagination that is essential to modernist inspiration. It is in such a condemnation, for example, that Leiris grounds his autobiographical project. In 'On literature considered as tauromachy', he insists on the fact that *Manhood* is not a work of fiction: it is 'the negation of a novel'. Comparing his autobiography to a sort of Surrealist collage or, rather, photomontage, he presents it as a collection of pieces of evidence: 'No element is utilized', he says, 'which is not of strict veracity or of documentary value.'[48] The same 'documentary' inspiration led Bataille to add a final chapter of 'Coincidences' to *Story of the Eye*: these memories serve to diminish the role taken in novelistic invention by the freedom of the imagination.[49]

In this sense, *Documents* is not a Surrealist journal.

It is an aggressively realist journal.[50]

'Imagination alone tells me what can be', wrote Breton in the 1924 *Manifesto*.[51] But *Documents* wanted neither the imagination nor the possible. In it, photography takes the place of the dream. And if metaphor is the most active figure of Surrealist transposition, the document constitutes its nemesis, aggressively anti-metaphorical. With it, the impossible, which is the real, chases away what can be.

A fetishist materialism

The unmitigated enthusiasm for fetishism that we find in *Documents* is without a doubt what distances us more than anything. For, if fetishism for Barthes's listener evokes the escapist tactics of rather 'soft', flirtatious, tingly perversions, for Bataille it defines the 'hard' requirements of the thing itself. Fetishism is an absolute realism: it unleashes real desires, in real spaces, with real objects. Not for an instant does Bataille oppose, as Marxists do, fetishism and use-value (for him there is no fetishism of the commodity); when he evokes fetishism, it is, on the contrary, always against merchandise. The fetish is the irreplaceable, untransposable object. 'I challenge', writes Bataille, 'any art lover to love a canvas as much as a fetishist loves a shoe.'[52] And Leiris begins his article on Giacometti by opposing true fetishism ('undisguised' fetishism) to what he calls the 'transposed fetishism' (or false fetishism) of works of art: 'It is only rarely that one finds in the realm of works of art objects (paintings or sculpture) capable of responding to the demands of this true fetishism.'[53] The transposed fetish is the fetish that no longer works as a fetish: it has been discarded and framed to be put on the market; it has been degraded to become a commodity. It is no longer used but collected. According to Leiris, Giacometti's Surrealist objects would be the first real fetishes to have reappeared in a long time in the studio of an artist in Paris. It is significant that it was not the ethnographers who used this concept, which nevertheless refers to primitive religions.

In April 1929, Emmanuel Berl published his pamphlet, *The Death of Bourgeois Thought*. *The Death of Bourgeois Morality* followed a few months later. Its conclusion, entitled 'Defence of materialism', proposed a materialism that deserves Bataille's label of *base materialism*, a materialism of an aggressive vulgarity which Berl presents as the proletarian weapon *par excellence*, the only ideological weapon of any weight against the bourgeoisie. Materialism, according to Berl, 'does not consist in giving an ontological value to the material in order to refuse it to everything else, but in first looking, in the infinity of causes which provoke a phenomenon, for the lowest, simplest causes ... Materialism', he continues, 'is therefore a way of depreciating. It indicates a certain taste for depreciation.'[54] Berl's words are close to

Bataille's. They echo those of a brief article, 'Materialism', published in the June 1929 issue of *Documents*, a few months before Berl's pamphlet, and started with an attack against the materialists who, having subjected the material itself to the idealist requirement of *devoir-être*, want to substitute in its place an 'ideal form of the material, a form that would come closer than any other to what the material should be'.[55]

But, despite various appeals to a proletarian populism, the inspiration of this materialism (Berl's and Bataille's) is more Heraclitean than Marxist. A materialism of use-value, it defines the material as what does not last.[56] It goes the way of all use-value, exhausted in its consumption. And it is not reborn from its ashes. No trace is left after the holocaust. Not even a memory. It is exhausted on the spot, does not survive itself. Bataille's materialism is not cumulative (whence the loss), it is a materialism of difference *à fonds perdus*, without representatives, without a future and without reserve, without sequel, without descendants, without any tomorrow. The material is expended integrally, without remains, without leaving anything behind, not a ghost, not an heir, not a double. A flash – then night.

Reprint

The significance of the reprint is not the same for a book as it is for a periodical. A novel is republished because it has had some success or because the time has come to rediscover it. With a journal, the transposition from the aorist to the imperfect alters the textual status of the object, its punctuality. Like an event condemned to linger on. To publish a facsimile of the *Fliegende Blätter* of 1929–30, in 1991, would be to set up a resemblance in more than one way with an exhibition of a primitive work of art in a Paris museum, be it a Museum of Man or the Louvre.

But it is for the kamikazes, for the most fleeting trackers of the avant-garde, those who have not even seen two winters, that the honour of the reprint is intended. The reprint recuperates, against its will, that which spat upon permanence. *Documents*, for example. Placed, as Leiris has said, under the sign of the impossible, it was not a journal destined to burn very long. The official ideological contract was an aesthetic of the irretrievable. There is, also, in the republishing of *Documents* – a phoenix in spite of itself – something of the same nature as, for example, the transformation of a slaughterhouse into a historical site. We other civilizations would have liked so much to be mortal. But, in the age of mechanical reproduction, it is too late. *Ceci*, after all, *ne tuera pas cela*. Who today would bet, like Hugo at the end of Sartre's *Dirty Hands*, on the irretrievable? Or, like Giraudoux's Judith, when she realizes with horror that the unmentionable pleasures she has known in Holophernes's bed are on the verge of being transformed into a pious story, into an edifying legend. Of being given as an example.

Translated by Liesl Ollman

Notes

1   Jean Babelon, 'Numismatique', in *L'histoire et ses méthodes*, ed. Charles Samaran, Paris, Gallimard, 1961, 329. Jean Babelon, a colleague of Bataille at the Bibliothèque Nationale's gallery of medals, was on the editorial board of *Documents* and collaborated on the journal.

2   It seems that, among the Chartists, the general opinion, around 1929, still predicted a fine career for Bataille as a numismatist. René Grousset, for example, in an article in *Documents*, refers respectfully to the 'numismatic studies of Mr G. Bataille' (René Grousset, 'A case of regression towards the barbaric arts,' *Documents* 2 [1930], 73).
    On Bataille's numismatics, see Denis Hollier, *La Prise de la Concorde*, Paris, Gallimard, 1974, 227–8. For an English version of this work see *Against Architecture: The Writings of Georges Bataille* trans. Betsy Wing, Cambridge, Mass., MIT Press, 1989.

3   Recollections of *Documents* published in Georges Bataille, *Oeuvres complètes* (*OC*), ed. Marmande, XI, Paris, Gallimard, 1988, 572.

4   One of the rare reviews provoked by the journal, a note which appeared in *Les nouvelles littéraires*, was to permit itself a play on words of the same type, facile and without malice, on the title: '*Documents* presents some very curious photographic 'documents' in its fourth issue.'

5   Bataille, 'L'Ordre de Chevalerie' (1922), *OC*, I, 100. See also the account (published in *Aréthuse* in 1926) of a volume of numismatics: 'These documents,' Bataille writes, 'often just as interesting from an archeological point of view as from an artistic one, cast into relief the effort taken to organize a magnificent network of circulation' (ibid., 107).

6   In the three first issues: 'Doctrines Archéologie Beaux-Arts Ethnographie'; from issue 4 on: 'Archéologie Beaux-Arts Ethnographie Variétés'.

7   The only contributor to *Documents* to defend art as such was the obscure prehistorian Henri Martin: he concluded his article on prehistoric sculptures by insisting that they respond to an intention that is not only 'cultic or symbolic'. One must also take into account, he writes, the 'imperious desire to satisfy a passion: that of Art' (Dr Henri Martin, 'L'art solutréen dans la vallée du Roc [Charente]', *Documents* 6 [November 1929], 309).

8   Michel Leiris, 'Revue des publications. Jean Brunhes, *Races*, documents commentés par Mariel Jean-Brunhes Delamarre, etc.', *Documents* 6 (1930), 104.

9   Carl Einstein, 'A propos de l'exposition de la Galerie Pigalle,' *Documents* 2 (1930), 104.

10 Bataille, 'Le cheval académique', *Documents* 1 (April 1929).

11 Several regular contributors were ethnographers, or on the verge of becoming ethnographers: Marcel Griaule, André Schaeffner, Michel

Leiris. And, among the occasional contributors, Maurice Leenhardt. We must also add Lévi-Strauss since he was the author of the article signed Paul Monnet in the issue devoted to Picasso (see his letter to Jean Jamin, July 1986). But it is true that, in 1930, Lévi-Strauss was still a long way from being an ethnologist.

12 In this sense, as Jean Jamin has convincingly shown, there has never been, even with *Documents*, a project that can properly be said to be common to both ethnographers and Surrealists (or, to take up the all too seductive phrase of James Clifford, there has never been a 'Surrealist ethnography'). There have only been, to quote the title of Alfred Métraux's article on Bataille, 'encounters with ethnographers', and these encounters have had a common resistance to commercial decontextualization as their terrain. The object of the present chapter is to situate the scene of these encounters and to mark out their limits. See Jean Jamin, 'L'ethnographie mode d'inemploi. De quelques rapports de l'ethnologie avec le malaise dans la civilisation' in *Le mal et la douleur*, Jacques Hainard and Roland Kaehr, eds, Neûchatel, Musée d'ethnographie, 1986. For a discussion of the articulation between aesthetics and anthropology in *Documents*, see also Rosalind Krauss, 'No more play' in *The Originality of the Avant-Garde and Other Modernist Myths*, Cambridge, MIT Press, 1985.

13 Marcel Griaule, 'Poterie', *Documents* 4 (1930), 236. What is essential in an object is not its form but its use. And it is rarely possible to deduce one from the other (it is an exception when the way something is used derives from its shape). This critique of formalist aesthetics turns up also in Paul Rivet: 'Ethnography should not content itself with a strictly morphological study of objects made by man. It must also study, and I do not hesitate to say that it must above all study, the techniques, which last longer than the forms and are less easily derived' (Paul Rivet, 'L'étude des civilisations matérielles: ethnographie, archéologie, préhistoire', *Documents* 3 [June 1929], 132).

The critique of formalism is moreover not made by ethnographers alone; we also encounter it with Carl Einstein: 'The moralists of pure form', he says, 'preach for the square, filled with drunkenness' (Carl Einstein, 'Tableaux récents de Georges Braque', *Documents* 6 [November 1929], 290).

14 'Beside the exhibited instrument should be displayed a photograph of its player; the mute object, and its position between the hands of the person who awakens and suddenly multiplies' (André Schaeffner, 'Des instruments de musique dans un musée d'ethnographie', *Documents* 5 [October 1929], 252).

15 Schaeffner, 'Des instruments de musique dans un musée d'ethnographie', 154.

16 This reflection on what a museum of use-value would be is not unrelated to the one which Heidegger was to develop a few years later (1935) in 'The origin of the work of art' with reference to Van Gogh's paintings representing shoes. 'The work belongs, as work, uniquely within the realm that is opened up by itself. For the work-being of the work is presented in, and only in, such opening up' (Martin Heidegger, 'The origin of the work of art' in *Poetry, Language, Thought*, trans. Albert Hofstadter, New York, Harper & Row, 1971, 41).

17 Leiris, 'Du musée d'ethnographie au musée de l'homme', *La nouvelle revue française*, 299 (August 1938), 344.

18 Marcel Proust, *Remembrance of Things Past*, trans. C. K. Scott Moncrieff and Terence Kilmartin, New York, Random House, 1981, 709.

19 For the origins of the Museum of French Monuments and the project of restoring (and even resuscitating) the fragments of the past by reconstituting their context, by shifting from a metonymical to a synecdochal presentation of exhibited objects, see the chapter dedicated to De Sommerard and to Alexandre Lenoir by Stephen Bann, *The Clothing of Clio* (New York, Cambridge University Press, 1984, 85 and 91). Bann's analyses fully justify the proximity of the two museums hosted in the Trocadéro: for the romantic museum (the Museum of French Monuments) the alterity is national and medieval, remote in time; for the modern (the Museum of Ethnography) it is exotic, remote in space.

20 Walter Benjamin, 'The work of art in the age of mechanical reproduction,' *Illuminations*, trans. Harry Zohn, New York, Schocken, 1978, 223, 224.

21 Ibid., 225.

22 Leiris, 'Civilisation', *Documents* 4 (September 1929), 221–22.

23 Bataille, 'L'esprit moderne et le jeu des transpositions', *Documents* 8 (1930), 490–1.

24 Bataille was working at the time on 'La valeur d'usage de D.A.F. de Sade', in which he denounces (to take up Jamin's expression) the 'mode d'inemploi' to which the admiration of literary circles has reduced Sade; Sade's use-value – if there is one – cannot be limited to the bibliophilic pleasure of collectors and connoisseurs. Bataille, 'La valeur d'usage de D.A.F. de Sade' in *OC*, II, 56. See also *Le bleu du ciel*, in *OC*, III, 428.

25 On the place left to fetishism by Heidegger's analyses, see Jacques Derrida, 'Restitutions' in *The Truth in Painting*, trans. Geoff Bennington and Ian McLeod, Chicago, University of Chicago Press, 1987.

26 Bataille, 'Van Gogh as Prometheus', *October* 36 (spring 1986), 60.

27 Georges Henri Rivière, 'Le musée d'ethnographie du Trocadéro', *Documents* 1 (April 1929), 58.

28 Paul Rivet, 'L'étude des civilisations matérielles: ethnographie, archéologie, préhistoire'. *Documents* 3 (June 1929), 132.

29 Rivière, 'Le musée d'ethnographie du Trocadéro', 58. It was probably not the Surrealists who claimed the entrance into the Louvre by primitive arts. In 1930, after the exhibition at the Pigalle Gallery, in order to save it from the cult of the exotic and the savage to which Surrealism had driven the fashion for primitive arts, Paul Guillaume was to declare black art to be ripe for the Louvre.

30 Desnos, however, expresses an identical resistance to another aestheticization, the one from which popular imagery benefits (or suffers): 'It is popular manifestations which suffer the most from these fleeting fads' (Robert Desnos, 'Imagerie moderne', *Documents* 7 [December 1929], 377). Same note in Bataille: 'Some very pathetic aesthetes, looking for some place to put their chlorotic admiration, flatly invent the beauty of the factories' (Georges Bataille, 'Smokestack', *October* 36 [spring 1986], 15).

31 Rivet, 'L'étude des civilisations matérielles', 133.

32 Griaule, 'Un coup de fusil', *Documents* 1 (1930), 46.

33 Schaeffner, 'Des instruments de musique', 252.

34 James Clifford, 'On ethnographic Surrealism', *Comparative Studies in Society and History* (October 1981), 52. The word sacrilege comes from Leiris's article: 'Spitting is the height of sacrilege' (Michel Leiris, 'Crachat', *Documents* 7 [December 1929], 381–2).

35 Leiris, 'De Bataille l'impossible à l'impossible *Documents*', *Brisées*, Paris, Mercure de France, 1965, 261.

36 Leiris, 'Métaphore', *Documents* 3 (June 1929), 170.

37 Clifford, 'On ethnographic Surrealism', 49.

38 Bataille, 'Informe', *Documents* 7 (December 1929), 382.

39 Marcel Mauss, 'Les techniques du corps' in *Anthropologie et sociologie*, Paris, Presses Universitaires de France, 1960, 383. This article followed that by Griaule and Leiris by several years.

40 Leiris, 'L'homme et son intérieur', *Documents* 5 (1930), 261.

41 Bataille, 'The big toe' in *Visions of Excess: Selected writings, 1927–39*, ed. and trans. Allan Stoekl, with Carl R. Lovitt and Donald M. Leslie Jr, Minneapolis, University of Minnesota Press, 1985, 20–1.

42 Bataille, 'The deviations of nature', *Visions of Excess*, 55.

43 Ibid.

44 Bataille, 'Human face', *October* 36 (spring 1986), 18.

45 Hans Reichenbach, 'Crise de la causalité', *Documents* 2 (May 1929), 108.

46 Carl Einstein, 'Pablo Picasso: quelques tableaux de 1928', *Documents* 1 (April 1929), 35. The same conclusion is drawn from Masson's paintings: 'We are tired of biological identity' (Carl Einstein, 'André Masson, ethnological study', *Documents* 2 [May 1929], 102). We encounter the same articulation of the biological and the aesthetic, the same identification of reproduction with representation in Henry-Charles Puech, who also interprets Picasso – and modern painting in general – in terms of a rebellion against the 'biological demand of representation' (H.-C. Puech, 'Picasso et la représentation', *Documents* 3 [1930], 118).

47 Bataille, 'X marks the spot', *Documents* 7 (1930), 437.

48 Leiris, *Manhood*, trans. Richard Howard, New York, Grossman Publishers, 1963, 157.

49 Bataille would later manifest the same insistence in 'La tragédie de Gilles de Rais': 'Such scenes are not the work of an author. They have taken place.'

50 Realist professions of faith are frequent. For example, Leiris: 'It is in my opinion utter nonsense to forget the fundamentally realist character of Picasso's work' (Leiris, 'Toiles récentes de Picasso', *Documents* 2 [1930], 62).

   See also Georges Ribemont-Dessaignes: 'I am a realist … There are people who talk about What-exists and What-does-not-exist, and who only believe in the latter, even as they deny its very existence … They are merely surrealists.' 'A painter is always a realist. I do not know of any who are not. Too bad for the surrealists: let them abandon all relations with painting' (Ribemont-Dessaignes, 'Giorgio de Chirico', *Documents* 6 [1930], 337, 338).

   And Desnos, in his review of *La femme 100 têtes*: 'For the poet, there are no hallucinations. There is the real' (Desnos, '*La femme 100 têtes*, par Max Ernst', *Documents* 6 [1930], 238).

51 André Breton, *Manifeste du surréalisme*, in *Oeuvres complètes*, ed.

Marguerite Bonnet, Paris, Gallimard, 1988, 312.

52 Bataille, 'L'esprit moderne et le jeu des transpositions', *Documents* 8 (1930), 49.

53 Leiris, 'Alberto Giacometti', *Documents* 4 (September 1929), 209.

54 Emmanuel Berl, *Mort de la morale bourgeoise* [1929], Paris, Jean-Jacques Pauvert, 1965, 174. With the crisis of Surrealism as background (and also, without doubt, the comings and goings of Suzanne Muzard between Breton and Berl), a brief dialogue took shape between Berl and Bataille. In 'Conformismes freudiens', Berl, while discussing what he calls contemporary 'fetishism' (which he condemns), mentions the name of Bataille: 'The phallus replaces the fig leaf. No more, no less. And, to put it in Georges Bataille's language, the idealism corrupting the fetish makes of it a *devoir être*' (Berl, *Formes* 5 [April 1930]).

The denunciation of *devoir-être* was one of the key features of Bataille's anti-Surrealist realism; see Bataille: 'If one says that flowers are beautiful, it is because they seem to *conform to what must be* [*ce qui doit être*]' (Bataille, 'The language of flowers', *Visions of Excess*, 12): and: 'Space would do much better, of course, to fulfill its duty [*faire son devoir*]' (Bataille, 'Espace', *Documents* 1 [1930], 41). On the contrary, André Breton: 'It is up to us to oppose to it together this invincible force which is that of *devoir-être*, that of human becoming' (Breton, *Position politique de surréalisme*, in *Manifestes du surréalisme* [Paris, Jean-Jacques Pauvert, 1962], 274).

55 Bataille, 'Materialism', *Visions of Excess*, 15. Bataille was to return to this critique of 'ontological materialism' in 'Base materialism and Gnosticism', *Visions of Excess*, 45.

56 'The material', Berl writes, 'is that which does not last ... Materialism therefore refuses all values of permanence, everything which clings to continuance' (Berl, *Mort de la morale bourgeoise*, 174).

11 Poussière/peinture
Bataille on painting

Briony Fer

In *Documents* in 1930, Bataille wrote a short commentary on paintings by Miró recently shown at the Galerie Pierre. He described how, in Miró's work, reality disintegrated into dust, a sun-shot dust (*poussière ensoleillée*). For Bataille, a metonymic chain, where one term migrates into another, is triggered by the metaphor of dust. It is as if a mass of grains or specks occupies the field of vision and forms a veil against the light. Vision is obscured, and yet the sight is ravishing. Forms are dissolved, almost like a modern form of chiaroscuro. Under these conditions, the pleasures of *not* seeing, or at least of not seeing clearly, are intense.

Dust and its network of associations are woven through Bataille's writing on modern painting, in particular his writing on Miró, Masson, Picasso and Dali. In this essay I am concerned with the ways in which this constellation of metaphors around dust relates to Bataille's view of the origins of modern painting in a psychic scenario of sexual difference, a scenario which does not so much illuminate as deal in shadows. My interest is in Bataille's sense that obscurity – as it is played off against insight and enlightenment – is a condition of modern painting. It is a question of how dust, as a metaphor, can migrate from waste, from matter, to 'dust in your eyes' (*une poussière dans l'oeil*) and a blurring of sight and of meaning, where meaning is necessarily opaque and impervious to light.

Those Miró paintings which prompted Bataille to write were the result of what is generally described as Miró's 'crisis' of 1929–30. After the extraordinary series of Dutch interiors which followed his trip to Holland in 1928, Miró abandoned painting for collage. His work in collage used neither coloured papers nor the decorative additions that had characterized the Cubist collages of Picasso or Braque. Rather the collages seem resolutely understated, with areas of brown paper or plain sandpaper interspersed with minimal drawing in pencil or ink. In comparison with the saturated colour which reached a pitch in Miró's reworkings of Dutch seventeenth-century paintings, the shift of interest could not have been more marked. To characterize this shift as a crisis usually implies that what followed was a negative interlude, a departure from the main concerns of modern painting which Miró would only resolve some years later and ultimately in the Constellation series of the late 1930s. Unlike Picasso's and Braque's Cubist collages, which have been seen as somehow more engaged with the concerns of modern art than even modern painting,[1] Miró's experiments appear as too much of an abnegation, both in the sense of a denial and of a loss or lack of something that had previously been present in the work.

For Bataille to take up Miró's work at just this point was remarkable for two main reasons. The first was primarily strategic and shows how the differences between Bataille and André Breton were articulated over the ground of practice. In December 1929, Breton had published the *Second Manifesto of Surrealism* in the last issue of *La révolution surréaliste*, in which he insisted on Surrealism's central commitment to a political programme. This had the effect of marginalizing those who did not share in it, like Miró, even though Breton had earlier claimed him as an artist at the heart of Surrealism. As Breton's interest waned, Miró was championed by Bataille in *Documents*. When Bataille engaged with Miró's work, it was not simply to take up an artist who had wavered from Breton's version of the Surrealist path. It was also, I will wish to claim, because there was some significant common ground between Miró's art and Bataille's thinking.[2]

Secondly, Miró's move away from painting towards collage and the *papiers collés* was symptomatic of his attitude towards painting itself at the period, and towards its decomposition. On his return from Holland in 1928, Miró began working on the interiors at the same time as his first collages. There was no neat break between one type of work and the other and he continued to work in these different veins. The idea that the art of picture making lies not in composition, as it is normally understood, but in decomposition, links these apparently contradictory ways of working. To use collage as painting's 'undoing' had been Miró's achievement during the last years of the decade. Maurice Raynal first quoted Miró in 1927 as saying 'I want to murder painting',[3] and this was reiterated by Tristan Tzara who later observed that Miró wanted to kill painting by its own means.[4] When Bataille wrote about Miró's work in *Documents* in 1930, he quoted the same remark. For Bataille, the desire to kill painting becomes a kind of confession, and the work which acts out the desire is, of course, a series of paintings. Six of these, including Figure 11.1, were reproduced in *Documents* alongside

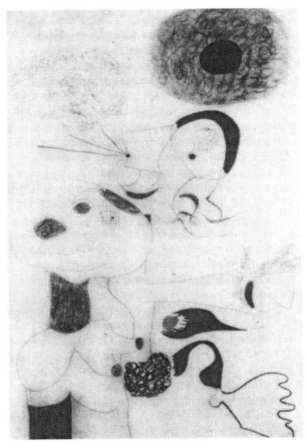

Figure 11.1 Joan Miró, *Peinture*, 1930, oil on canvas. Beyeler Collection, Basle.

Bataille's text. Whilst this so-called crisis in Miró's work has been regarded as a temporary diversion from the path of modernist painting, it is significant that Bataille took it to be exemplary of modern painting and of its sadistic impulse. Rather than a digression, then, from the concerns of modern painting, annihilation and obliteration *were* the concern of modern painting.

Doing violence to representation forms the basis, for Bataille, of any representational act. The short piece on Miró followed his long review of G. H. Luquet's recent book, *L'art primitif*, in which he discussed the idea of alteration (*altération*) as the basis for drawing. *Altération* involved not only the change from one state to another but also a succession of changes, each destroying the preceding state. In the act of drawing, a clean piece of paper or a bare wall is in effect 'spoilt' and so transformed into something else – a horse or a head, for example; the drawing process, as it continues, subjects the basic figure to further deformations (*déformations*). Art proceeds 'by successive destructions. And so in so far as it liberates *libidinal* instincts, these instincts are sadistic'.[5] Bataille discussed children's drawings in these terms, illustrating several by Lili, the nine-year-old daughter of the painter André Masson. He also used Abyssinian children's graffiti from church pillars and doors. These were characterized by their use of ambiguous forms which could be read in several different ways at once, like a play on words or a pun. The value Bataille attributes to drawing is as a kind of 'prehistory' of art, where art's unconscious is to be found. In the simple tracing of a line, he sees the underlying mechanisms at work in representation. For Bataille, the interest of the term *altération* is its two senses – 'a partial decomposition analogous with that of corpses and at the same time the transition (*passage*) to a perfectly heterogeneous state corresponding to ... the sacred, found for example in the ghost'.[6] Its dual aspect is both material and immaterial, present and absent. The metaphors of decomposition and decay, of corpse and ghost, may have their origins in a prehistory but are perpetually in play, like the prehistory of the modern unconscious.

Bataille's later account of the work of Manet develops the idea that modern art is characteristically sadistic; that the impulse within modernism is to do violence to the text by obliterating the text. In his book on Manet (1955) Bataille argued that both *Olympia* and *The Execution of Maximilian* show the way a painting and a text, such as the narrative of prostitution or assassination, 'part company'. 'In both cases', he wrote, 'the picture *obliterates* the text, and *the meaning of the picture is not in the text behind it but in the obliteration of that text*.'[7] This is not simply because the narrative is incoherent in the paintings, although it is true that their various elements often fail to add up, but something more. Cancelling out is always a violent manoeuvre. 'All we have', he goes on to say with reference to *Olympia*, 'is the "sacred horror" of her presence – presence whose sheer simplicity is tantamount to absence.'[8] This state of absence, of indifference and silence, is characteristic of modern painting. Rather than reveal the flat surface of painting, in Bataille's view it is more significant that the bare canvas is destroyed, or a text destroyed, in a series of destructive moves or cancellations. This renders other modes of interpretation, which depend on finding a focus, a source, a psychological centre or a text, inappropriate ways of looking at Manet's work – for the destruction of the subject was Manet's achievement as a modern painter. With Manet began the repudiation of meaning and the obliteration of the original text. Yet it is Goya who is the crucial precursor to modernism: 'Modern painting', Bataille wrote, 'attains through *absence* what Goya, in a world freighted with solemnity and grave respect, attained through *excess*.'[9] Goya's terrifying dreams prefigure the 'core of inner, underlying violence' around which modern art is fashioned.[10]

According to the trajectory traced by Bataille, the exemplary moments in the history of art are those which combine erotic and sadistic impulses – Delacroix, Manet, Moreau and Surrealism. Indeed, in his last published work, *Les larmes d'Eros* (1961), Bataille came to see Surrealism as a kind of modern Mannerism. The book's title was taken from a painting then attributed to Rosso, the Italian Mannerist painter who worked at Fontainebleau for François I, under whose patronage was produced the erotic art of the French High Renaissance. In Rosso's *Venus weeping over the death of Adonis* Venus is depicted standing over the body of the beautiful Adonis, the object of love who has been killed by the wild boar. It encapsulates in that moment the connection between desire and death. The central metaphor here of the tears which fill the field of vision is an extension of Bataille's earlier ideas on art with which this essay is primarily concerned. His language also echoes Freud's on the two classes of instincts. Freud had always acknowledged that the sadistic impulse was present in the sexual instinct and related to narcissism.[11] He called the sexual instinct Eros, the preserver of life, and distinguished it from the death instinct 'the task of which is to lead organic life back to the inanimate state', with sadism as its representative. Eros, on the other hand, 'by bringing about a far-reaching combination of the particles into which living substance is dispersed, aims at . . . preserving life'.[12] Never completely separate, these two classes of instincts could be 'fused, blended, alloyed'. The metaphorical language of animate to inanimate, combination and dispersal, is already in Freud, but in Bataille that fusion takes on ecstatic form.

Like the modern literary text, modern painting rehearses the cruelty of sacrifice on its own means of representation. From this point of view the history of art from Lascaux on represents so many layers of a modern unconscious. This does not so much universalize the art of the past so much as metaphorize its effect as prehistory. For Bataille, it is this sacrifice that is obsessively repeated in painting in the destruction of objects 'in a field of attraction induced by a flashing point (*pointe*) where solid forms are destroyed, where these objects available in the world . . . are consumed as in a blazing mass (*brasier*) of light'.[13] Here the image of flashing light which dissolves form by making it difficult to see is brought together with *un brasier de lumière* – a burning, blinding source of light. We encounter here, as in Bataille's earlier text on Miró, a light of immobilizing intensity which obscures the objects in vision.

Whilst the sun for Bataille is the most elevated of conceptions, it is also emasculating. Because of our incapacity to look at the sun, which elicits horror and which blinds, such elevation is always and unavoidably combined with a sudden fall from grace. It is this paradoxical state which characterizes modern painting and which links it to the Oedipal scenario and the compulsively repeated theme of castration. As he puts it in 'Rotten sun', published in *Documents* in 1930, 'In contemporary painting . . . the search for that which most ruptures the highest elevation, and for a blinding brilliance, has a share in the elaboration or decomposition of forms, though strictly speaking this is only noticeable in the paintings of Picasso.'[14] The fall, of course, restores things to ground level and to the base material of dust and dirt.

What Bataille noticed in Miró's work later in 1930 both related to this same process of decomposition and took on a specific character of its own. Just as it is possible to see how his view of successive destructions enacted in Miró's work related to his general view of art, it is also important to acknowledge how his experience of Surrealist painting shaped his later formulations. In *Painting* (Figure 11.1) Miró used drawing to suggest ambiguous forms, like in the graffiti which Bataille had commented on in his review of Luquet's book. Here the female body appears to be made up of so many extensions, disconnected one from the other. A line may trace the figure of an eye but also cancel or scratch it out. Alongside the sinuous tracing of lines, there are scumbled, textured surfaces. These are ambiguous too, like a sun that is erased or in eclipse. A scribbled patch hovers next to denser areas of paint. It covers over, almost, the bare canvas beneath. Many of the paintings exhibited at the Galerie Pierre appear to be a series of cancellations, with different forms of crossing out, even scribbling over, being used (see Figure 11.2).

Bataille remarked, in the article with which this chapter begins, on the extreme lengths to which Miró had taken the principle of decomposition. But there was also something particular in Miró's work which made the metaphor of dust so vivid: 'Joan Miró started out from a representation of objects so minute (*minutieuse*) that to some extent it reduced reality to dust.'[15] This is qualitatively different from the kind of violence involved in the work of Picasso (for instance, in *The Three Dancers* from 1925), or indeed that of Masson or Dali, the other artists with whom Bataille was primarily concerned at this time. It is a form of erasure that lends itself to a dissolution into minute tiny particles, a rather exquisite scattering of apparently random marks. In this context, the metaphor with which I first began, of 'sun-shot dust', relates to that sense of the flashing light in a climactic moment of sacrifice, or the live coals decomposing on a brazier. It suggests not the clarification of form or enlightenment but the obscuring of vision through a cloud of powdery dust – pulverized yet fragile.

The effect of Miró's decomposition is dispersal into 'a throng of decomposed elements and even more agitated'.[16] The surface of painting at once scintillates and decomposes – understood as the undoing of the composition – in a storm of minute particles, like phosphorescent powder strewn across it. The risks involved for the painter are constantly invoked by Bataille's stress on the extreme lengths to which Miró had taken the process, and the gamble, the risk of extinction, is always present. For Bataille, 'Decomposition has been pushed to such a point that there remain no more than a few unformed marks on the lid (or on the tombstone, if you wish) of a box of tricks.'[17] The idea of the surface of a painting as a lid suggests that it covers up something else, that it conceals its contents, which, like the corpse in the graveyard, lie beneath. It is a surface which attracts, which is both obscuring and yet irresistible, which invites speculation yet resists explanation or fixed meaning. It is, like the tombstone, the part above ground, just.

The 'box of tricks' alludes to Pandora's box. Beneath the lid traced with a few unformed marks, evil must lie. According to the myth, Pandora, as a figure of destructive femininity, was so curious to see what the box given to her by the gods contained that she let out all the evils of the world. The symbolic connection between a box and a tomb is familiar from Freud's theory of dreams, but here, in Bataille's formulation, the surface of painting denotes both these metaphors at

Figure 11.2 Joan Miró, *Composition*, 1930, oil on canvas. Photo Musée de Grenoble.

once. Latent in Bataille's almost incidental reference to the 'box of tricks' is the sense that the woman is revealing secrets, and knowledge has to be equated with the tomb and with death. This is not just a question of the woman conventionally associated with death – but the woman associated with secrets, and it is the secrets which mortify. To pursue such knowledge is to court certain danger: 'Then the little coloured and deranged (*aliéné*) elements proceeded to a new irruption, next they disappear once again today in these paintings, leaving only the traces of you know not what disaster.'[18] Having violently ruptured the surface, the unformed marks are just traces in the dust. Elsewhere, Bataille described what he termed Masson's 'rodeo', about to 'bite the dust' (*mordre la poussière*).[19] The expression reinforces the conjunction of dust with death, familiar already in the sense of dust (*poudre*) as the mortal remains of the body.

'Dust' was one of Bataille's entries in the 'Critical dictionary' published in *Documents* in October 1929. Storytellers, he wrote, had not imagined that Sleeping Beauty awoke coated in a thick layer of dust. Of course, she would have been covered in sinister spiders' webs, for dust uniformly invades every kind of human habitation 'as if it were a question of preparing attics and old rooms for the impending entrance of obsessions, phantoms, grubs.'[20] Dust evokes dirt, spectres and nocturnal terrors of abandoned houses and it renews itself continually. If Sleeping Beauty conventionally stands for a feminine ideal of passive perfection, here she is subject to worm-eaten and rancid decrepitude. Women servants, continued Bataille, may use the vacuum cleaner to clean those provincial houses, like philosophers and thinkers who try to clean up with logic, but the dust persists. Woman as a servant, or as a mother, is charged (and I mean charged in both senses of responsibility and impugned guilt) with the management of dirt. Dirt and cleanliness are the woman's prerogative.[21]

Bataille's fantasy, each corner of which is a dust-trap, embodied the worst nightmares of the hygienist movement; after all, Le Corbusier had claimed in *Towards a New Architecture* in 1923, 'Every man today realizes his need of sun, of warmth, of pure air and clean floors.'[22] Whilst the machine aesthetes celebrated the factory, Bataille spoke of the factory not as a place of beauty but of 'lugubrious filth',[23] and factory chimneys emitting 'sinister convulsions' of smoke. Dust engendered a language of dirt, nastiness and filth – precisely the language not only so distasteful to the hygienists and advocates of a machine aesthetic but also to Breton himself. Breton made central to his aesthetic the idea of involuntary convulsions, but in the service of 'convulsive beauty'. Dismissing Bataille in the *Second Manifesto*, he invoked the last lines of Bataille's essay 'Human face', and Bataille's call 'To run absurdly with *him* – eyes suddenly dim and filled with unavowable tears – towards haunted provincial houses seamier than flies, more depraved and ranker than barbers' shops'.[24] The drawing together of metaphors of dust and tears was for Breton so telling of Bataille's 'vulgar' materialism. Breton attempts here to assert control over such abject material as well as over dissident figures such as Bataille.

One of the images which illustrated the essay 'Human face' was an old photograph of a bourgeois marriage. On the surface so respectable, this was, for Bataille, the scene of a buried psychic scenario of perversion. It was in respectable provincial attics and garrets, after all, that one found the wasp-waisted corsets which have become 'the prey of flies and mites, the hunting ground for spiders'.[25] By association with the female body, these old corsets are the site of psychic detritus and waste. He likened leaving these old rooms to parting from the maternal breast 'where everything had been arranged by vain phantoms, not excepting the rancid dust'.[26] Old homes, and the mother as the ultimate 'home', are the object of ambivalent feelings of fascination and repulsion. The photograph, as Bataille sees it, is a picture not just of a provincial wedding, but of a mother and a father as monsters which engender violence and impurity, and where beneath the veneer of order there is trauma. It is the psychic scenario between the child and its mother and father that Bataille sets up as the frame in which modernity is played out. And the mother's body is invoked by a fragmented part, the corset or the breast – they seem interchangeable – as an incoherent terrain of desire and fear.

Just as the provincial attic had acted as an exemplary site of repressed bourgeois sexuality in 'Human face', so the attic of the museum figured in the 'Critical dictionary' (Figure 11.3). Two photographs entitled 'Attics: Mannequins, debris and dust' (*Greniers: Mannequins, debris et poussières*) accompanied the entry on 'Dust'. The stores of the museum in which its contents gather dust become, like the history of art, a metaphor for the modern unconscious. This is a museum of the mind, or as he wrote elsewhere, the museum serves as a 'colossal mirror' to every aspect of the psyche, a place whose contents were only formed in the minds of its spectators. The birth of the museum also coincided with the development of the guillotine.[27] It was thus associated, by sleight of hand, with violent death and dismemberment, by decapitation.

In the photographs, African sculptures of male figures haphazardly rest on each other and sculpted heads are strewn on the floor. This is a place where you might easily find a decapitated head at your feet. Here

Figure 11.3 Greniers: Mannequins, débris et poussières, Documents 5,
October 1929.

Figure 11.4 Salvador Dalí, *Le jeu lugubre*, 1929, oil and collage on card.
Private collection.

you can find the debris of the modern unconscious – made up of so many dismembered parts, enveloped in dust, like a film or screen which both coats and obscures solid form, as it decomposes and crumbles. What interests me here is the distinction in the photographs between dismemberment (in the sculpted figure as disarticulated mannequin) and decomposition, as formless decay or dissolution. Both these aspects come together in the photographs, perhaps more vividly here than anywhere else. So far I have concentrated on the chain of associations set up by Bataille's notion of decomposition. Now I want to comment on the associations triggered by dismemberment as the separation, rather than the dissolution, of parts. Of course, these two chains often tend to collapse in the event of Bataille's writing, but it is a vivid distinction none the less.

In his essay 'Sacrificial mutilation', Bataille took, again, the male body, that of the artist, as the site of dismemberment. The case history with which he begins deals with a thirty-year-old Sunday painter, one Gaston F., who fixed his eyes on the sun and received the order to cut off his thumb. There is a parallel drawn between the motif of the sun and the pictures of sunflowers which Van Gogh repeatedly painted. Such a preoccupation with sun imagery can only be regarded as a pathological obsession, connected with Van Gogh's self-mutilation of cutting off his own ear, a part of himself. The sun is not so much decomposed, scattered, dispersed or polymorphous – as were its effects in my earlier discussion – as cut up and dismembered. This scenario can be regarded as one of castration anxiety, in which the sun, as a paternal metaphor, blinds, threatening sight and is linked to the loss of a member – the thumb or the ear, which serves as a substitute for the castrated penis.

The theme of castration, to which Bataille himself frequently returns, is central to his interpretation of Dali's painting *Le jeu lugubre* (Figure 11.4). In his essay, which takes the same name as Dali's painting, he declares at the outset, 'Intellectual despair results in neither weakness nor dreams, but in violence'.[28] In the context of Bataille's writing on art, 'The "Lugubrious Game"' continued the theme of mutilation which he had identified even in his earlier writing on the eleventh-century St Severs Apocalypse – that prehistory characterized by dislocation, alteration and destruction. The violence done was to painting and to thought, as he wrote of Picasso, 'when Picasso paints, the dislocation of forms leads to that of thought'. And where Picasso's were hideous, Dali's were 'frighteningly ugly'.[29] Bataille was writing about Dali's work following his exhibition at the Galerie Goemans in November 1929 and so a few months before Miró's show at the Galerie Pierre in 1930. Already the conflicts with Breton had surfaced over Dali. Under

Breton's influence Dali refused to let Bataille reproduce an illustration of *Le jeu lugubre* in *Documents*, so Bataille had to make do with a schematic drawing in which he mapped out the psychoanalytic scenario involved.

The figure at the centre of Dali's painting explodes into minute parts and the body is dismembered. The picture parodies the traditional form of an Assumption, where it is now not the Virgin whose spirit rises upward, but desire – and only towards punishment and castration. Even the title 'Le jeu lugubre' was indicative, for Bataille, of the underlying theme of the painting – of castration, of cutting and being cut. According to Bataille, the act of castration is expressed in the exploding central figure, whose body, from the waist up, is 'entirely torn off'.[30] The statue on the left is a figure who contemplates his own castration with even a certain satisfaction. It is the ignominy of the scenario which Bataille stresses as he attacks Breton's idealized view that, with Dali, 'it is perhaps the first time that the mental windows have been opened really wide'.[31] Dreams are soiled, like the pants of the male figure in the bottom right-hand corner. The picture invokes memories of the absent mother, the Virgin Mother, whose apotheosis is redrawn here as a male fantasy on the theme of castration.

The title Bataille gave to the first draft of this essay was 'Dali screams with Sade'. In the first version Bataille made more explicit references to Freud's theory of dreams. In particular, he mentioned the mechanism of dream-work which underlies his reading, where beneath the surface are found 'the terrible things' of which Sade had written.[32] With the change of title, though, he brought into the foreground a different aspect. 'Lugubre', although sometimes translated in Dali's work as 'dismal', means lugubrious or gloomy, but also has the sense of the ominous or dire – that sense which Freud captured when he offered 'lugubre' as one of the French terms for the 'uncanny' in his famous essay.

It is in the context of Freud's notion of the uncanny that I want to draw together some of the strands that have emerged in this discussion of Bataille's writing on art. For in Freud's essay on the uncanny we find a similar set of metaphors at work. In the analysis of Hoffman's story of the Sandman, the crucial elements are the beautiful, lifelike automaton Olympia and the Sandman who throws bits of sand or burning coals into children's eyes. The themes which Freud brings to the surface concern sight and insight, sight and thwarted sight, and sight and castration. The structure of the narrative also combines the two mechanisms: of dismemberment in the automaton Olympia and of terror of the sand or burning coals being thrown into one's eyes.

There is a certain symmetry here of the metaphors of automaton/ mannequin and dismemberment on the one hand, and of sand/dust and thwarted sight on the other. There is also, of course, an asymmetry: between the female automaton, the fair Olympia, and the male figures of African sculptures found in the *Documents* photograph, even though they may be feminized as mannequins in the subtitle (Figure 11.3). It does not seem to me, however, that this asymmetry – the displacements between male and female, non-Western and Western – eclipses the point. For it is what is done to representation, and not simply its iconography, which matters here in the destructuring metaphors of fragmentation, which explode into tiny particles; through such metaphors, I have suggested, sexual difference is brought into play. In the reduction to powder, in obliteration, the Oedipal scenario is played out on the surface of painting – not behind it, or somehow elsewhere – and it is framed as a trajectory of the male spectator (Bataille) and staged in painting itself.

In Freud's essay, the uncanny denotes both a state of strangeness and a mechanism of estrangement. Freud talked of ghosts and spirits and the way in which some languages, such as English, only capture a sense of the *unheimlich* house by the word 'haunted'. The uncanny, the *unheimlich*, denotes the unhomely, that which is secretly familiar and has been repressed. 'Dismembered limbs, a severed head, a hand cut off at the wrist ... feet which dance by themselves ... all these have something', wrote Freud, 'particularly uncanny about them.'[33] For Freud, dismemberment is linked to the fear of castration. In this context, the female figure of Olympia in Hoffman's story is only a projection. The hero Nathaniel's obsessive love for the doll is narcissistic, and only symptomatic of his father fixation which makes it impossible for him to love a woman.

There are two chains of migrating metaphors in Freud's analysis of the story. One is the figure of sight, from the fear of sand in one's eyes through the prosthetic objects of spectacles and spyglass; the figure of sight ultimately refers to the sight of the mother's genitals, which threatens the boy's castration. The other is the migration of sand to coals, and coals to sand, through the introduction of the Sandman as the one who throws 'handfuls of sand' into children's eyes; the sand becomes burning coals as Coppelius, the family friend whom the young Nathaniel had imagined was the Sandman, seized him and threatened to drop 'bits of red-hot coal from the fire into his eyes'.[34] It turns out that the boy's father is killed in an explosion, which fulfils in Freud's analysis the boy's Oedipal desires. These two chains come together in the optician Coppola, the later incarnation of the Sandman; he is a maker of spectacles, whose name, Freud notes, was associated with the word 'coppella' or 'crucible' and 'coppo' or 'eye-socket'.[35]

In Freud's analysis, the Olympia figure is ultimately only an alibi for the main drift of the story – of the Sandman who threatens the boy with castration and who is ultimately responsible for the uncanny effect. Freud's suppression of the Olympia element has the effect of privileging the father–son axis and the main rivalry between the boy and his father. On that axis, the feminine is always subordinated to the paternal metaphor.[36] It is this psychic scenario which is played out in Bataille's view of modern painting. Its dual aspects for Bataille are dismemberment and decomposition – as two drifts in modern painting represented by Dali and Miró respectively.

We find sight or insight set against obscurity – dust in your eyes – where the constant threat is punishment by the Law of the Father. In this context, femininity is a blindspot, but in the context of an Oedipal fascination not with seeing but with not seeing and with lack. For Bataille, femininity is a secret or knowledge that threatens untold disaster, the destructive femininity of Pandora's box. The inside of that box, like the female genitals, is an object of fear – it is an *unheimlich* place with a frightening, uncanny effect. It is the opposite of what Freud talked of as the ultimate *heim*, the mother's body. 'In this case', wrote Freud, 'the *unheimlich* is what was once *heimisch*; the prefix "un" . . . is the token of repression.'[37] The uncanny is something secretly familiar but buried, and the uncanny effect of the Sandman is linked to the castration complex in childhood, where the mother's lack threatens castration. Absence is loss, the lack of something, and that absence is threatening to the boy and initiates the trauma of sexual difference, marked by both desire and fear. That absence of meaning invoked by the fragmentation and decomposition of painting also invokes desire and fear of what lies in that dangerous realm beneath the lid, in the shadowy terrain of the unconscious.

I do not mean to suggest, finally, that the lid can be lifted, or the dust swept aside, to reveal what is beneath in a clear light. My point has not been to expose an underlying truth, but only to lay out the topography, or the drift, of metaphors as they occur in Bataille's language on painting. Although Bataille's language erases feminine desire and pleasure, his formulation of a male sexual economy occupies the shadows, where meaning and identity fail. And in the metaphor of dust, both the surface and the obscurity of modern painting exist in some kind of relationship to each other and to a psychic fantasy of the Oedipal origins of modern painting, in which categories are scattered and dispersed. In this sense, dust acts as a pivotal metaphor – for painting and its origins, for meaning and the impossibility of meaning. Dust in the eye, and obscurity in the field of vision, then, are not obstacles to explanation or truth, but a condition of modern painting.

Notes

1   For the centrality of collage in the modernist aesthetic, see Clement Greenberg, 'Collage' in *Art and Culture*, Boston, Beacon Press, 1961, 70–83. For Greenberg, it was in about 1930, that is after the first experiments with collage, that Miró 'precipitated the integral elements of his style'; 'Review of an exhibition of Joan Miró', *The Nation*, 7 June 1947, in C. Greenberg, *The Collected Essays and Criticism*, 2, Chicago, University of Chicago Press, 1986, 154.

2   In personal terms, Miró had always been closest to Leiris and those associated with him. In 1927, he painted a kind of abstract group portrait called *Musique, Seine, Michel, Bataille et moi*. In October 1929, Leiris's article on Miró was published in *Documents* with illustrations of a Dutch interior from 1928 and three other reworkings of Old Master portraits. Whilst Bataille's view of art is more often linked with Masson and Dali, this essay attempts to show the possibilities for interpretation opened up by the juxtaposition of Bataille and Miró. For important work on Bataille and Miró, see David Lomas's forthcoming Ph.D. thesis on Surrealism, to be submitted to the Courtauld Institute, University of London.

3   Maurice Raynal, *Anthologie de la peinture en France de 1906 à nos jours*, Paris, Editions Montaigne, 1927, 34.

4   Tristan Tzara 'Le Papier Collé ou le proverbe en peinture', *Cahiers d'Art*, 6, 2, 1931, discussed by W. Jeffet in *Joan Miró, Paintings and Drawings 1929–41*, London, Whitechapel Art Gallery, 1989, 29.

5   Bataille, 'L'art primitif', *Documents* 7, 1930, in *Oeuvres complètes* (*OC*), 1, Paris, Gallimard, 1970, 253.

6   What Bataille terms the 'sacred' here is his interpretation of what Otto calls the 'tout autre', a reference omitted in my quotation. Note in 'L'art primitif', *OC*, 251.

7   Bataille, *Manet* [1955], London, Macmillan, 1983, 62.

8   Ibid.

9   Ibid., 50.

10   Ibid., 51.

11   Sigmund Freud, *Beyond the Pleasure Principle* (1920), in *On Metapsychology*, 11, London, Pelican Freud Library, 1984.

12   Freud, *The Ego and the Id*, ibid., 380–1.

13   Bataille, 'L'exercise de cruauté', *OC*, XI, 482.

14   Bataille, 'Rotten Sun' in *Visions of Excess: selected writings, 1927–39*, ed. and trans. Allan Stoekl, with Carl R. Lovitt and Donald M. Leslie Jr, Minneapolis, University of Minnesota Press, 1985, 58. In *Documents* 3, 1930, the essay was illustrated by Picasso's *Three Dancers*, 1925.

15   Bataille, 'Joan Miró: peintures récentes', *OC*, I, 255.

16   Ibid.

17   Ibid.

18   Ibid.

19 Bataille, 'André Masson labyrinthe' [1946], *OC*, XI, 35.
20 Bataille, 'Poussière', *Documents* 5, October 1929, *OC*, I, 197.
21 See Cathérine Clement's discussion in 'The Guilty One', in H. Cixious and C. Clément, *The Newly Born Woman*, Manchester, Manchester University Press, 1987. It is also interesting to compare with Bataille's the retelling of the Sleeping Beauty tale by Cixous, ibid., 66.
22 Le Corbusier, *Towards a New Architecture* [1923], London, The Architectural Press, 1970, 257.
23 Bataille, 'Cheminée d'usine', *OC*, I, 206.
24 André Breton, *Second Manifesto of Surrealism* [1929], in *Manifestos of Surrealism*, Michigan, Ann Arbor Press, 1972, 181, quoting virtually word for word Bataille's last lines of 'Figure humaine', *OC*, I.
25 Bataille, 'Figure humaine', ibid., 185.
26 Ibid., 181.
27 Bataille, 'Musée', *OC*, I, 240, and see D. Hollier's discussion of the museum and the slaughterhouse in *Against Architecture: The writings of Georges Bataille*, Cambridge, Mass., MIT Press, 1989, xii–xiii.
28 Bataille, 'The "Lugubrious Game"', 1985, in *Visions of Excess*, 24.
29 Ibid., 27.
30 Ibid., 29.
31 Breton, 'The first Dali exhibition' [1929], in *What is Surrealism? Selected writings*, ed. F. Rosemont, London, Pluto Press, 1978, 45.
32 'Dali hurle avec Sade', 219. It was Sade who wept 'larmes de sang' over his lost manuscripts, such as 'Cent vingt journées' (Sade Correspondence, quoted in *La littérature et le mal* which Maurice Heine had recovered and brought back to Paris in 1929. For a discussion of 'Le "Jeu Lugubre"' and the theme of castration see D. Hollier, *Against Architecture*, 122.
33 Freud, 'The "Uncanny"', *Art and Literature*, 14, The Pelican Freud Library, 1985, 366.
34 Ibid., 349.
35 Ibid., 352.
36 Kristeva acknowledges Bataille in her reworking of the notion of abjection in terms of the maternal axis; her writing on the maternal metaphor both extends and cuts against the grain of Bataille's Oedipal drama. See Julia Kristeva, *The Powers of Horror*, New York, Columbia University Press, 1982. See also Susan Rubin Suleiman's discussion of Bataille and femininity in *Subversive Intent, Gender, Politics, and the Avant-Garde*, Cambridge, Mass., Harvard University Press, 1990, 72–87.
37 Freud, 'The "Uncanny"', 368.

12 Fêting the wound

Georges Bataille and Jean Fautrier in the 1940s

Sarah Wilson

By the early 1950s the 'Informel' as a style dominated European painting. Was it clearly 'derived from what Georges Bataille had named the "formless" [*informe*] in the 1920s', as the art historian, Serge Guilbault has confidently opined?[1] Bataille's relationship with the painter and sculptor Jean Fautrier is central to Guilbault's assertion, which must none the less be challenged.

The shift from the 1920s and 1930s to a world scarred by the Second World War is reflected in Bataille's shift from a renegade Surrealism to an alliance with a more existentialist ethos. The leading Surrealist dissident before the war, Bataille continued to dissect the Surrealist corpse, charting its spiritual fall from grace during the 1940s. In 1945, reviewing Jules Monnerot's sociological analysis of Surrealism, *La poésie moderne et le sacré*, in *Combat*, he agreed that the movement was essentially religious in aspiration: 'This work brings serious study, as it should, into a domain which rejects superficial forms, only admitting form at its most profound.' Despite its evident failings, Bataille concluded (and his polemics with the movement had been notoriously fierce), Surrealism had engendered a revolution, bringing a 'morality of revolt' into consciousness and literature.[2] Yet with the revelation of the concentration camps, followed by Hiroshima and the entry into a nuclear age, retrospective analyses like Monnerot's became redundant as an explanation of man in a world with new and terrible monuments: 'Like the pyramids or the Acropolis, Auschwitz is the doing, the sign of man. The image of man is henceforth inseparable from that of the gas chamber', Bataille was to write in 1947.[3]

Was existentialism a means of personalizing this terrible drama? Beyond the question of its philosophical derivations and all its variants, it attempted to bring the weight and blackness of the whole world into a paradigmatic individual experience. Through this focusing, one could argue, it became a retreat from the implications of collective guilt and responsibility and the ideal of political action with which Bataille had been so engaged at the moment of Contre-Attaque and which had so remarkably failed in France.

Bataille's reflections upon the mysteries of inner experience and the outer world of forms involved a profound complicity with certain artists. In the prewar period, he had a close relationship with the dissident Surrealist André Masson, who illustrated *L'anus solaire*, 1931, *Sacrifices*, 1936 and the journal *Acéphale*. Indeed, it is in the article on Masson of 1946, in a climate already dominated by the existentialist/Communist debate, that Bataille attempts to redefine 'engagement' while speaking of the work of art: 'If we speak of engagement we can define it in two ways. To be "engagé" means to engage in a specific activity, a revolution, a war, political reform, agricultural or industrial production. But what engages me could also be a totality . . . each work by André Masson *is* a totality.'[4]

Bataille's whole thrust is eschatological, remote, in fact, from the world of Masson, but related intimately to the rest of his writing during the Occupation and its aftermath. The 'interior debate' that he announces 'has only sense if experienced in the depths of night, in the affliction once produced for the faithful by the representation of God'. Nietzsche was first to announce the death of God. 'With God dead, I must *replace* him.' Either man is now free to serve man and no longer God, Bataille argued, or the void is a revelation of man's potential to be 'a *totality*, no longer at the service of other men'.[5] It is not without significance that Jean-Paul Sartre was concurrently writing about Masson who, in 1946, was working on the décor for his play *Morts sans sépulture*.[6] Intertextually speaking, a veritable battle for souls was being waged: while the German painter Wols 'chose' Sartre in 1945, and became for the philosopher the exemplary existentialist painter,[7] Bataille's relationship and his work was with Jean Fautrier (who, like Wols, was a pioneer exhibitor at the Galerie René Drouin in the Place Vendôme, birthplace of the newest postwar art). The major difference between the two painters during the early 1940s was the profoundly erotic content of Fautrier's work.[8]

The paths of terror and horror pursued in Fautrier's work trace extraordinary parallels with Bataille. Yet the two men did not meet until 1942. Their collaboration lasted until 1947. Fautrier had illustrated Dante, and would be working with Jean Paulhan, Paul Eluard, Francis Ponge and André Frenaud during the early 1940s.[9] He would agree to illustrate Bataille's two most erotic texts, *Madame Edwarda* and *Alleluiah, catéchisme de Dianus*, published in 1945 and 1947 respectively.[10]

Fautrier was no ordinary School of Paris artist: his singularity was that he had completely escaped the co-ordinates of the Parisian situation at the outset of his career. Taken as a child to London where he trained, he had remained untouched by late Cubism or Surrealism; his sombre realism in the 1920s aligned itself with the current painters of the 'return to order'. Yet far from seeking a classical or Latin ideal, Fautrier had a fascination for ugliness and deformity. His genetically inbred *Tyroliennes en costume de dimanche* (*Tyroleans in Sunday costume*) of 1925, arranged with the stiffness and banality of a ritual photograph pose, may legitimately by compared with one of Bataille's first *Documents* articles, 'Figure humaine', which evokes the horror of the personages of our immediate precursors arranged before the local photographer. This 'shameful ascendancy', far from signalling 'a to some extent pathological degradation', demonstrated indeed 'the very principle of our most civilized and most violent mental activity'.[11] One could likewise compare Fautrier's *Idiot* of 1925, a touching study of a retarded boy from the Salpetrière hospital, with Bataille's texts on monstrousness, the freaks of nature, in *Documents* 2.[12] Fautrier's early sculpture – totally without parallel at the time, while relating to Degas' rough wax 'ébauches' and Degas' own interest in lumpy adolescence and sexual pain – are of exemplary ugliness.[13] The moulded matter of the clay became analogous to the inchoate, thickly worked impasto in small landscape whose precedents must be found in the irridescent, dissolving forms of Monet's late water-lily paintings.[14] More Bataille-like, however, and conceived at the time of Bataille's reflections upon high and low, upon the 'Soleil pourri', the rotten sun, and the blinding of the sun in blood and night, is Fautrier's own evocation of night. His blackened palette overwhelmed the motifs of landscape and still life; light and dark became symbolic, metaphysical.[15] The metaphysical became conjoined to the erotic in Fautrier's portrayal of nudes, in works infinitely more disturbing than the 'filles' of a Moise Kisling or the 'maisons closes' of a Jules Pascin ... The convention itself, the cliché of the brothel, was re-examined as a rite of passage with the Other, an encounter with the Sacred, a metaphysical event and exemplar of man's state, as it would be for Bataille in *Madame Edwarda*.

It is Fautrier's exploding and as it were 'reinforming' of the conventional genres, comparable with Bataille's 'rewriting' of the essay, the novel of initiation, the pornographic tale, that makes the parallel between the two men remarkable. The conventional still-life, the 'nature morte', became a depiction of slaughter and evisceration; rabbits, suspended by the neck – not upside down to drain as in the classic depictions of a Chardin or a Derain – have inevitable

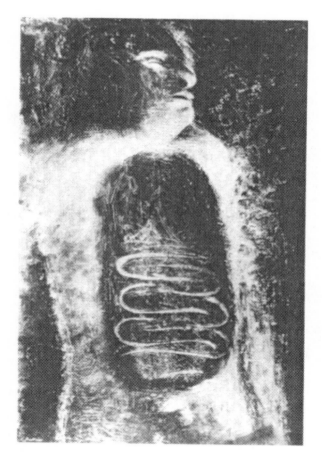

Figure 12.1 Jean Fautrier, *L'homme ouvert*, 1928–9, oil on canvas. Musée des Beaux-Arts, Dijon. Donation Pierre Granville.

Figure 12.2 Jean Fautrier, *Enfer, Chant IV, c.* 1930, lithographic inks on paper. Madame Florence Malraux, Paris.

anthropomorphic connotations (one recalls Bataille on the slaughter-house). Fautrier was moving towards the painting of the wound.

In his famous 'The big toe' article, published in 1929, Bataille refers to 'vicissitudes of organs, the pullulating of stomachs and larynxes, the bloody and involuntary palpitations of the body to which we are involuntarily subject'.[16] Fautrier painted *L'homme ouvert* or *L'autopsie* (*The Open Man* or *The Autopsy*), in 1928–9.[17] Now the painting itself became 'all wound', like the body of Bataille's Chinese torture victim:[18] the exposure of the viscera expressed a condition of 'life in death'.

By this time Fautrier was working an encaustic, waxy material, mixed into his paint, that became analogous to flesh. For *L'homme ouvert*, like a real anatomist himself, Fautrier worked on the flat – as though above a veritable corpse, physically engaging, as it were, with the entrails of his life-size victim. He then, literally, raised the body, as though from the dead, to an erect position – to hang it on the wall, assuming the power of the life-giving Creator.[19] Conceived as flat, as low, Fautrier's nude women, painted as though on a mattress, appeared on the wall as though suspended in a weightless limbo. Women – from breasts to big toe – left the horizontal/vertical axis. They corresponded to the bodies depicted in another source which interested both Fautrier and Bataille, from the point of view not only of colour and form, but more crucially, to use Bergson's phrase, 'matière et mémoire', 'matter and memory', that of prehistoric cave painting. The caves of Altarmira in Spain, of Eyzies in France, and the work of the Abbé Breuil and his colleagues were well known at the time: the cave was a womb-like environment, corresponding to the curves and roundnesses of the animals depicted, the space preceding (and refuting) any notion of rectilinearity, as did the small fertility goddess sculptures like the many-breasted 'Dame de Lespugue', so important for Fautrier's female nudes. In the cave sign-system, the wound itself became elided with the female sex and the notion of Woman. The cave was the very matrix of the birth of art and of its magical and eschatological force: a place where death spoke to posterity.[20]

It was through a failed project to illustrate Dante's *Inferno* – hell – that Fautrier elaborated what he would retrospectively agree to call 'la peinture informelle', 'Informel painting', a broad art movement of which he was the almost unacknowledged leader in the postwar period. The concept of figuration itself fell into limbo in Fautrier's *Enfer* (*Inferno*) lithographs. The thirty-four drawings in lithographic ink required no less than thirty lithographic stones to create the desired colour effects. Dante described the Shades who appeared and dis-appeared on the edge of the river Styx, begging for release into life or death; here Fautrier's 'filles' are reduced to residual forms, finally to mere stripes.[21]

Bataille's brief and contemporaneous description of the 'informe' – the Inform – in *Documents*, 1929, was of its power as a 'term serving to declassify'. Yet his images of crushed spiders and philosophy as a 'mathematical frock-coat' are simple metaphors for an attack on the straightjacket of conventional philosophy: its inadequacy to describe the universe or to convey inner experience, its desire to match specific signs with definable significations.[22] He says no more. Fautrier, on the other hand, sets up a dialogue between life or limbo, and death, the classical and the contemporary, exterior and interior worlds; he pushes contemporary debates about figuration versus abstraction to new frontiers. His inchoate forms posited an original matter and a paternity[23] remote from the Cubist/primitivist/Surrealist concerns of *Documents* (see Figure 12.2). His elaboration of the concept of striation would converge with Bataille's own correspondences between the wound, the sex and the scar, reappearing as form and matter in the artist's *Otages* (*Hostages*) paintings of the 1940s.

When Fautrier and Bataille did meet it was at perhaps the most intense moment in France's history since the Revolution. Once again, terror, far from being a historical notion, or even an incitement to riot – as in Bataille's Contre-Attaque period of the late 1930s – was part of the tissue of life and death.[24] Jean Paulhan, the writer and editor of *La nouvelle revue française*, was finally responsible for introducing the writer to the artist in 1942. All three would consider the engagement of literature with the politics and the morality of terror in a context extending beyond the Occupation of France to the atrocities committed in the name of the 'épuration'.[25] In 1942 Paulhan decided to borrow a selection of paintings, including *L'homme ouvert* (*The Open Man*), for a private display of the artist's works in his apartment.[26] The insufficiencies of Fautrier's only lifetime biographer and the 'limbes' – the frontiers, rather than the limbo – of scholarly territory are such that very little is known about that introduction, the frequency of their meetings and the intensity of the Bataille/Fautrier friendship during the 1942–7 period, apart from some of Fautrier's technical correspondence with his editor.[27]

In 1941, Bataille's first edition of *Madame Edwarda* appeared under the pseudonym Pierre Angélique, dated 1937 as a protective measure.[28] He wrote it during September and October 1941, at a moment of intensified hostage taking and reprisal shootings in France (precisely the catalyst for Fautrier's *Otages* series) and just before the writing of 'Le supplice', part of *L'expérience intérieure*. 'I could not have written "Le supplice" if I had not already offered the lubricious key to the piece. All I wanted to describe in *Edwarda* was a movement of independent ecstasy', he said.[29] Yet the analogy between the sexual encounter and torturer and his victim relentlessly recalled the external world – not formless, 'informe', but filled with repeated and specific atrocities which pierce the privacy and erotic tension of Bataille's text.

Bataille had started writing his intimate journal, *Le coupable* (*Guilty*), in September 1939 at the outbreak of war – a contemplation of the relationship between erotic and mystical experience. A constant recollection was the death of his lover Laure (Colette Peignot) in November 1938: 'Pain, horror, tears, "délire", orgies, fever and then death were the daily bread that Laure shared with me.' She died in fury and hate, raging against him in the knowledge of his burning and secret adultery.[30] While he immediately took up with Denise Rollin, his soul was in torment: the war anticipated and celebrated in *Acéphale*, the promise of ecstatic annihilation, was now a question of the banalities of everyday versus the profound anguish of unknowing, of terror of potential betrayal, which in itself became banal – the quotidian of every being in occupied France – life at the limits of the unimaginable. In both *Le coupable* and *L'expérience intérieure* there is an insistent yearning for confrontation with God, who can be 'anéantissement', death itself, or can be replaced by abject humanity as in the case of Madame Edwarda, the prostitute who shows her wound, her sex, to the narrator saying 'You see – I am God'.[31]

Madame Edwarda as a text constantly slides into the eschatological. At the very moment when she insists that the narrator kiss and lick her sex, her 'guenilles' or rags, the palimpsest in Bataille's mind, evoked in the text *L'expérience intérieure*, is the female Saint Angèle de Foligno's *Book of Visions* that he read concurrently with the writing of *Le coupable*: 'Christ called me to put my lips on the wound in his side. I felt for the first time a great consolation mixed with a great sadness, for I had the Passion before my eyes.'[32] In *Madame Edwarda*, the narrator says: 'At last I kneeled, trembling, and put my febrile lips on the living wound.'[33] The crucial trope in 'Le supplice' is the moment of 'lama sabachthani', Christ's cry from the cross: 'Why hast Thou forsaken me?' Bataille reflects upon Saint John of the Cross: 'We should imitate in God (Jesus) the fall from Grace [*déchéance*], agony, the moment of unknowing ["*non-savoir*"] of the "lama sabachthani".' Drunk to the very dregs, Christianity is the absence of salvation, despair of God. . . . The agony of God in the person man is fatal, the abyss into which he is vertiginously invited to fall. The agony of a god has only to explain sin. It justifies not only the sky (sombre incandescence of the heart) but

Figure 12.3 Jean Fautrier, vignette for *Madame Edwarda*, 1945, heliogravure. Cabinet des Estampes, Geneva.

hell (childishness, flowers, Aphrodite, the laugh).[34]

For *Madame Edwarda*, Fautrier created 31 engravings in an edition of only 88 numbers. The slim publication of 1945 was dated 1942, again as a precautionary measure. 'Jean Perdu', Fautrier's pseudonym, signified a loss of identity or the lost hope of the unredeemable sinner, in ironic contrast, perhaps, to Bataille's angelic ascendance as 'Pierre Angélique'. For a work of darkness, Fautrier's engravings were paradoxically in orange – the colour of hot flesh, the sun – fittingly using the photographic process of 'héliogravure'.[35] Each vignette is a coupling; in the case of the moment in the taxi there are two male figures involved – yet these are hardly figures but a line of knots, 'sexes entrelacées' (see Figure 12.3). For Bataille/the narrator, the encounter is a torture; the body is as though delivered to the executioner. Fautrier's figures are tipped, writhing, constantly sliding, echoing both Bataille's sexual rhythms and his description of metaphysical and horizontal 'glissement' (slippage). While whole figures are indicated, the mélange of lines indicates Bataille's 'indifférence'; in some cases the vignette itself becomes the sexual organ. The Roman reference is still present in Fautrier, recalling the pornographic graffiti and 'tintinnabulae', votive, winged penises, at Pompeii, and at the same time Bataille's statement in *Le coupable*: 'the idea that my body itself and my head had become a monstrous penis naked and bloodshot – an idea so absurd that I would faint with laughter.'[36]

Just so, the englobing of the universe as sexual organ had been used as a trope by Fautrier in his illustration to Robert Ganzo's poem 'Orenoque' in which the Orinoco river and the sex of a woman become one: 'I know not where I am plunging and I know not where you finish.' The representation of woman as landscape is subsumed here – into the rosy 'fente', the slit, and the 'parties velues', the velvety dark surrounding the fronds of a pubic landscape.[37]

The Bataillian night, the 'vertige', the slipping into annihilation, are replicated in Fautrier's lines, engraving presence as arabesque into inky night with *Le cadavre de la femme* (*The Woman's Corpse* – 'cadere' is to fall) of 1942, used later to illustrate Jean Paulhan's text *Fautrier l'enragé*.[38] But the 'fente' is also 'déchirure' and 'blessure' – the sex is a wound. As Bataille said in 'Le supplice' in January 1943: 'We are perhaps the wound, the malady of Nature.' He advocates 'a fêting of the wound' – 'faire de la blessure une fête'.[39] At the very time Fautrier was working on *Madame Edwarda*, he was also creating his *Otages* (*Hostages*) paintings and sculptures which contained a shocking mélange of eroticism and cruelty (see Figure 12.4).[40] The voyeurism inherent in both the circumstances of their genesis and in

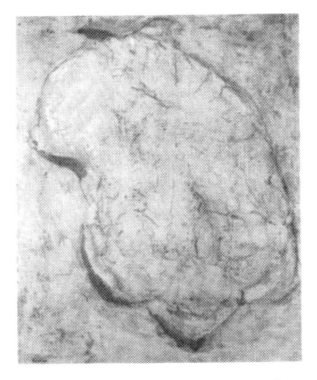

Figure 12.4 Jean Fautrier, *Otage: La toute jeune fille*, 1943, oil on paper mounted on canvas. M. Sami Tarica, Geneva.

Figure 12.5 Jean Fautrier, vignette for *Alleluiah, catéchisme de Dianus*, 1947, lithograph. Cabinet des Estampes, Geneva.

the uncomfortable response of the spectator to such paintings stems from the way in which Fautrier had turned 'blessure' into 'fête', and even more precisely in the direct evocation of Watteau's *Fêtes galantes*. Pink flesh and petticoats in the countryside which became subsumed in Fautrier's painterly matter, fused with the memories of scarred torsos of raped and mutilated victims in the forest of Chateaubriand.[41] 'The shot victim replaces the Crucified one, the anonymous man replaces the painted Christs' said Francis Ponge in his remarkable 'Note sur les Otages' of 1945.[42]

Fautrier's painting *L'ecorché* (*The Flayed Man*), 1943, again a reactualizing, a *détournement* of an artistic convention, evokes the erotic contortions of Edwarda or, alternatively, the Nazi's hostages struggling to escape death in the mud and the grass. The elevation to the vertical of such a painting, made again on the flat with its rough surface of raised pastes ('hautes pâtes') sprinkled with powdered paints and crystals, again evokes cave art, this time with all the topicality of the discovery of the Lascaux caves in September 1940.[43] The other, limbless shapes of Fautrier's hostages such as *La juive* (*The Jewess*), 1943, have their prehistoric model in the Dame de Lespugue.[44]

Bataille's hope was to publish *Alleluiah, catéchisme de Dianus* in time for Fautrier's *Otages* show at the Galerie René Drouin in November 1945.[45] Had this come to pass, the links between eroticism and torture, the wound and the fête in Fautrier's works, would have been set in a context definitively related to Bataille. Francis Ponge indeed made the connection with 'Lord Auch', Bataille's previous erotic pseudonym, in his 'Note sur les Otages' referring to *Histoire de l'oeil*, 'sperm, urine, production, dejection' and Fautrier's excremental metaphors, but Bataille as the author of 'Le supplice', the 'Pierre Angélique' of *Madame Edwarda*, is absent from his critique.[46]

Alleluiah did not appear until early 1947, the book made as a collaboration between Auguste Blaizot and Fautrier working together on the artist's press at Chatenay-Malabry. The artist's interlaced signs mixed erotic arabesques with the anguished grimaces of the *Otages* (*Hostages*) series. In *Alleluiah*, the grass is filled with the 'Otage' sign, the ⊙ – which also becomes a forest of tiny sexes (Figure 12.5). The vertical axis of *Alleluiah* as a text of the divine and the obscene is insisted upon at the outset: 'Your face is noble but the parts hidden under your dress bear no less truth than your mouth – those parts that are secretly open to ordure.' The head 'open to the stars' versus the slit, the 'fente', is paralleled by the glacial peaks which give onto the abyss and herald the significant change in Fautrier's palette after 1945.[47] While Fautrier may have addressed the paean of his own thoughts and lines to

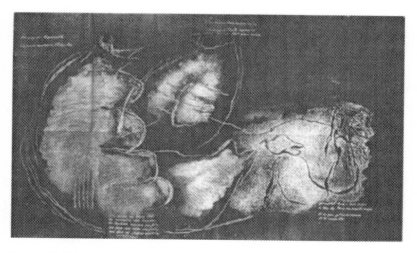

Figure 12.6 Jean Fautrier, *La femme de ma vie*, 1948, lithograph, first state. Madame Madeleine Malraux, Paris.

his companion, Jeanine Aeply,[48] Bataille wove his invocation to a Diana, Diane Kotchoubey, with his Roman pseudonym, Dianus, a name in itself containing Dionysus and Dionysus the Areopagite, 'the flavour of a bearded woman and a dying god'.[49] Yet Laure is still present as memory and as language in *Alleluiah*: Bataille's passage on the nudity of the breasts and obscenity of the sex derives from Laure's own *Histoire d'une petite fille*.[50] For both writer and artist, memory and language, memory and form come together, mingling with the unformed chaos and mystic despair of inner experience.

Fautrier's nude arabesques, reminiscent of the tracings of the prehistoric archeologists, his 'frottage' (rubbed) infills with their rough, cave-like textures,[51] could not fully express his profound reading of Bataille. In 1948, the night of *Alleluiah* re-emerged as the soft, purple ground for *La femme de ma vie* (Figure 12.6), Fautrier's illustrations for the poem by André Frenaud. Here we enter the actual wound, the 'déchirure', the 'fente' of the conclusion of *Alleluiah*, the night of palpitating hearts, lungs, viscera of the body in anguish and ecstasy: 'To be silent, to die slowly in the conditions of a complete, an entire "déchirure". From there, slipping into the depths of silence and with an infinite perspective, you will know from what infamy the world is made.'[52] The night of blood of the 'épuration' would prolong the infamy of guilt, torture, death and betrayal throughout the 1940s.[53]

Only in 1951 was the term 'Informel' coined; Fautrier's priority was from the start acknowledged, a priority he attempted to recuperate dramatically with the exhibition 'Fautrier, 30 years of Informel painting' held in 1957, supplemented by a show including his *Enfer* lithographs.[54] A new European audience felt his impact, yet in a world where the crucial conjunction with Bataille was hardly remembered. The 'Informel', Michel Tapié's term, was imbued with a neo-Dadaist ideology that was expanding to embrace new fields of mathematics, science, music. It became a mode involving late Surrealist, Orientalist and action-painting references that spread to an international community.[55] Most specifically, this Informel lacked the tragic and erotic dimension of Fautrier's intense and private creation of the 1940s. The recent attempt to elide Bataille's 'informe', defined in the 1920s, with the Informel movement, in terms of shapelessness and 'spittle' ('le crachat'), bringing other artists of the 1940s, such as Wols, into the equation, is surely reductive.[56] It does injustice firstly to the individuality and wide-ranging sources of the myriad gestural painters concerned. More specifically, it ignores the implications of the intellectual and personal exchanges between Fautrier and Bataille, the impact of Bataille's erotic texts of the 1940s and the existential and mystic shiftings in Bataille's own thought epitomized by *L'expérience intérieure*. The elision also ignores Bataille's own interest in the very public debate between Surrealism and existentialism in the 1940s, where notions of poverty, residual matter and emotion, authentic voice and action, were attached to the latter philosophy, in all its manifestations. The 'informe'/Informel connection – never made in the 1950s – none the less bears witness to the appropriating drive that characterizes contemporary reassessments of Bataille.[57] Fautrier's role must both extend certain arguments and offer a focus for greater precision.

Fautrier's art is a majestic supplement to the erotic and terrible universe of Bataille. They came together at a moment when the world itself underwent a convulsive spasm of destruction, when millions of anonymous bodies perished. Breaking the straitjacket of language and of form – a possibility both had indicated in 1929 – they attempted to reach out to the world of inner experience. Their achievement in the 1940s heralded a rupture, the birth of a new epoch.

Notes

1 See Serge Guilbaut ed. *Reconstructing Modernism: Art in New York, Paris and Montreal, 1945–1964*, Cambridge, Mass., MIT Press, 1990, 50, 59. For an overview of the Informel, consult Enrico Cripolti, *L'Informale: Storia e Poetica, In Europa, 1940–1951*, 1, Assisi and Rome, 1971 (no mention of Bataille).

2 Bataille, 'La révolution surréaliste', *Combat*, 14–15 April, 1945, in *Oeuvres complètes (OC)*, XI, Articles, 1944–49, Paris, Gallimard, 1988, 17–18. See also 'La réligion surréaliste', lecture of 2 February 1948, etc., in *OC*, VII, 1976, 381–407. Bataille also wrote in the catalogue of the Exposition Internationale du Surréalisme at the Galerie Maeght in 1947.

3 Bataille, 'Jean-Paul Sartre, réflexions sur la question juive', *Critique*, 12, 1947, 471–3.

4 Bataille, 'André Masson', *Labrynthe*, 19, Geneva, 1 May 1946, 8, in *OC*, XI, 36, 564.

5 *Ibid.*, 38. See also Bataille, 'Le surréalisme et sa différence avec l'existentialisme', *Critique*, 2 July 1946, and his lecture 'Surréalisme et existentialisme' given at the Tribune Franco-Belge in Brussels 11 and 12 May, 1949 of which no transcript exists. (See *OC*, VII, 606–7.)

6 See André Masson, 'Balance faussée', *Les temps modernes*, 29, February 1948, 1,381–94, 1948. Sartre's text on Masson, 'L'artiste est un suspect' written at the same period appeared with Masson's *Vingt-deux dessins sur le thème de désir*, ed. La Diane Française, 1961, and as 'Masson' in *Situations*, IV, Paris, Gallimard, 1964, 387–407.

7 See my section 'Under the sign of Sartre' in 'Paris post war: in search of the Absolute', *Paris Post War: Art and existentialism, 1945–1955*, Tate Gallery, London, 1993, 35–6. The problem of existentialism as a popular

cultural movement as well as a specific philosophy, and the fact that there
was never such a term as 'existential art', is also discussed.

8   One should mention that in 1940, the exiled German Surrealist Hans
Bellmer had made etchings for Bataille's *Histoire de l'oeil* (indeed, he
would illustrate *Madame Edwarda* in 1966); Bellmer's diaphanous,
transparent anagrammatic drawings matched Bataille's earlier, metamor-
phic texts. For Fautrier, see *Fautrier 1925–1935*, Stedlijk Museum,
Amsterdam, 1986; *Jean Fautrier, les estampes*, Cabinet des Estampes,
Geneva, ed. Rainer Michael Mason, 1986; *Jean Fautrier 1898–1964*,
Musée d'Art Moderne de la Ville de Paris, Paris, 1989.

9   See my essay, 'Jean Fautrier, ses écrivains et ses poètes' in *Ecrire la
peinture*, Philippe Delaveau ed., Paris, Editions Universitaires, 1991,
241–9. (Fautrier's deep friendship with Paul Eluard, concurrent with the
Bataille relationship, is underestimated (p. 245), as I was ignorant of
correspondence in the possession of M. Jean-Paul Ledeur at the time.)

10   The Bataille–Fautrier relationship is not discussed in *October*, 36, Georges
Bataille number, spring 1986, Michel Surya's biography *Georges Bataille,
La mort à l'oeuvre*, Paris, Librarie Séguier, 1987, or the catalogue *Georges
Bataille, une autre histoire de l'oeil*, Cahiers de l'Abbaye, Sainte-Croix,
69, March–June, 1991.

11   See *Tyroliennes en habit de dimanche*, 1921–2 in *Jean Fautrier
1898–1964* cat. 1 (exhibited at the Salon d'Automne of 1922 and the
Galerie Visconti, 1924), and Bataille, 'Figure humaine', *Documents* 4,
September, 1929, 195–6. (Compare Bataille's 'La laideur belle ou la
beauté laide dans l'art et la littérature', *Critique*, 34, March, 1949, 215–20,
an article on Lydie Kretovsky, 'Le problème spirituel de la beauté et la
laideur'.)

12   See Fautrier's *Idiot*, 1925, in *Jean Fautrier, Gemalde, Skulpturen end
Handzeichnungen*, Josef–Haubrich–Kunsthalle, Cologne, 1980, 5, and
Georges Bataille, 'Les écarts de la nature', *Documents* 2, 1930.

13   Four studio sales of Degas' sculpture were held at the Galerie Georges
Petit in 1918 and 1919; a major sculpture retrospective took place at the
Galerie A. A. Hébrard from May to June 1921.

14   Monet's mural-scale *Nymphéas* paintings were finally revealed to the
public installed in the Orangeries in 1927.

15   See Bataille, 'Soleil pourri' in *Documents* 3, 1930, 173–4 and Marcel
Zahar, 'Fautrier or the powers of darkness', *Formes*, II, 7, July 1930
(English edition).

16   Bataille, 'Le gros orteil', *Documents* 6, December 1929, 297–302.

17   Previously dated 1929, the painting is dated 1928 in *Jean Fautrier,
1898–1964*, 65, without explanation.

18   Bataille's 'young and seductive Chinese man delivered up to the executioner' (photographs by Carpeaux, *Cent morceaux* of 1905, published by
Dumas in his *Traité de psychologie*, Paris, 1923) reappears in 'Extase', part
of the 'Post-scriptum au supplice', *OC*, V, 140.

19   Compare Bataille's elaboration of lowness, 'basesse' and the weightless
and axial disorientation of Jacques-André Boiffard's famous photographs
for 'Le gros orteil'.

20   See the substantial bibliography in Morin-Jean, *Les artistes préhistoriques*,
part of the populist series 'Les grandes artistes', Paris, Henri Laurens,

éditeur, 1933, 125; and Bataille, *Lascaux, ou la naissance de l'art*, Geneva, Albert Skira, 1955. André Leroi-Gourhan's reading of paleolithic art as the 'mise-en-scène' of sexual difference confirmed the intimations of Bataille and Fautrier; see *Préhistoire de l'art occidental*, Paris, Mazenod, 1965.

21 See Rainer Michael Mason, 'L'Enfer, 1930' and Marcel-André Stalter, 'Les lithographies pour l'Enfer de Dante' in *Jean Fautrier: Les estampes*, 26–37, 173–7 for extensive description and discussion, including vexed dating problems. My deepest thanks to Madame Madeleine Malraux, Paris, who has allowed me to see the *Inferno* lithographs so many times.

22 Bataille, 'L'Informe', part of 'Chronique Dictionnaire', *Documents* 7, December 1929, 382, concluding, with obvious irony: 'On the other hand to conclude that the universe does not resemble anything and is nothing but *informe* comes down to saying that the universe is something like a spider or gobbet of spit'. The extended anthropological analysis of the 'Crachat' (spittle) and the word 'Débacle' which precede Bataille's fifteen-line paragraph are by Marcel Griaule and Michel Leiris.

23 Fautrier's paternity: Rembrandt, Turner, Rodin (displayed with Monet in the Orangeries), Degas, Monet.

24 See for its topicality Bernard d'Astorg, *Introduction au monde de la Terreur: de Saint-Just, Sade et Blake a Ernst Junger*, Paris, Editions du Seuil, 1945, dedicated to Jean Paulhan.

25 Paulhan produced *Les fleurs de tarbes, ou la Terreur dans les lettres*, in 1941. See my reading of terror and *épuration* (which does not discuss Bataille) in 'Humanism and terror', part II of 'Paris post war' in *Paris Post War*, 27–8, 48.

26 Telephone conversation with M. André Berne Joffroy, Paris, 15 June 1993. *The Opened Man*, dated 1929 by Berne Joffroy in *Jean Paulhan à travers ses peintres*, Grand Palais, 1974, 562, was admired by Eluard in May 1943 (see letter 34 in catalogue). It was taken by Fautrier from his dealer Jeanne Castel for the display some time in 1942–3, where it hung in Paulhan's dining room, rue des Arènes. (This private exhibition which had a considerable impact on Paulhan's NRF circle, including Bataille, is not mentioned in the Paris retrospective catalogue, 1989. Castel died before she could recover the canvas.)

27 Palma Bucarelli's biography *Jean Fautrier, pittura e matiera*, Editions Saggitori, Milan, 1963, written with the artist's active collaboration, is unfootnoted. Both facts and assertions must be verified from alternative sources. Bataille's unilluminating letter to August Blaizot is quoted in *Jean Fautrier: Les estampes*, 49 in the *Madame Edwarda* section, 49–53. See also Castor Seibel, 'Bataille et Fautrier: Vers la liberté de l'impossible' (reprinted in *Jean Fautrier: Les estampes*, Geneva, 1986, 65–6) and Dominique Lecoq, 'Fautrier/Bataille: dialogue des enragés' in *Jean Fautrier-Etienne Martin*, Billom–Saint Loup, 1985 (Bataille 6), a document unknown to the author at the time of the Bataille conference and generously communicated in June 1993, by M. Jean-Paul Ledeur.

28 Pierre Angélique, *Madame Edwarda*, Editions du Solitaire (Robert Chatté), fifty examples, 1941 ['1937'].

29 Unsourced quotation in Michel Surya, *Georges Bataille*, 501.

30 Bataille, *Le coupable*, *OC*, V, 504 (notes to p. 257), a passage juxtaposed

with Laure's violent letter to Bataille in Michel Surya, *Georges Bataille*, 265.

31 Pierre Angélique, *Madame Edwarda*, illustrated by Jean Perdu, Paris, Le Solitaire, 1945 ['1942'], 20.

32 See Anglèle de Foligno, *Le livre de l'expérience des vrais fidèles*, Paris, Droz, 1927 (duplicate French and Latin texts). Ernest Hello's translation is quoted without page reference by Michel Surya, *Georges Bataille*, 309. Compare this 'écriture feminine' with Bataille (the saint 'se dit angélique', *OC*, V, 123), in particular his shock at discovering Laure's writing which then enters his own, and the slippage of sexual identities between masculine and feminine in his erotic texts (mirrored in Fautrier's art).

33 Pierre Angélique, *Madame Edwarda*, 20.

34 Bataille, 'Le supplice', *L'expérience intérieure*, 61. Fautrier's own 'lama sabachthani', an engraving made at the beginning of his career in 1923, inscribed with the words from Saint Matthew's Gospel, 'My God, My God. Why hast thou forsaken me?', was in fact of Saint Andrew's rather than Christ's cross (*Jean Fautrier: Les estampes*, 16, p. 21: *Mon Dieu, Mon Dieu*, 1923). Compare Bataille's vision of experience as a Saint Andrew's cross in *L'expérience intérieure*, 146.

35 See Rainer Michael Mason, *Madame Edwarda*, in *Jean Fautrier: Les estampes*, 49–56, for reproductions and all bibliographic and technical details.

36 Bataille, *Le coupable*, erased passage, restored as note to p. 276, *OC* V, 517.

37 See Robert Ganzo, *Orenoque*, Paris, Librarie Auguste Blaizot, 1942 [1945], 15, reproduced in *Jean Fautrier: Les estampes*, 39–44, especially the colour plate, p. 181 (inverted) of aquatint 67.

38 Ibid., no. 236, p. 113, *Le cadavre de la femme*, 1942.

39 Bataille, 'Le supplice', 1943 Gallimard edition of *L'expérience intérieure*, 'prière d'inserer' (in manuscript notes dated 24 January 1943), *OC*, V, 422. See also Bataille on the 'Fête' in 'Schema d'une histoire des religions' part 6, *OC*, VII, 314.

40 'Les otages: Peintures et sculptures de Fautrier', Paris, Galerie René Drouin, 26 October–17 November 1945, preface by André Malraux.

41 Compare with Bucarelli's account of Fautrier, the 'voyeur della morte', *Jean Fautrier, pittura e matiera*, 50, Louis Aragon's *Les martyrs de Chateaubriant: Quelques uns des 60,000 fusillés du Parti Communiste*, Bourg, undated, 13: 'I have before my eyes a report concerning the Vallée des Loups, the territory of innumerable executions never mentioned . . .'

42 See Francis Ponge, 'Note sur les Otages', January 1945, Paris, Edition Seghers, 1949, in *OC*, X, 453, 456. The resonances of 'épuration' and vengeance in this text are contextualized in Wilson, 'Humanism and terror', Part II of 'Paris Post War', *Paris Post War*, 27, and the *Hostages* illustrated and discussed by Frances Morris, ibid., 89–103.

43 I discuss the Bachelardian and Bergsonian implications of the 'raised pastes' ('hautes pâtes') of Fautrier and Dubuffet in 'Matter and memory: A new primitivism', part V of 'Paris Post War', *Paris Post War*, 33–4.

44 See *L'ecorché*, 1943, and *La juive*, in *Fautrier 1898–1964*, 111, p. 122 and 99, p. 116.

45 Rainer Michael Mason's citing of *Alleluiah*, the text, in a letter of 19

November, 1944 (*Jean Fautrier: Les estampes*, 73), predates Bataille's letter to Queneau of November 1945 cited by Dominique Lecoq (*Jean Fautrier-Etienne Martin*, 1985, 18). Bataille's text is erroneously claimed to have been written in 1946 in *OC*, V, 572.

46 Francis Ponge, 'Note sur les Otages', 462–3. Serge Guilbaut's assertion (see note 1) is constructed on the strength of Ponge's reference to 'Lord Auch' here.

47 Bataille, *Alleluiah, catéchisme de Dianus*, with nine original drawings, lithographs and vignettes by Jean Fautrier, Librairie Auguste Blaizot, 1947, 10. Fautrier's initial inspiration was Turner's Alpine scenes; his own *Glacier* paintings of 1926 structurally inform later paintings with their new aerial, snowy, blue and white palette.

48 Fautrier illustrated *Lespugue*, a poem by Robert Ganzo describing prehistoric couplings in glacial landscapes, in 1942 (jointly published by the two men), dedicating his own work to Jeanine Aeply, his companion.

49 See Bataille, *OC*, V, 437 (note to p. 41). 'Dianus' was first used as a pseudonym for the publications of the first fragments of 'Le coupable' in *Mesures*, April 1940 (edited by Jean Paulhan).

50 See Dominique Lecoq in *Jean Fautrier-Etienne Martin*, 19.

51 Fautrier first used this soft drawing technique while working with Robert Ganzo on *Lespugue*, 1942. Ganzo had accompanied the expedition which discovered the steatopygous Aurignacian fertility goddess at Lespugue (Haute-Garonne) in 1922.

52 Bataille, *Alleluiah*, 57 (a different version from that in *OC*, V, 415). See also André Frenaud and Jean Fautrier, *La femme de ma vie*, Paris, Auguste Blaizot, 1947, discussed with illustrations in *Jean Fautrier: Les estampes*, 88–95.

53 Pierre Assouline's *L'épuration des intellectuels*, Brussels, Editions Complexe, 1985, is particularly shocking within the broader context of the *epuration* at large.

54 'Fautrier, 30 années de figuration informelle', preface by Pierre Restany, Galerie Rive Droite; graphic work with *Enfer* lithographs Galerie André Schoeller, 15 November–15 December 1957; 'Fautrier – 30 Jahre informelle Malerei', Galerie 22, Dusseldorf, 1958.

55 See my prolonged discussion of the terms 'informe' and 'Informel' in context in the section 'The open work' in Wilson, *Paris Post War*, 45–6, 51–2, where I point out that Enrico Crispolti's seven-page discussion of the origins and usage of the term 'Informel' in *L'Informale, storia e poetica* (see note 1), 47–54 and important discussions of the 1960s, make no mention of Bataille.

56 Serge Guilbaut backs his assertion of the 'informe'/Informel direct link (see note 1) by referring to Rosalind Krauss's article 'Corpus Delicti', *October*, 33, summer 1985, 31–72. Her fascinating discussion of Surrealist photography in the 1930s, using 'informe' (after Salvador Dali) as a metaphor for special effects of distortion and blurring, has no bearing at all on painting after 1945, nor, *pace* Guilbaut, is Bataille's 'crushed spiders' reference of 1929 an adequate key to the reading of Wols, whose work has its origins in the drawings of Yves Tanguy, Georg Gross and Paul Klee.

57 The Tapiès historian, Manuel Borja, attempted to effect the 'informe'/

Informel conjunction in 'A note on Tapiès', *Art Forum*, 24, 2, 1985, 113. However, Katya Garcia-Anton confirmed in conversation with the artist that Tapiès began to read Bataille only recently, on Borja's specific instigation. See Garcia-Anton, *Antoni Tapiès: nationality and identity*, M.A. report, Courtauld Institute of Art, University of London, 1993, pp. 1–3 and p. 4, notes 7–8.

Index

Lightning Source UK Ltd.
Milton Keynes UK
UKOW04f1808221215

265260UK00001B/25/P